TOWARDS THE MANAGED ECONOMY

ROGER MIDDLETON

TOWARDS THE MANAGED ECONOMY

Keynes, the Treasury and
the fiscal policy debate of the 1930s

METHUEN · LONDON AND NEW YORK

FOR ELLEN

First published in 1985 by
Methuen & Co. Ltd
11 New Fetter Lane,
London EC4P 4EE

Published in the USA by
Methuen & Co.
in association with Methuen, Inc.
29 West 35th Street,
New York NY 10001

© 1985 Roger Middleton

Typeset by
Scarborough Typesetting Services
and printed in Great Britain at the
University Press, Cambridge

All rights reserved. No part of this book may be reprinted or reproduced or utilized in any form or by any electronic, mechanical or other means, now known or hereafter invented, including photocopying and recording, or in any information storage or retrieval system, without permission in writing from the publishers.

British Library Cataloguing in Publication Data

Middleton, Roger
Towards the managed economy: Keynes, the treasury and the fiscal policy debate of the 1930s.
1. Great Britain – Economic policy – 1918–1945
I. Title
330.941'083   HC256.3

ISBN 0–416–35830–6

Library of Congress Cataloging in Publication Data

Middleton, Roger
Towards the managed economy
Bibliography: p.
Includes index
1. Great Britain – Economic policy – 1918–1945. 2. Fiscal policy – Great Britain – History. 3. Keynesian economics – History. 4. Great Britain. Treasury – History.
I. Title
HC256.3.M418   1985
339.5'2'0941   84–29607

ISBN 0–416–35830–6

CONTENTS

List of figures	vii
List of tables	viii
List of symbols and conventions	x
Acknowledgements	xi

1	**Introduction**	1
2	**Mass unemployment and the interwar British economy**	10
	1 Unemployment	10
	2 The British economy 1929–39	18
	3 Policy issues and policy constraints: a conspectus	27
3	**The Treasury, economic policy and public expenditure**	31
	1 The Treasury and economic policy	31
	2 The course of expenditure	37
	3 The Treasury and expenditure control	47
4	**The revenue departments, taxation and policy**	57
	1 The revenue departments	57
	2 The course and structure of receipts	62
	3 Revenue forecasting	69
	4 Taxation and economic activity	70
5	**The budget and budgetary policy: introduction**	78
	1 Budget definitions	78
	2 Fiscal window-dressing	80
	3 Budgetary orthodoxy	83
	4 Crowding-out	92

6	**Budgetary policy 1929–39**	96
	1 Budgetary history	96
	2 The transition of budgetary policy	109
	3 Conclusions	120
7	**An assessment of changes in fiscal stance 1929–39**	122
	1 The measurement of fiscal influence	122
	2 The constant employment budget balance	124
	3 Constant employment GDP	125
	4 The characteristics of the fiscal system	127
	5 The fiscal stance 1929–39	132
	6 Conclusions	142
8	**The 'Treasury view' and public works**	144
	1 The case for public works	145
	2 The 'Treasury view' 1929–30	149
	3 An *IS–LM* model of the 'Treasury view'	155
	4 The 'Treasury view' 1931–9	165
	5 Conclusions	171
9	**Conclusions**	173

Appendices

I	Dramatis personae	191
II	The actual and adjusted budget definitions	193
III	The estimation of constant employment receipts and expenditure	196
	Notes	204
	Bibliography	213
	Index	233

FIGURES

1.1	The British economy 1924–32 and 1975–82	2
1.2	A taxonomy of interwar economic historiography	8
2.1	Employment and unemployment 1921–38	11
2.2	Fluctuations in real GDP and unemployment 1924–37	22
2.3	Real GDP and components 1929–39	23
3.1	Expenditure ratios 1920–38	42
3.2	Fluctuations in gross domestic fixed capital formation 1920–38	47
4.1	Effective rates of tax: personal and corporate income 1920–38	64
7.1	Budget balance as % of GDP 1929/30–1939/40	134
8.1	*IS–LM* representation of Keynesian models	156
8.2	*IS–LM* representation of monetarist models	157
8.3	*IS–LM* representation of the 'Treasury view'	161

TABLES

2.1	Regional unemployment rates (insured persons aged 16–64), Ministry of Labour Divisions, 1923–37	14
2.2	Regional employment growth (insured persons aged 16–64), Ministry of Labour Divisions, 1923–37	15
2.3	Growth of GDP, labour, capital, total factor input and total factor productivity 1856–1973	21
2.4	Economic indicators 1929–39	25
2.5	Balance of payments: current account as % of GDP 1929–39	28
3.1	Public expenditure by economic category as % of GDP, selected years, 1913–37	38
3.2	Observed elasticities of public expenditure growth relative to GDP growth (current prices) 1924–37	41
3.3	Cyclical behaviour of expenditure ratios 1920–38	42
3.4	Gross domestic fixed capital formation by sector 1929–38	46
4.1	Public sector receipts by economic category as % of GDP, selected years, 1913–37	62
4.2	Central government revenue as % of GDP 1929/30–1939/40	65
5.1	Central government budget balance: conventional and adjusted definitions 1929/30–1939/40	81
6.1	Central government receipts, expenditure and budget balance: conventional and adjusted definitions 1929/30–1939/40	97
6.2	Budget summary 1929/30–1932/3: published forecasts and results	98

TABLES ix

6.3	Outlay on unemployment benefits 1929/30–1931/2	99
6.4	Expenditure on debt service 1929/30–1939/40	102
6.5	Budget summary 1933/4–1936/7: published forecasts and results	103
6.6	The financing of defence expenditure 1935/6–1939/40	106
6.7	Budget summary 1937/8–1939/40: published forecasts and results	108
6.8	Central government budget accounts: Great Britain, France, Germany and United States 1929/30–1932/3	111
7.1	Actual and constant employment GDP 1929/30–1939/40	126
7.2	Response of central government receipts to trend growth in real GDP 1929/30–1939/40	128
7.3	Response of budget balance to cyclical variations in real GDP (selected years) and autonomous expenditure 1929/30–1939/40	130
7.4	Central government receipts, expenditure and budget balance: actual and constant employment 1929/30–1939/40	135
7.5	Summary figures of defence expenditure 1929/30–1939/40	140
8.1	Liberal Party's 1929 public works programme	147
8.2	Composition of insured unemployed April 1929	151
9.1	Effects of a 'Keynesian type' public works programme	177

TABLES – APPENDICES

II.1	Expenditure adjustments: sinking fund payments and government expenditure charged to capital 1929/30–1939/40	194
II.2	Revenue adjustments: non-recurrent receipts included in 'Ordinary and Self-Balancing Revenue' 1929/30–1939/40	194
III.1	Central government receipts at constant employment 1929/30–1939/40	197
III.2	Elasticities of Customs and Excise duties with respect to GDP	198
III.3	Central government expenditure: actual and constant employment 1929/30–1939/40	202

SYMBOLS AND CONVENTIONS

1. Dates: / is used for financial years, e.g. 1931/2 for the financial year ended 31 March 1932;
   – is used for two or more calendar years, e.g. 1931–2 for the two calendar years 1931 and 1932.
2. Rounding: in many of the tables estimates are given in such a way that components may not add exactly to totals.
3. Symbols:
   .. = not available;
   — = nil.

ACKNOWLEDGEMENTS

This study, like many first books – too many perhaps – arose out of a Ph.D. dissertation. Accordingly, I first want to thank Professors Robert Neild and Leslie Pressnell, who acted as supervisors; Susan Howson, George Peden and Stephen Drayson who read early drafts of the dissertation and did much to improve the final product; and the ESRC, Houblon-Norman Fund and University of Durham for financial support.

In revising this earlier study I have been greatly assisted by my former colleague, Martin Jones, who generously read and made many useful comments on my manuscript at a time when he was preoccupied with the writing of his own version of Britain in the 1930s; Methuen's academic readers; my past interwar economic history special subject students at Durham University; seminar groups and lecture audiences at Birmingham, London, Nottingham and Sheffield Universities, where I presented early drafts of chapters 3, 5, 7, 8 and 9; and Ellen Wratten, my wife, who attended to the book's style and content, drew the figures and carried much of the burden of proof reading. The usual disclaimers apply about any remaining errors of fact, analysis or interpretation.

My thanks are also due to Margaret Hall and Judith Willis for their typing expertise; John Ashworth for computing advice; and Charles Feinstein who kindly lent me the working notes to his 1972 study. Finally, for access to copyright material and permission to quote from it, I am grateful to Steve Broadberry, the Commissioner for HM Customs and Excise (departmental papers), the Confederation of British Industries (FBI papers), the Controller of HMSO (Crown copyright), Mary Daly, Tim Hatton, Martin Jones, Alasdair Lonie, Terry Thomas, James Trevithick and the University of Birmingham (Chamberlain papers). I apologize to any holder of copyright whom I have failed to contact or trace.

Roger Middleton

CHAPTER ONE

INTRODUCTION

The object of this study is threefold. First, to examine the form and impact of British fiscal policy in the 1930s. Secondly, to investigate the theoretical, political and bureaucratic determinants of that policy. And thirdly, to assess the degree to which official economic thinking – supposedly enshrined in the infamous 'Treasury view' – had come to accept Keynesian prescriptions for deficient demand and mass unemployment by the eve of the Second World War.

The book thus focuses upon the origins of modern economic management in Britain. Whilst this subject continues to be much debated by economists and economic historians, as yet no real consensus exists, particularly on the issue of Keynes's influence upon the Treasury. Throughout, the book is addressed to this and related questions. It seeks to lay bare the misconceptions of earlier works in order to advance our understanding of the 1930s fiscal policy debate. But it also has a broader purpose: to demonstrate to readers concerned with the current policy debate, as well as that of the 1930s, that changes in official economic thinking rarely derive from theoretical considerations, though clearly they are informed by them. Thus the 1930s policy debate should be of interest to those who have long harboured the suspicion that policy prescriptions which – at the theoretical level – appear to transcend reason almost invariably have political and bureaucratic foundations sufficiently powerful to ensure their continuance even in face of a sustained theoretical attack.

* * *

The achievement of full employment since the war (to, say, 1970) has generally been attributed – Matthews (1968) is here the one, prescient exception – to the success of Keynesian demand management, this appearing to vindicate the case for fiscal expansion put by Keynes and others between the wars. It is a major contention of this book that the Keynesian condemnation of interwar policy-makers has been both misdirected and myopically over-confident. As the interwar economic historiography developed there was absent any appreciation that the period was increasingly being viewed through the filter of the practical success of demand management since the war, and that the effect of this filter was not only to blur our image of the interwar period but also to generate an undue optimism about the permanence of the gains effected by the Keynesian revolution. For example, as recently as the early 1970s, the following judgement was widely expressed and appeared well founded: 'It seems safe to predict that unemployment will never again be more than a fraction of the amount suffered between the wars' (Stewart 1972, 296–7).

In so far as history reflects current concerns as well as a genuine interest in the past for its own sake, then this study cannot evade our current crisis of unemployment. The numbers unemployed today are rather more than a 'fraction' of interwar levels, indeed they are actually comparable to the *worst* of the earlier depression period. Our current depression, the seriousness of which is revealed by figure 1.1, and its initiation by the retreat from demand management to the Thatcher

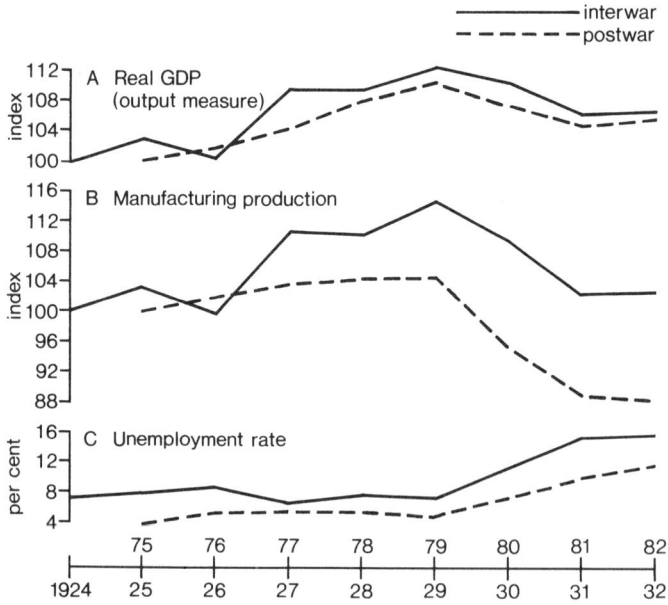

Figure 1.1 The British economy 1924–32 and 1975–82
Sources: 1924–32: Feinstein (1972, tables 6, 51, 57). 1975–82: HMSO (1983, 6, 28, 36).

monetarist experiment (Blackaby 1979; Buiter and Miller 1981), can hardly fail to alter the filters through which we view the 1930s depression and policy debate. Conversely, our attitude towards the present depression is very likely informed by our understanding of its predecessor. That this understanding is frequently suspect has proved an additional motive for the writing of this book.

Thus, in examining the 1930s policy debate, parallels with more recent periods are pursued whenever legitimate. The attractions, both political and intellectual, of budgetary orthodoxy during periods of economic crisis are investigated. So also are the results of eschewing deficit-financing in face of mass unemployment. Here a cyclically-adjusted budget measure is used to show that governments, at times of rising unemployment, ignore at their peril the effects of automatic stabilizers upon budgetary stability. More broadly, the study suggests that there are marked similarities between the questions facing both economists and policy-makers in the 1930s and 1980s, and that *our strategy towards the present might usefully be informed by a knowledge of the past.*

As with other recent studies of interwar economic policy, the government policy documents from the Public Record Office (PRO) have been the main source for information about policy-making. I have, however, been mindful of the problems associated with this source, in particular that 'To concentrate on the State papers is to concentrate on the administrative processes of policy-making rather than on the causes and effects of policy' (Booth and Glynn 1979, 315). Consequently, the PRO papers have been supplemented by the use of certain private papers, namely those of the Federation of British Industries (FBI), Neville Chamberlain (CP) and Maynard Keynes (KP). This study also rests upon a reading of the period's financial press and a thorough review of the extensive secondary literature.

* * *

This study divides into three parts, arranged as follows. In chapter 2 the interwar unemployment problem and the economy's cyclical and trend course are surveyed: from this certain policy constraints are identified. Chapters 3 and 4 also consider background issues: the Treasury's institutional position and the expenditure side of the budget in the case of the former; and the revenue departments and taxation in the case of the latter.

The following three chapters constitute the second part of this study. Chapter 5 considers the interwar budget accounts and budgetary practices as well as the light that these cast upon our interpretation of adherence to budgetary orthodoxy; it also introduces the related issues of the 'Treasury view' and 'crowding-out'. Chapter 6 summarizes 1930s budgetary history. In particular, it details how the financial demands of the rearmament programme of the later 1930s resulted in important changes in the budget as a policy instrument. Using the constant employment budget measure, the fiscal stance of the authorities and the way in which this was influenced by the characteristics of the fiscal system are discussed in chapter 7.

The final part of the book examines the fiscal policy debate from a broader perspective. Chapter 8 is devoted to public works and the 'Treasury view'. The theoretical differences between Keynes and the Treasury are examined, and an interpretation of the 'Treasury view' propounded which, for the first time, integrates theoretical, political and bureaucratic factors in order to show how, and why, by 1939 at least, there was still little common ground between the Treasury and Keynesian views. Chapter 9 concludes by examining questions of a more enduring nature, ones relevant to both the 1930s and present conditions. The political–psychological attractions of balanced budgets in the 1930s are discussed; the unsatisfactory form of economic debate in Britain, the administrative ethos of the British civil service, and connected economic–political issues also receive attention in our explanation of why demands for sound finance have proved the most robust recurrent theme in twentieth-century British economic policy.

Before proceeding to our task, however, let us first complete our introduction to the 1930s fiscal policy debate, its main issues and its various interpretations. From this we can then identify key questions for later consideration.

* * *

The history of the 1930s fiscal policy debate has hitherto been largely a Keynesian history (see, for example, Stewart 1972 and Winch 1972). It has been founded both upon a personal sympathy with Keynes, for having to endure such a sustained combat against an obscurantist Treasury, and upon the judgement that if only Keynes's policy prescriptions had been adopted the interwar unemployment problem would have been satisfactorily resolved. Thus Joan Robinson (1976, 71), a leading exponent of the 'new' economics,[1] typically described the debate as 'the familiar tale of the hard-fought victory of the theory of effective demand'.

It follows that in studying the interaction between economic thought and policy between the wars, research should have primarily focused upon the gradual evolution of Keynes's policy prescriptions and theoretical writings. Culminating in the *General Theory* (Keynes 1936), and finding eventual acceptance and expression by the Treasury in Kingsley Wood's 1941 budget (*Hansard* 1941; HMSO 1941) and the 1944 *Employment Policy* White Paper (HMSO 1944), this Keynesian explanation has been couched in terms of the Treasury, guided solely by economic objectives, succumbing by the force of reason to the theoretical correctness of the 'new' economics.

In this view, the gradual refinement of Keynes's theories holds the key to an understanding of the 1930s policy debate. Accepting Keynes's (1933, 350) accusation that the Treasury and wider opinion were 'trying to solve the problem of unemployment with a theory which is based on the assumption that there is no unemployment', then by inference policy must change as the developing 'new' economics systematically undermined the Treasury's classical economic foundations for its policies. For example, the first biography of Keynes, by Harrod (1951, 340), typifies this approach, as instanced by the following account of a lecture given by Keynes to the Liberal Summer School of 1924:

> Watching his enthusiasm on the one side and the comparative apathy of his audience on the other, I felt that there was some missing clue, something unexplained. . . .
> There was indeed a missing clue. The task of discovering that clue was to occupy the next twelve years of his life. What was lacking was an explanation in terms of fundamental economic theory of the causes of unemployment.

As Skidelsky (1975b, 89) rightly comments: 'The implication here is that had this "missing clue" been discovered in 1924, the Keynesian Revolution would have taken place there and then.'

This essentially Keynesian history thus suffers from a particular developmental bias, an undue prominence given to theory. It is not so much incorrect as incomplete, for it excludes the political dimension of these developments. During the 1930s the Treasury objected to the 'new' economics, and more generally to those advocating a more enlightened and active stabilization policy, on grounds not only economic in character but more fundamentally political and administrative. Similarly, the acceptance of the 'new' economics during the war years is explicable in terms of a change in political attitudes and prevailing administrative conditions, as well as the conversion to the Keynesian theoretical position.

Our reappraisal of this policy debate, however, needs to be conducted with extreme caution, lest either we swing too far to the opposite extreme and discount theory altogether or alternatively interpret Keynes's concern with theory too narrowly. Certainly Keynes thought deficiencies of theory the fundamental problem, but he was far from oblivious of his political surroundings. Rather, as we shall see, more important problems were the manner of Keynes's interpretation of the theoretical debate, and certain political presuppositions which guided both his conduct of the debate and the form of his policy advice.

Accordingly, the interpretation offered here of the 1930s fiscal policy debate is one founded upon a synthesis of the political and administrative, as well as the more normally cited economic–theoretic, constraints to acceptance of Keynesian principles of budgetary policy. No particular originality is claimed for this approach; rather, that it merely revives and makes explicit what hitherto has been muted or implicit in the literature of the period, though it does permit a more informed, and very different, specification of the issues of theory that actually divided the 'new' economics and the official orthodoxy.

The admission of a substantial element of non-economic considerations to this study broadens considerably the issues requiring discussion. The breadth and diversity of questions thus raised can best be introduced by reference to the most frequently suggested fiscal stimulus of the period, that of a large-scale loan-financed public works programme. At this stage we can classify the various issues associated with such a proposal under four broad headings:

1 Economic–philosophical
2 Political
3 Administrative
4 Technical

As regards the economic–philosophical issues, had this policy been adopted questions would have been raised about the viability of the belief in the powers of spontaneous rejuvenation of the free market economy. The policy might have acted as a precedent, encouraging entrepreneurs to seek broader state assistance, and thereby threatened a debilitation of entrepreneurial independence. This independence, of course, was perceived as an essential foundation of the minimalist state. Broader questions would also have been raised about the power of the state and its command of resources; with a larger proportion of final demand now not subject to ordinary market disciplines, the scope for resource misallocation, and thus growth inhibiting actions, was accordingly more pronounced, with obvious implications.

The political dimension results from the decision to pursue such a policy, which in turn must invariably have resulted from a greater priority being ascribed to reducing unemployment than was in fact the case during the interwar period. Thus we need to investigate why, in Lloyd George's words, unemployment was never treated 'in the same spirit as the emergencies of the War' (Liberal Party 1929, 6). We need to admit the possibility that, after the experience of the inflationary boom of 1919–20 and its attendant labour unrest, the authorities might actually have preferred some measure of unemployment as a means of disciplining organized labour. We need also to acknowledge the interwar Treasury's preference for policy instruments which, in a sense to be defined later, were 'politically neutral'. These served both a practical purpose, that of limiting the criticism of existing policies, and a broader political principle, that of avoiding discrimination between individuals and groups which might undermine the free market economy.

The administrative issues, that 'All policies have conditions of existence outside the minds of those who determine policy' (Tomlinson 1981b, 4), necessitate study of the principal institutions responsible for formulating and executing policy. Accordingly, chapter 3 is devoted to a study of the Treasury and local government relations.

Finally, a discussion of institutions raises certain technical issues, in particular those concerning the volume and quality of economic information available to policy-makers. If Grant's (1967, vi) judgement be correct, that 'Britain between the Wars was not only a country of excessive unemployment but of inadequate statistics', then we need to consider the implications of this for fiscal policy. In so doing, it will become apparent that the effects of bureaucratic conservatism were not confined to economic information, that it affected a whole range of other technical issues, and thereby acted as a powerful constraint upon the adoption of more active and ambitious macroeconomic policies.

* * *

The economic context within which a Keynesian fiscal stimulus would have had to operate is also of importance. We need, therefore, to introduce the issue of the performance of the real economy between the wars.

This is best done through Broadberry's (1982) taxonomy of the interwar economic historiography, a compendium of which is given in figure 1.2. Here a distinction is drawn between two genera (pessimists and optimists) and two species or variants (old and new). The terms 'pessimist' and 'optimist' refer to assessments of the efficiency of the market mechanism in resource allocation and thus to the justification for policy intervention, 'pessimists' for example judging the market inefficient and the economy as thus requiring a demand stimulus. The 'old' and 'new' of the taxonomy refer to the chronology of the historiography and the methodology upon which it is founded. Thus the 'old', for example, is characterized by a traditional, largely non-quantitative methodology, whereas the 'new' (mirroring the new of the so-called 'new economic history') is inspired by econometric investigations and recent developments in Keynesian macroeconomic disequilibria theory (see Malinvaud 1977).

From the end of the Second World War until the early 1960s or thereabouts, the old pessimists' interpretation of the interwar period went unchallenged: it was the orthodoxy that the economic performance of the interwar British economy was seriously deficient, that the high unemployment of the period was a clear manifestation of market failure, and that a Keynesian fiscal stimulus would have been entirely appropriate. The old optimists were not of this opinion, their challenge to the prevailing orthodoxy being founded upon certain new statistical series

Genus	Species	Principal authors	Interwar growth performance	Acceleration of rate of structural change	Efficiency of market mechanism	Deficient demand/ involuntary unemployment	Role for Keynesian macro-economic policies	Benefit-induced unemployment
Pessimists	old	Arndt 1944; Lewis 1949; Youngson 1969	Poor	No	Poor	Yes	Yes	No
Optimists	old	Richardson 1961, 1965; Matthews 1964; Aldcroft 1967	Good	Yes	Good	Some	Little	No
Optimists	new	Benjamin and Kochin 1979	Good	—	Good	Cyclical	No	Yes
Pessimists	new	Hatton 1980, 1983; Tunzelmann 1982; Broadberry 1982, 1983	Poor	No	Poor	Yes	Yes	No

Figure 1.2 A taxonomy of interwar economic historiography
Source: Derived from Broadberry (1982).

which suggested a much improved growth performance. Contemporaneously, there was initiated what was to become the infamous old–new industries debate (see Alford 1972, ch. 2), the old optimists claiming that the period saw an acceleration in the rate of structural change, with heavy unemployment as a largely unavoidable consequence. In this view, therefore, heavy unemployment was a manifestation of market efficiency, rather than the converse. Consequently, Keynesian remedies were now inappropriate, indeed largely counterproductive as they would have inhibited structural change and worsened the performance of the real economy.

The interpretation of the interwar economy offered by the old optimists, though questioned to a degree, initially found substantial favour, so that it had almost become the new orthodoxy by the later 1960s. Its hegemony, however, proved short-lived – rather ironically as it transpires. For the challenge from the new pessimists was in part a reaction to the new optimists; the result, a growing body of literature which has sought to reaffirm the traditional belief in the efficacy of the Keynesian solution to interwar unemployment.

The form of this most recent phase of the debate is as follows. The new optimists are represented by Benjamin and Kochin (1979), their reaffirmation of the old optimists' belief in market efficiency being couched in terms of an explanation of interwar unemployment as benefit-induced rather than as a consequence of accelerated structural change. The new pessimists' literature is in part a reaction to this; it also has a rather longer lineage, deriving from pre-existing doubts about the old optimists' thesis.

The debate continues, though mainly through the medium of conferences and unpublished papers, so that its effects upon the broader literature have as yet been slight (see, however, Broadberry 1983 and Hatton 1983). Whilst the issues raised above are treated more fully in chapter 2, we should note at this stage that the existence of this debate widens considerably the questions requiring attention in this study. In addition to the question normally addressed, could Keynesian policies have been adopted in the 1930s, we now need to question more seriously whether they would have mitigated unemployment and what the consequences would have been for broader economic performance.

CHAPTER TWO

MASS UNEMPLOYMENT AND THE INTERWAR BRITISH ECONOMY

Next to war, unemployment has been the most widespread, most insidious, and most corroding malady of our generation: it is the specific social disease of western civilization in our time.

(*The Times*, 23 January 1943)

An analysis of the magnitude and characteristics of interwar unemployment is a necessary prelude to our investigation of policy. This is undertaken in the first section of this chapter; the second surveys the cyclical and trend course of the British economy 1929–39; and the final section discusses certain policy constraints which resulted from Britain's economic difficulties.

1 UNEMPLOYMENT

Without in any sense seeking to diminish the historical significance of this experience of mass unemployment, three points should be made at the outset of this study.

1 As was recognized as early as 1950, 'the persistence of heavy unemployment [may legitimately have] given the interwar years a bad name', but the concentration on this one feature of the period has also served to obscure the contemporaneous progress in productivity and real wages (Allen 1950, 464).

MASS UNEMPLOYMENT AND THE INTERWAR ECONOMY   11

2 Contemporaries tended to misunderstand and in some ways exaggerate unemployment in statistical terms (Booth and Glynn 1975).
3 The conventional indicators of unemployment are imperfect and potentially misleading, both as a basis for the investigation of the causes of unemployment, and as a means of identifying appropriate policy responses. Ideally, they should be supplemented by study of unemployment and vacancies (U/V analysis), unemployment duration and frictional unemployment (Worswick 1976).

Macro labour market

The courses of employment and unemployment are given in figure 2.1 for the period 1921–38. Two different series are presented for unemployment: (A) Feinstein's (1972) estimates based on the total working population; and (B) the national insurance returns, the former being a revision of the latter which did not cover the whole of the labour force.

The national insurance series is an imperfect indicator of interwar unemployment. On the one hand, its incomplete coverage results in an understatement of the numbers unemployed. On the other, as Census data reveal, the rate of unemployment for insured persons was nearly

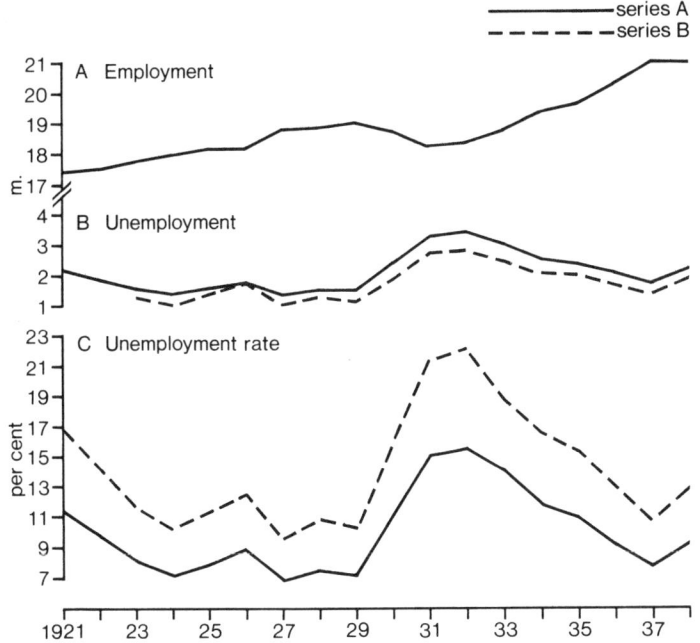

Figure 2.1 Employment and unemployment 1921–38
Sources: Series A: Feinstein (1972, table 57). Series B: HMSO (1971, tables 160, 163).

one-third higher than that for the labour force as a whole, so that the series overstates the unemployment rate. Thus, throughout the rest of this study, Feinstein's series is used, this being a reasonably accurate representation of unemployment amongst the total labour force. On occasion, however, it is also necessary to use the more limited national insurance series since this was the most important monthly macroeconomic indicator available to interwar governments.

Both series in figure 2.1 show the marked cyclical fluctuation of the unemployment rate: the range of variations for series (A) is from a low-point of 6.8 per cent in 1927 to a peak of 15.6 per cent in 1932, while the figures for series (B) are 9.7 and 22.1 per cent respectively. The average rates of unemployment for the period 1921–38 will therefore also differ significantly as between the two series, being 10.0 per cent for (A) and 14.2 per cent for (B).

The trend rate of unemployment between the wars undoubtedly exceeded that of the prewar period, though by how much is difficult to determine with any precision as there are major statistical problems associated with the available unemployment series (Beveridge 1944, 72–3; Garside 1980, ch. 1). Furthermore, the usefulness of comparisons between the two periods is lessened by an appreciation that pre-1914 unemployment was a fundamentally different phenomenon, that of chronic non-Keynesian labour underutilization (Matthews 1968, 564–5). Whatever the precise position might be, the interwar period stands in stark contrast to the postwar record – an average unemployment rate between 1948–70 of only 1.7 per cent (Wood 1972, table 1). The concern felt by contemporaries for the high level of unemployment was thus not without foundation. The unemployment problem cannot be explained away by reference to the inadequacies of the data; the economic loss of unemployment was of too great a dimension (T. Thomas 1981, 333–5).

With these preliminary comments in mind, the point should now be made that, whilst there was an immense economic loss as a result of mass unemployment and while Keynesian stabilization theory would suggest that this could have been reduced or eradicated by deficit-financing, *the unemployment problem was not monolithic, nor monocausal* (Beveridge 1936). In particular, it is contended that it is erroneous to interpret the period solely in terms of deficient demand, for such interpretations seek a uniformity of experience which was non-existent and fail to take full account of the varied and changing characteristics of interwar unemployment. These will now be explored in some detail, beginning with the relationship between population and labour supply.

A study of Feinstein's series for civilian employment reveals two features of interest: first, that it was not until as late as 1935 that the level of employment prevailing in 1920 was again obtained; secondly, that over the whole period 1920–38 total civilian employment grew by 7.4 per cent but the total working population grew by a far greater amount (by 14.0 per cent). Thus, on trend, unemployment rose: from 1.4 million in 1924, to 1.5 million in 1929 and 1.8 million in 1937 (unemployment rates moving in line, at 7.2, 7.3 and 7.8 per cent respectively).

A comparison with prewar trends provides a partial explanation for this upward shift in the trend of unemployment. First, changes in labour supply need to be taken into account. The rate of growth of the working population is a function of the rate of growth of the total population, changes in the age distribution of the population, and changes in age- and sex-specific participation rates. Before 1914 the rate of growth of the working population had approximately equalled that of the growth of total population: at annual averages of 0.99 and 0.85 per cent respectively over 1880–1914. During the interwar years population growth declined quite sharply,[1] to an annual rate of growth of 0.46 per cent over 1920–39. If prewar trends had continued, a fall in the rate of growth of the working population would have resulted. Such trends, however, did not continue: against the 9.2 per cent increase in population over 1920–39 there was actually a 14.1 per cent rise in the working population (Feinstein 1972, tables 55, 57).

The divergence between these two rates stemmed from two influences:

1 The fall in the birth-rate led to an increase in the proportion of the population of working age: from 63.8 per cent in 1913 to 69.5 per cent in 1939 (Feinstein 1972, table 56).
2 There was a rise in the proportion of women taking paid employment: female participation rates rising from 32.6 per cent in 1921 to 35.8 per cent in 1938 (LCES 1972, table F).

Therefore, as Aldcroft (1970a, 136) concluded, 'had the pre-war relationships between the two variables remained the same the growth of the labour force would have been lower and unemployment less severe'.

While it is clear that unemployment was exacerbated by the action of demographic and sociocultural trends upon labour supply, more complex issues arise when considering labour demand. For example, much of the literature on the interwar period, and particularly that of the old optimists (see pp. 18–19), incorporates rather imprecise notions of the unemployment problem as in part the consequence of improved productivity performance. Thus Aldcroft (1970a, 135), following Matthews (1964), maintained that interwar unemployment was exacerbated by an upward shift in the trend rate of growth of total factor productivity (TFP) relative to the period 1899–1913 (when the principal stimulus to GDP growth had been the labour input). Although the recent revisions to Matthews's original data (Matthews et al. 1982) now suggest that the growth of TFP between the wars was only marginally higher than before the war (see table 2.3, p. 21), Aldcroft's proposition requires more fundamental questioning.

Table 2.1 Regional unemployment rates (insured persons aged 16–64), Ministry of Labour Divisions, 1923–37

	1923	1929	1932	1937*
London	10.1	5.6	13.5	6.3
South east	9.2	5.6	14.3	6.7
South west	10.6	8.1	17.1	7.8
Midlands	10.7	9.3	20.1	7.2
North east	12.2	13.7	28.5	11.0
North west	14.5	13.3	25.8	14.0
Northern†	..	..	..	17.9
Scotland	14.3	12.1	27.7	15.7
Wales	6.4	19.3	36.5	22.3
Inner Britain‡	..	6.3	16.0	5.9
Outer Regions‡	..	12.9	28.5	14.5
GREAT BRITAIN	11.6	10.3	21.9	10.6

Sources: Daly (1979, table 1); Beck (1951, table 18).

Notes:
* The administrative divisions were rearranged in August 1936, thereby precluding exact comparison between the 1937 figures and earlier years.
† The northern division, created in August 1936, with Newcastle as its nodal point, was based upon parts of the old north-eastern and north-western divisions.
‡ Figures are for June each year. Inner Britain is here defined as Greater London, the south and the midlands; the outer regions as northern England, Wales, Scotland and Northern Ireland.

Verification of such a labour displacement thesis requires information about the form of technical progress: whether Hicks neutral, capital- or labour-saving (Heertje 1977). Only if the latter can be established will labour displacement result. Such empirical evidence as is available for interwar Britain suggests that technical progress was indeed Hicks non-neutral, but capital- rather than labour-saving, there being a capital-saving element in TFP growth which kept down investment in some sectors (Matthews *et al.* 1982, 541). Thus the case for technologically-induced unemployment is not proven, though further research is needed before more definite conclusions can be drawn. In particular, information is required about the price elasticity of demand for output, from which to test the implicit counterfactual to the old optimists' case: that a lower growth of TFP would not have impaired price competitiveness – with consequent effects upon exports and import penetration – or investment,

Table 2.2 Regional employment growth (insured persons aged 16–64), Ministry of Labour Divisions, 1923–37

	% change in employment			
	1923–29	1929–32	1932–37	1923–37
London	20.4	−1.9	22.9	45.2
South east	26.9	0.3	25.3	59.4
South west	17.0	−2.3	22.1	39.6
Midlands	11.0	−8.8	30.8	32.4
North east	5.1	−12.4	24.0	14.1
North west	8.7	−12.1	17.2	12.0
Northern	−1.4	−21.6	31.3	1.6
Scotland	4.8	−13.2	22.6	11.6
Wales	−15.4	−18.9	25.1	−14.2
GREAT BRITAIN	10.0	−8.9	23.9	24.3

Source: Calculated from Fogarty (1945, table 5).

which *inter alia* were the determinants of GDP growth and labour demand.

Regional/industrial labour markets

Although serious when viewed at the macro level, the interwar unemployment problem was made more acute by its uneven incidence as between regions and industries. Indeed, this is increasingly seen as its most important feature. These disparities were a vivid manifestation of the serious structural problem confronting the interwar British economy: the secular decline of the staple industries (coal, cotton and other traditional textiles, iron and steel, shipbuilding and mechanical engineering). The regional problem resulted from their location, a strong concentration in only four regions: north-east and north-west England, south Wales and lowland Scotland.

Regional employment trends are summarized in tables 2.1 and 2.2. The regional disparities are immediately apparent from both the figures for unemployment and employment growth, disparities which widened over time. These trends reflected both the high levels of unemployment in the declining staple industries (concentrated in the outer regions)[2] and the pattern of location of the new, expanding industries of the period, one strongly directed towards regions with already lower than average unemployment (inner Britain).

The regional problem thus assumed two dimensions: the very high rates of unemployment of the industries centred on these depressed regions and their below average rates of employment growth. In addition, cyclical factors were also of importance in contributing to the regions' problems. The outer regions were heavily committed to producer goods industries which, as with investment in GDP, experienced the most pronounced cyclical fluctuations in output and employment. By contrast, the more prosperous regions of inner Britain had more diversified industrial bases – in particular a growth of consumer goods industries – and this lessened their susceptibility to the worst effects of cyclical depression.

The extreme concentration of unemployment on the staple industries, with its consequences for certain regions, forms the centrepiece of recent arguments which have sought to question the traditional view of interwar unemployment as primarily demand deficient and as unduly high as compared with the preceding period. Thus Booth and Glynn (1975, 617) contend that 'National average rates of unemployment during most of the interwar period were probably not significantly higher than the rate which prevailed before 1914', account being taken of the cyclical unemployment of 1920–2 and 1929–33 and the regional problem.[3] This reinterpretation has been carried too far, for Booth and Glynn understate the increase in interwar over pre-1914 unemployment (Hatton 1977), while, in any case, it is debatable whether one can abstract away from the two depression phases in this manner. Nevertheless, the regional problem is of great importance, having implications for the effectiveness of stabilization policies. These can be introduced by a study of the dynamics of the interwar labour market.

It is axiomatic that the number of people on the unemployment register rises or falls as the flow of newly unemployed coming onto the register exceeds or falls short of the flow of people leaving the register to take up employment, and that the duration of unemployment is consequently as important an indicator of labour market conditions as the absolute numbers unemployed. As Cripps and Tarling (1974, 289) stress:

> An understanding of the dynamics of this process is important both for judging policies designed to mitigate the evils of prolonged unemployment and for interpreting the unemployment statistics as a measure of the pressure of demand in the labour market.

Thus, the true significance of Britain's interwar unemployment problem lay not only in the high absolute levels of unemployment in certain depressed regions but in the prolonged nature of this unemployment and its worsening as the period progressed.

Although no data are available prior to 1929, Ministry of Labour figures collected thereafter show that the average duration of unemployment rose significantly over the 1930s (Beveridge 1944, table 8); while other evidence suggests that this deterioration was in fact evident from the early 1920s onwards (HMSO 1928). In September 1929, 89.1 per cent of the total had been unemployed for less than 6 months (short-period unemployment) and only 4.7 per cent for more than 12 months (long-period unemployment). By August 1937, however, short-period unemployment stood at 65.7 per cent of the total while long-period unemployment had grown to 24.3 per cent, and had in fact worsened over the recovery period (from 16.4 per cent in 1932). In terms of absolute numbers, the long-period unemployed had grown from 45,100 in 1929 to 287,821 in 1937, by which date they had become 'the most serious element in the problem of unemployment' (Beveridge 1937a, 11). As Beveridge (1944, 66) rightly commented, 'The legacy of the Great Depression was a host of long-period unemployed – nearly 300,000 men and women in enforced idleness – for whom continuous money payments were a manifestly inadequate provision.'

The policy implications of this long-period unemployment problem stemmed from its regional nature. For example, in 1937, 83.8 per cent of those unemployed at 21 June in London (which had a mean unemployment rate for the year of 6.3 per cent) had been unemployed for less than 6 months and 71 per cent for less than 3 months, while in the northern region (mean unemployment rate of 17.9 per cent), only 36.6 per cent had been unemployed for less than 3 months and 47.6 per cent for less than 6 months, with 40.3 per cent unemployed for over 12 months (Beveridge 1944, 66–7, table 9; Middleton 1985).

In broad measure, all the depressed areas experienced similar problems to those of northern England: regional unemployment rates significantly in excess of the national average, and characteristics of unemployment in these areas – by age and skill, as well as duration – such as to cast doubt on the effectiveness of a centrally directed stimulus to aggregate demand as a *sufficient* solution for these areas' problems. This becomes clearer when unemployment is viewed at the sub-regional or local level, the level at which the disastrous effects of an unsatisfactory industrial structure were most pronounced.

The astronomical rates of unemployment recorded in certain towns at the depth of the depression (January 1933) are well known – for example, 91 per cent in Saltburn and 77 per cent in Jarrow (McCrone 1969, 91). Less well known, and infrequently cited, was the accompanying long-period unemployment problem for many depressed area towns. This was vividly brought to the public's attention by a Pilgrim Trust (1938, 75) survey of November 1936 which found that, even after four years of strong national recovery, 71 per cent of the unemployed in Crook and 45 per cent in the Rhondda had been unemployed for five years or more, as compared with only 3 per cent in the prosperous southern town of Deptford.

The structural problems confronting the British economy, made manifest in the case of these and other depressed area towns, and the search for possible solutions, forced interwar governments against a range of problems far wider in scope than those posed simply by the desirability or otherwise of a management of demand. To the economic authorities, the desirability of a revival of demand at local levels was not in doubt. More questionable was whether the existing industrial base of many of these areas was capable of responding, to the degree required, to a general stimulus of demand; and if not, whether government should assume direct responsibility for industrial reconstruction or whether it should retain its previous *laissez-faire* stance.

The still current problem of declining staple industries was first faced by interwar governments. Having begun to widen their responsibilities for economic and social affairs in the early years of the century, a *laissez-faire* stance would have been both inappropriate and politically unrealistic. Yet the characteristics of interwar unemployment made comprehensive solutions more difficult. Of course, at the same time, its seriousness made them more imperative. Of vital concern also were the cyclical course of the British economy and the various constraints upon policy, subjects to which we now turn.

2 THE BRITISH ECONOMY 1929–39

As a result of detailed study in recent years, the record of the interwar economy is well known and need not be recounted in any detail. Accordingly, the following discussion is limited in scope, and focuses upon those features of the economy which are pertinent to the issues considered in later chapters. It begins with a fuller discussion of an issue first raised in the introduction: that of the performance of the real economy.

Reference was made earlier to the fact that the persistence of heavy unemployment acted to obscure other more favourable developments of the period. The traditional interpretation (the old pessimists') undoubtedly paid excessive attention to the declining staple industries. Hence the current view, one generally accepted until recently, is that the period 'was by no means as black as has been painted' (Lomax 1964, 15), for substantial progress was made, at both micro and macro levels.

In this view, one particularly associated with the work of Aldcroft and Richardson (the old optimists), stress is placed upon, on the one hand, the growth of the new consumer goods industries and the enlargement of the service sector, and, on the other, the acceleration of the underlying growth rate. Put simply, the old optimists contend that the improved growth performance derived from a combination of these structural changes at the industry level and an upward shift in TFP associated with more rapid technological change (see pp. 13–14).

A clear implication of this view is that the heavy unemployment of the period was a manifestation of market efficiency (i.e. technological unemployment), there being no necessity for a Keynesian policy intervention, though rigidities in the labour market are admitted in the explanation of the regional problem's persistence. The dismissal of the Keynesian solution to interwar unemployment has also been put by Benjamin and Kochin (1979), the new optimists. Their reasoning and line of enquiry, however, an investigation into the effects of unemployment benefits upon aggregate labour supply, differs markedly from that of the old optimists; as do their conclusions. While admitting that cyclical factors operated upon unemployment during the depressions of 1920-2 and 1929-32, they argue that the persistence of mass unemployment

> was due to the operation of an unemployment insurance scheme that paid benefits that were high relative to wages and available subject to few restrictions. We estimate that the insurance system raised the unemployment rate by five to eight percentage points on average and that in the absence of the system unemployment would have been at normal levels through much of the period.
> (Benjamin and Kochin 1979, 441)

It is claimed that the insurance system both encouraged workers to enter the labour force, so as to register as unemployed, and also provided pecuniary incentives to substitute leisure and job-searching for work. Their thesis rests upon two foundations: a time-series regression relating unemployment to the deviation of output from trend and the benefit–wage ratio (the replacement rate); and cross-sectional evidence on the impact of the insurance system upon unemployment amongst juveniles and married women.

Benjamin and Kochin's (1979, 474) contention that 'The army of the unemployed standing watch in Britain at the publication of the *General Theory* was largely a volunteer army' not surprisingly evoked much adverse comment, with their econometrics forming the focus for debate. Such has been the wealth of critical work directed against this thesis that we need only mention a selection of the counter-arguments available from the large and varied menu on offer. Thus, for example, Ormerod and Worswick (1982, 402-7) have shown that the results for the coefficient on the benefit–wage ratio are highly sensitive to the sample period chosen, while Irish (1980) has cast further doubt upon this key coefficient by demonstrating that it loses its statistical significance if other trend variables, such as population, are included in the regression. Their model cannot explain the (very pronounced) regional unemployment pattern (Jones 1983); while their cross-sectional evidence is also open to serious doubt (Hatton 1980). The full Benjamin and Kochin thesis has not survived the comprehensive scrutiny to which it has been subject.

While few would question that the insurance system generated some voluntary unemployment, for there is survey evidence available to this effect (Pilgrim Trust 1938), the balance of evidence suggests that the effect was limited.

It remains to comment upon the old optimists' interpretation of the interwar British economy, one that has been much criticized by the new pessimists. In particular, the importance of the new industries, the centrepiece of the arguments about structural change and improved productivity growth, have seriously been called into question. More generally, there are considerable difficulties associated with growth calculations between the wars because of the wide amplitude of cyclical fluctuations. Whilst growth might have been respectable as compared with earlier or later periods, the point remains that demand still failed to grow at a rate sufficient to match the growth of the labour force.

A thoroughgoing reappraisal of the Aldcroft–Richardson view has yet to be undertaken. Nevertheless, serious doubts have been raised about its essentials. Two aspects in particular require further comment since they relate to policy issues.

First, Aldcroft (1966, 234) contends that 'the sharp contraction of some of the older industries was a positive long-term advantage', since by releasing resources they permitted an acceleration of structural change, and the creation of a development block of new, high-growth, industries which underlay the rapid recovery from the 1929–32 depression. As Howson (1975, 63) comments:

> The flaw in this argument is the assumption of a limited stock of resources, limited in the aggregate by exogenous technical progress and within that aggregate 'over-committed' to the production of the old staples by 'structural' factors. Technical progress and structural factors are not independent of aggregate demand and with one million unemployed there could have been more expansion in the new industries even if the old were not declining, if aggregate demand had been growing sufficiently to create profit expectations favourable to investment in the new industries (primarily domestic-based).

Furthermore, the Aldcroft view ignores the facts that:

1. in terms of employment, investment and output, the new industries were still of limited quantitative significance even by the later 1930s, and their contribution to the absorption of labour released by the staple industries was overshadowed by the employment growth of the service sector (Dowie 1968; Buxton 1975);
2. a recovery of the staple industries would have stimulated demand for the products of the new industries, both directly (induced demand) and indirectly through the operation of the multiplier process on aggregate demand;

3 since the external balance was precarious throughout the 1930s, a recovery of the export industries was necessary to prevent an external constraint to increased domestic demand (see pp. 27–8, 178–9).

The authorities' preoccupation with a revival of the staple industries was thus not misplaced. Nor it seems was Keynes's concern with aggregate demand and the necessity for its enhancement.

Secondly, quantitative reference should be made to the interwar growth performance. The problems presented by such an exercise are particularly acute in the case of the interwar period. Apart from the perennial problem of attempting to isolate the trend from the cycle, cyclical fluctuations were particularly marked during this period, thus presenting difficulties in the selection of suitable initial and terminal dates for intertemporal comparisons. Indeed, much of the initial overstatement of interwar growth stemmed from Aldcroft's choice of a 'variety of base years and sub-periods which distort[ed] the long-term trend' (Alford 1972, 20).

The only legitimate dates for intertemporal comparisons are 1924 and 1937 (with an intermediate date of 1929), years of broadly comparable capacity utilization. On this basis, the most recent estimates – reported in table 2.3 – suggest that real GDP grew on average by 2.2 per cent per annum between 1924–37, a result that compares favourably with earlier periods, especially when account is taken of the economic loss resulting from the persistence of mass unemployment.

Table 2.3 Growth of GDP, labour, capital, total factor input and total factor productivity 1856–1973 (annual % growth rates)

	GDP	Labour*	Quality adjusted labour†	Capital	Contributions to TFI — Quality adjusted labour	Capital	TFI	TFP
1856–73	2.2	0.0	1.4	1.9	0.8	0.8	1.6	0.6
1873–1913	1.8	0.9	1.7	1.9	1.0	0.8	1.8	0.0
1913–24	−0.1	−2.3	−0.4	0.9	−0.3	0.4	0.1	−0.2
1924–37	2.2	1.5	2.1	1.8	1.5	0.5	2.0	0.2
1937–51	1.8	0.1	1.1	1.1	0.7	0.4	1.1	0.7
1951–73	2.8	−0.5	0.1	3.2	0.1	0.9	1.0	1.8

Source: Matthews *et al.* (1982, tables 2.1, 4.7, 16.2).

Notes:
* Labour measured in man-hours.
† Adjustments for changes due to age, sex, nationality and education of labour force, and changes in intensity of work.

Whilst, on trend, the behaviour of GDP approximated to that of earlier periods, cyclical fluctuations were far more pronounced. Matthews *et al.* (1982, table 10.1) calculate that the amplitude of GDP fluctuations was nearly twice as strong 1920–37 as 1873–1913, and between two and four times as strong as postwar cycles (1951–73), the primary explanation being the strong cyclical behaviour of exports. In addition, even after allowance for lags, proportional fluctuations in employment in the postwar period (to 1973) have been not much more than one-half of those in GDP, while in the interwar period employment fluctuated by about as much as GDP. The seriousness of interwar cycles is clearly evident from figure 2.2, the range of fluctuations in GDP (over 12 percentage points) being far greater than any postwar experience.

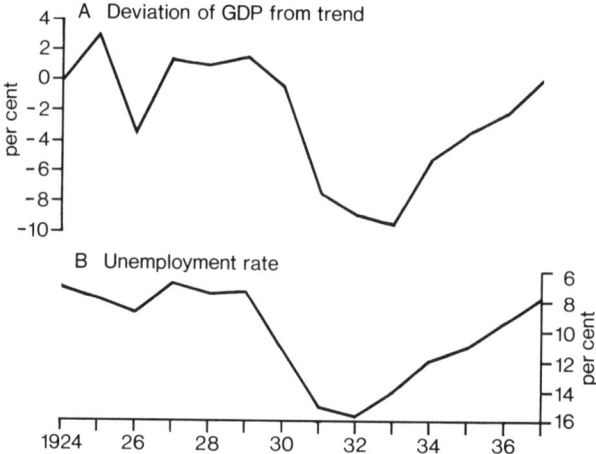

Figure 2.2 Fluctuations in real GDP and unemployment 1924–37
Source: Calculated from Feinstein (1972, tables 5, 57).
Notes:
A: GDP measured at 1938 market prices. The deviation of GDP from trend is measured as the percentage by which actual GDP varied from what it would have been had GDP grown constantly at the observed average rate of growth between 1924 and 1937.
B: Numbers unemployed as a percentage of the civilian working population.

Turning now to the more limited period under review (1929–39), the general picture of cyclical movements is summarized in figure 2.3 which records annual figures for real GDP and its components. Three subperiods, or cyclical episodes, can be delineated: depression 1929–32, recovery 1932–7, recession and rearmament 1937–9. The main features of each episode are now considered in turn.

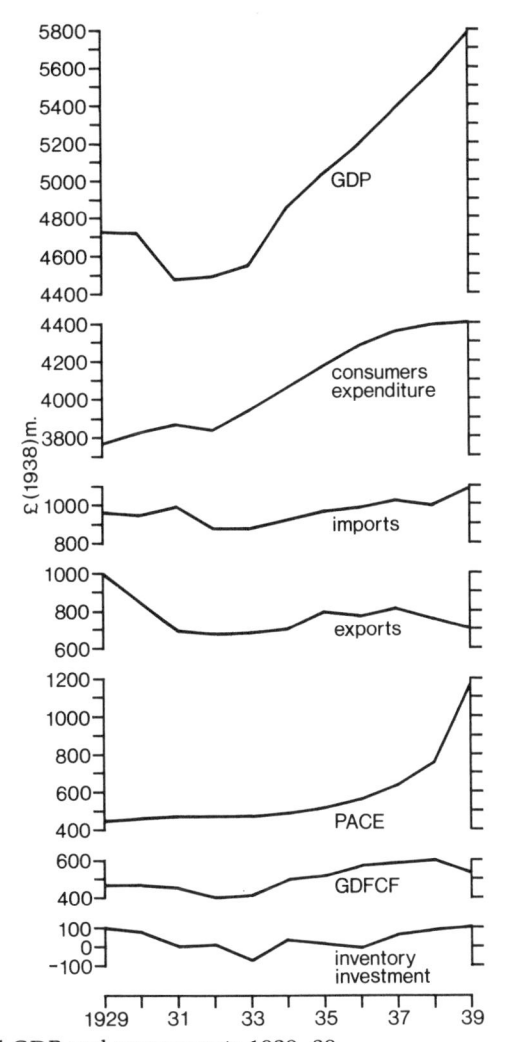

Figure 2.3 Real GDP and components 1929–39
Source: Feinstein (1972, table 5).

Depression 1929–32

The generally accepted interpretation of this episode is that the 'economic blizzard of 1929–32 was something that struck Britain from outside' (Sayers 1967a, 53), depression being transmitted from the US – first, through an indirect effect, whereby the curtailment of US foreign lending from mid-1928 led to a reduction in purchasing power of those countries which had a large demand for UK exports; secondly, and more directly, by the cutting of US import demand for UK goods once depression had become established in the US (Corner 1956).

Exports both led at the upper turning-point (1929 III) and experienced the most pronounced losses over the subsequent depression period. As table 2.4 shows exports fell by 32.2 per cent over 1929–32 as compared with a fall of only 4.9 per cent in GDP (the falls at current prices were much greater, respectively 47.3 and 9.5 per cent). Depression was not initiated by the bursting of a domestic boom; Britain had in fact failed to share fully in the world boom of 1925–9. Furthermore, as Richardson (1967, 6) argues, the relative weakness of the previous upswing was to be a major factor moderating the depression after 1929.

The mildness of the depression can be seen from table 2.4, depression being only serious in the indicators for unemployment and exports. There were no autonomous internal sources of falling income, and a high floor to activity was ensured by the continued growth of consumers expenditure, a result of the downward inflexibility of wages and favourable movements in the terms of trade.

Furthermore, the UK depression was mild compared with the experience of other industrial economies: industrial production and incomes fell less than half as much as in Germany and the US. The experiences of unemployment, however, were fairly similar. Unemployment (series B) rose from a lowpoint of 9.6 per cent in June 1929 to a maximum of 23.0 per cent in January 1933, an increase of over 1.8 million to 2.979 million insured unemployed. When adjusted for seasonal factors, the actual maximum of cyclical unemployment was reached in 1932 III, the lower turning-point for other economic indicators.

Given the severity of the depression experienced by the export trades, and their geographical concentration, the most serious impact of the depression came at the regional level (tables 2.1 and 2.2). As is argued later, the form of the depression posed problems for any attempt to stabilize demand by conventional (Keynesian) measures.

Recovery 1932–7

Following the abandonment of the gold standard in September 1931 there occurred a short-lived recovery (1931 III–IV), evident particularly in the export industries. The contemporaneous tightening of monetary and fiscal policy ensured that this recovery was not supported by a domestic stimulus and thus proved unsustainable, depression forces being temporarily re-established from early 1932.

It was not until 1932 III that recovery became properly established. The subsequent upswing (to 1937 III) was both strong and of (historically) long duration. Over 1932–7 GDP grew by 20.4 per cent, industrial production by 45.8 per cent and employment by 14.1 per cent. Unfortunately, the

Table 2.4 Economic indicators 1929–39 (% changes)

	1929–30	1930–1	1931–2	1929–32	1932–3	1933–4	1934–5	1935–6	1936–7	1932–7	1937–8	1938–9	1937–9
A. National income and components (constant 1938 prices)													
1 GDP	−0.1	−5.1	+0.3	−4.9	+1.1	+6.8	+3.8	+3.1	+4.3	+20.4	+3.0	+3.9	+7.0
2 Consumers expenditure	+1.5	+1.1	−0.6	+2.0	+2.6	+2.9	+2.8	+2.9	+1.7	+13.5	+0.8	+0.5	+1.4
3 Imports	−1.4	+3.8	−10.8	−8.6	+0.1	+4.4	+4.9	+2.5	+3.6	+16.5	−2.2	+8.9	+6.5
4 Exports	−13.9	−19.4	−2.2	−32.2	+1.3	+3.8	+12.8	−2.9	+5.1	+21.1	−6.5	−7.5	−13.6
5 PACE	+2.5	+2.4	0.0	+5.0	+1.1	+2.3	+6.8	+9.1	+11.6	+34.5	+19.5	+51.4	+80.9
6 GDFCF	+0.4	−1.9	−12.8	−14.1	+3.3	+21.8	+4.0	+9.1	+3.4	+47.5	+1.4	−10.5	−9.2
B. Other													
7 Industrial production (constant prices)	−4.3	−6.5	−0.4	−10.8	+6.6	+10.0	+7.6	+9.0	+6.0	+45.8	−2.7	..	..
8 Employment	−1.6	−2.7	+0.5	−3.7	+2.2	+3.2	+1.5	+3.0	+3.4	+14.1	0.0	+3.8	+3.8
9 Unemployment:													
(series A)	+60.0	+37.5	+3.0	+126.7	−8.8	−16.1	−7.7	−12.5	−14.3	−47.1	+22.2	−40.9	−27.8
(series B)	+58.3	+42.1	+3.7	+133.3	−10.7	−16.0	−4.8	−15.0	−17.6	−50.0	+35.7	−26.3	0.0
10 Retail prices	−3.7	−6.5	−2.8	−12.4	−2.8	+0.7	+1.4	+2.9	+5.6	+7.8	+0.7	+3.3	+3.9
11 Terms of trade	+9.2	+9.9	+0.7	+20.8	+2.8	−2.7	−1.4	−2.8	−5.8	−9.7	+9.2	−1.4	+7.6
12 Gross profits	−11.9	−10.1	−4.4	−24.3	+9.5	+8.5	+8.9	+12.2	+6.7	+54.9	−4.0	..	..

Sources: (1)–(6) calculated from Feinstein (1972, table 5); (7) ibid., table 8; (8)–(9) as figure 2.1; (10) Feinstein (1972, table 65); (11) ibid., table 64; (12) ibid., table 26.

reduction of unemployment was not as impressive: from a (seasonally unadjusted) peak of 2.979 million (23.0 per cent) in January 1933 insured unemployment fell to a minimum of 1.404 million (9.7 per cent) in September 1937 (the comparable figure for June 1929, the previous upper turning-point, was 1.176 million).

Although impressive when viewed in aggregate terms, the recovery was uneven in its rate of progress and affected different sectors to varying degrees, characteristics which were to have important implications for economic policy. The first stage of recovery, from 1932 III to 1933 IV, saw a vigorous revival of activity, and by the end of 1933 'the economic situation was more favourable than at any time since June 1930. Abroad, on the other hand, the economic outlook remained bleak' (Richardson 1967, 28). The recovery was thus initially domestically based, the export trades remained depressed – a reflection of the slow revival of world trade and the not unconnected increasing economic nationalism of the period. At a national level, the unemployment rate fell from 23.0 per cent to 17.5 per cent over January–December 1933, but this fall was extremely uneven as between the various regions. Against a 23.2 per cent reduction in the aggregate numbers of insured unemployed, the regional figures were 32.4 per cent for London and 34.3 per cent for the south east, but only 18.8 per cent for the north west and 9.3 per cent for Wales (HMSO 1971, table 162).

These disparities continued throughout 1934, a year in which the rate of recovery slackened as the initial stimulatory forces became exhausted, exports failing to rise as an offset to the reduced growth of domestic demand. Recovery was resumed, however, from the spring of 1935 and tended to assume different characteristics from the preceding phase. First, costs began to rise with increasing intensity from late 1935 and shortages of skilled labour developed. Secondly, world trade began to recover and the export industries to revive, thereby ensuring a more broadly based reduction in regional unemployment rates. Finally, residential construction, which had been crucial in the upturn, started to slacken, but a revival of non-residential construction and producer goods output acted as an offset so that recovery was able to continue unabated until 1937 III. There then occurred a short, sharp recession.

Recession and rearmament 1937–9

As with the turning-point of 1929–30, exports played a crucial role in initiating the downturn of 1937–8, and for depressing demand thereafter (Phelps Brown and Shackle 1939, 125). From the behaviour of GDP in table 2.4 it is not immediately apparent that 1937–8 constitutes a recession period. The course of unemployment, however, portrays a different and more illuminating picture. In fact, the downturn of 1937–8 was sharper than that of 1929–30, but the recession was not general (J. A. Brown 1940). While export volumes and consumer durables were both seriously affected, output of some industries continued to grow under the stimulus of the rearmament programme.

Insured unemployment rose from a lowpoint of 1.404 million (9.7 per cent) to a (seasonally unadjusted) peak of 2.134 million (14.2 per cent) in January 1939. The recession had, however, run its course by mid-1938, although a definite upturn was not evident until 1938 IV. Thereafter, recovery proceeded rapidly and, as is shown in later chapters, was largely determined by fiscal operations.

3 POLICY ISSUES AND POLICY CONSTRAINTS: A CONSPECTUS

It remains in this final section to discuss some broader aspects of the British economy of the 1930s, their relation to policy issues, and the way in which certain economic conditions – conditions largely unrelated to theoretical questions – were to constrain policy.

First, the course of the British economy should be placed in an international context. The mildness of the depression in Britain, as compared with the experience of other industrial economies, has already been noted. Mention should also be made of the fact that recovery occurred earlier in Britain than in many other countries, was stronger and more complete (Richardson 1967, ch. 12). In particular, the case of the US economy under the Roosevelt administration was instructive: its limited recovery was taken as an object lesson by the British authorities of the dangers associated with unorthodox policies.[4] It therefore also served to reinforce the authorities' commitment to orthodox policies in Britain.

The precarious external balance was also to limit policy and the scope for complete economic recovery (see table 2.5). Contrary to the Aldcroft–Richardson view that the traditional interpretation of the interwar period placed undue emphasis upon poor export performance, the behaviour of exports – both on trend and over the cycle – was the most disturbing feature of the economy at that time, and one of the most potent constraints to the achievement of full employment.

Exports consisted primarily of capital and high-income goods, overseas demand for which was highly income elastic. The area composition of British exports also made demand potentially unstable. Imports, on the other hand, were still dominated by foodstuffs and raw materials, the income elasticity of which was much lower. An autonomous fall in world incomes, therefore, led to an immediate worsening of the British balance of payments. For example, the depression phase saw a move from a £96 million current account surplus in 1929 to a deficit of £103 million in 1931 (a deterioration of 4.4 percentage points of GDP, quite unparalleled with anything of post-1945 experience), though this reflected changes in net

Table 2.5 Balance of payments: current account as % of GDP 1929–39

	Exports	Imports	Merchandise trade balance	Invisible balance	Current balance
1929	18.0	23.6	−5.6	7.6	2.0
1930	14.3	20.3	−6.0	6.8	0.8
1931	10.6	18.0	−7.4	5.0	−2.4
1932	9.9	15.0	−5.1	3.9	−1.2
1933	10.0	14.5	−4.5	4.3	−0.2
1934	10.2	15.1	−4.9	4.4	−0.5
1935	11.4	15.3	−3.9	4.4	0.5
1936	10.7	16.0	−5.3	4.7	−0.6
1937	11.6	18.0	−6.4	5.5	−0.9
1938	10.1	15.2	−5.1	4.1	−1.0
1939	8.4	13.4	−5.0	0.8	−4.2

Source: Calculated from Feinstein (1972, tables 3, 37).

invisible earnings as well as the merchandise trade account. In these circumstances, a reflation of British domestic demand (uncoordinated with an international reflation),[5] might have involved serious consequences for the balance of payments, and considerable risks for the continued pre-eminence of London as a world financial centre.

Nor, on trend, was the export position satisfactory. Over the period 1924–37, exports of goods and services fell by 12.2 per cent, while imports rose by 17.5 per cent and GDP by 27.7 per cent (at constant prices). Accordingly, the importance of the foreign trade sector declined: the export/GDP ratio, which had been 0.244 in 1913, fell from 0.218 in 1924 to 0.209 in 1929, and to 0.150 in 1937 (Feinstein 1972, table 5). The full significance of Britain's deteriorating export position is evident when viewed in the context of world trade: UK exports as a proportion of total world trade fell from 13.9 per cent in 1913 to 10.2 per cent in 1937, and in world manufactures from 29.9 per cent to 22.4 per cent (Aldcroft 1970a, 247).

Since the current balance was also deteriorating over this period, from a surplus of 9.3 per cent of GDP in 1913 to a deficit of 0.9 per cent in 1937, and since at least one million were unemployed throughout, a higher level of domestic demand could only have been sustained by measures to rebuild Britain's export industries and/or curtail imports. Even after 1931, when tariffs partially insulated the domestic economy and a more flexible exchange rate policy was possible, a trade-off between full employment and external balance – such as has plagued the post-1945 economy – was a distinct possibility.

A second possible constraint to the achievement of full employment concerned the elasticity of aggregate supply and the related question of the seriousness of Britain's structural unemployment problem. Contemporary economists assumed a practically horizontal supply function in the early stages of recovery,[6] an assumption borne out by the stability of prices over 1932–5. From mid-1935 onwards, however, costs and prices began to rise with increasing intensity – the Board of Trade index of wholesale prices increasing by 27 per cent between July 1935 and its peak in July 1937. This was a reflection not only of rising import prices but also the development of structural imbalances in labour markets, there being sufficient excess demand in some sectors to force up wages despite the continuance of heavy unemployment in many other sectors (Richardson 1967, 31–2, 39, 232). By the time the upper turning-point had been reached in 1937, 'there [were] widespread complaints of shortages of labour and delays in production' (Beveridge 1937b, 181), and this at a time when there were still 1½ million or so unemployed nationally.

Supply constraints thus came into operation long before anything approaching full employment had been attained. Indeed, Richardson (1967, 22) has argued that:

> the similarity between the unemployment levels of 1929 and 1937 suggests that cyclical unemployment had been eliminated by the middle of 1937 and that the continuance of heavy unemployment is to be explained by other causes rather than a failure of recovery.

In this view, cyclical full employment had been reached by 1937 III, and a further stimulus to aggregate demand (irrespective of whether it was private or public sector induced) would not, at least in the short term, have led to further increases in aggregate output. Rather, supply constraints would have ensured that the additional demand was exhibited in rising prices.

Underlying such an argument is the distinction between structural and cyclical unemployment. Although it is difficult to establish satisfactory criteria for the empirical testing of the structural and cyclical components of total unemployment (Howson 1981, 269–73), a practical distinction can be drawn between them. Structural unemployment can be defined as that form of unemployment specific to certain industrial sectors and resulting from technological and market forces which are exogenously determined. Cyclical unemployment, on the other hand, is more general and more readily responsive to changes in aggregate demand (Thirlwall 1969, 20–1).

It should not be inferred, however, that structural unemployment cannot be reduced by an aggregate demand stimulus. Neither economic theory, nor general experience since 1945, would warrant such a conclusion. Nevertheless, it is also clear that certain qualifications need to be made about the efficacy of an aggregate demand stimulus in the circumstances of the interwar period. The serious nature of the regional problem made these circumstances in some sense unusual, while the subsequent continuance of regional imbalances in unemployment rates in the postwar period – when the average pressure of demand has been significantly higher than prewar – suggests that there is no automatic mechanism whereby a spatially uniform equilibrium results in all sectors of labour markets.

This line of enquiry has largely been neglected to date,[7] and while no detailed analysis is here attempted, reference should at least be made to certain relevant considerations.

1 Income multipliers for disadvantaged regions are generally smaller than their national counterparts (Archibald 1967).
2 The depressed areas were handicapped by an unfavourable industrial base, one dominated by declining industries dependent upon export markets.
3 Although migration from the depressed to the more prosperous areas was not insubstantial, there was a discernible 'mismatch' between the labour shed by the staple industries and that required in the expanding sectors.
4 The prolonged nature of unemployment in the depressed areas resulted in a marked deterioration in the quality and potential employability of this substantial constituent of total interwar unemployment. Here, as with the previous difficulty, substantial retraining and government assistance would have been required, existing provisions being manifestly inadequate (Burns 1941, 263–77).

Such issues are explored further in chapter 8, where they are related to official views on the constraints that might lessen the efficacy of deficit-financing and public works schemes. Before turning to policy issues, we conclude that while, *ceteris paribus*, a stimulus to aggregate demand was an appropriate remedy for Britain's interwar unemployment problem, it seems also that this would have had to be supplemented by both selective demand management measures and action to lessen supply constraints.

CHAPTER THREE

THE TREASURY, ECONOMIC POLICY AND PUBLIC EXPENDITURE

A review of the Treasury and public expenditure is a necessary first step in any investigation of both budgetary policy and its impact on the course of economic activity. This chapter begins with a discussion of the Treasury as an institution, its functions and the wider forum in which economic policy was formulated. The course and pattern of public expenditure are then surveyed, and their behaviour related to the trend and cyclical path of GDP. Finally, there follows a discussion of expenditure control and the suitability of existing arrangements for demand management purposes.

1 THE TREASURY AND ECONOMIC POLICY

Amongst the many charges that have been levelled against the Treasury, perhaps the most important has been, and continues to be, the criticism of its inherent scepticism towards new ideas, its reactive character and almost anti-intellectual bias (Brittan 1964, 33, 39–40). It is because of this, and as a reaction to the supposedly unenlightened policies of the interwar years, that there were frequent complaints regarding the dominance of the Treasury in economic affairs.

The achievement of this dominant position by the Treasury has a long lineage, but need not concern us here. It is sufficient to note two developments of the immediate postwar period which strengthened the Treasury's subsequent influence. First, its authority as the central department of state was heightened by the appointment in 1919 of Sir Warren Fisher as both

Official Head of the Civil Service and Permanent Secretary of the Treasury, a position which permitted great personal – and also wider Treasury – influence over staffing and policy matters (Peden 1979a). Secondly, its financial control was tightened by a number of administrative reforms instituted to augment and modernize the existing system of control which had been largely unchanged since the Gladstonian reforms of the 1860s (see pp. 48–9).

Two questions suggest themselves: first, the consequences of Treasury pre-eminence for the acceptance of the 'new' economics; and secondly, the validity of the traditional interpretation of the authority and influence exercised by the Treasury. The former question is considered in later chapters. With regard to the latter, much confusion has arisen in interpreting the development of Treasury thinking.

Previous studies have all too often viewed the Treasury from an extremely narrow perspective (for example Winch 1972; cf. Hutchison 1968). Thus there has been a tendency to interpret economic policies as deriving largely from economic forces, rather than being the outcome of the continual interplay of political and economic forces operating at a number of levels of government and ultimately being resolved as much with reference to the political expediency of a policy as to its economic efficacy. To take but one example. The Treasury has repeatedly been accused of unnecessarily restricting the growth of expenditure between the wars, and for misguidedly enforcing rigorous economy cuts in 1921–2 and 1931–2 – occasions when the stabilization objective demanded the opposite course. Yet as one official, active in the 1930s, put it many years later:

> The idea that it was a strong Treasury holding down spending between the wars misunderstands what was happening. It was in fact an economic doctrine permeating everywhere – Parliament, ministers, officials, press – everyone. Even to labour and trade union people the economic laws seemed clear-cut. They really believed these economic laws and were ready to cut expenditures.
> (cited in Heclo and Wildavsky 1974, 203)

Furthermore, nor is the accusation well founded that expenditure growth was excessively constrained, at least when measured against income growth. The observed elasticity of public expenditure growth relative to GDP growth was 1.60 for the interwar period (1924–37) and only 1.21 for the period 1960–76.[1]

The fact that the Treasury was compelled to respond to a variety of pressures – Parliamentary opinion, the City, industrial interests, and the reconciliation of conflicting departmental interests – as well as to the strictly economic needs of the time, made Treasury officials cautious in their outlook. They sought to avert risks wherever possible, and were deeply sceptical of the demands of politicians and economists, such as Lloyd George and Keynes, who the Treasury believed failed to take account of the full ramifications of the policies they were advocating.

These characteristics applied to all spheres of policy formulation and execution. One area in which this bias towards risk aversion was particularly evident was in the Treasury's attitude towards new directions in budgetary policy. For example, during the interwar period, the proposal was frequently made that, as a measure to stimulate demand, the authorities should reduce income tax, even though it necessitated initially unbalancing the budget, because it would greatly stimulate economic activity which, in turn, by acting on endogenous budget items (notably the income tax yield and outlay on unemployment benefits), would more than fully compensate for the initial deficit. (This was one of Keynes's favoured remedies for unemployment; it was also a popular policy choice with progressive Conservative MPs such as Harold Macmillan – see Keynes 1933 and *Hansard* 1933c.) The Treasury contemptuously termed this the 'act of faith theory', for they felt that the potential benefits (if any) of such a policy were far outweighed by the accompanying risks (PRO 1932m). It is at this point that adherence to budgetary orthodoxy assumed a political significance, a theme explored in chapter 5.

The locus of Treasury authority within Whitehall was its institutional position at the financial and political centre of government. This position rested on the control of expenditure, for it was this which endowed the Treasury with political power, and made it the most politically conscious of all the departments. This followed not only from the fact that 'Most actions of government have financial aspects which automatically bring them into the Treasury's orbit' (Chester and Willson 1968, 284), but also from certain essential features of bureaucratic government, whereby 'political institutions are [not] mere filters through which economic forces are automatically translated into policies . . . as though these filters have little if any effect upon the outcomes' (A. Robinson 1978, 9).

In general, Chancellors of the Exchequer during the interwar period had little direct experience of financial policy questions.[2] In these circumstances it might be supposed that Treasury power was strengthened; for example, Amery's (1955, 81) comment about Neville Chamberlain: 'the Treasury and City influences were too strong for a Chancellor . . . who, unlike Horne, never really understood monetary problems'.

The official papers show this view to be fallacious. Chancellors were not mere ciphers, the vehicle whereby Treasury officials transmitted policy advice to the Cabinet. Although there were occasions in which Chancellors did not immediately concur with Treasury advice on important policy issues, there was no question of a Chancellor (or the Cabinet) acquiescing in a policy which they deemed unacceptable. Where a Chancellor was initially unconvinced by the correctness of a policy (e.g. Churchill and the return to the gold standard in 1925), it is quite clear that in order to gain the eventual assent of the Chancellor the Treasury officials had to construct extensive justifications for a policy (Moggridge 1972, 64–79). Treasury officials, then, derived their authority and influence not from the weakness of Chancellors in technical questions, but from their political strength within Cabinet and Parliament.

As a result of Fisher's administrative reforms, which consolidated and strengthened the Treasury, a wider range of policy questions came into the Treasury's domain. In addition, changes brought about by the First World War, and longer term trends which had been in operation before 1914, led to a significant widening of the Treasury's responsibilities in economic affairs. The 'Treasury's traditional areas of responsibility – budgetary control and debt management – changed both in substance and in magnitude', while at 'the same time, the Treasury's responsibilities extended into new areas which either did not exist before the war, or else were not regarded as being the concern of central government' (Newman 1972, 340). Yet the Treasury has repeatedly been criticized for the 'lack of any perception of the impact which [their] administration might have on the economy, [and for] the absence of any idea of the macroeconomic implications of their actions'.[3]

Such a conclusion may have been permissible in the years before the Treasury papers were made available to researchers, for undoubtedly there was a paucity of material with which to judge the Treasury's interwar performance. Yet the foregoing assessment was made in 1972, and as such, is totally unacceptable. It erroneously assumes, both that it is permissible to view the interwar Treasury by the standards of modern economic management and that prevailing political conditions can be discounted, conditions which prior to the late 1930s were unpropitious to the development of those very objectives of economic management against which policy is here being appraised.

Similarly, to cite Heath's (1927, 1) minimalist definition of the Treasury's role, as being the 'Department which, subject to the control of the executive and to the authority of Parliament, is responsible for the administration of the public finances of the country', and from this to argue – as Fry (1969, 26) does – that the failures of interwar policy are hardly surprising, is to create a misleading impression of the actuality of Treasury responsibility for the economy. In formal terms, these responsibilities may have been narrowly defined, but the point at issue is the actual nature of Treasury responsibility and its implications for the economy.

It is studies such as Fry (1969) and Newman (1972), which seek to view the Treasury as operating in a vacuum, unrelated and unresponsive to prevailing political conditions, that have generated much confusion and misunderstanding of the Treasury's economic position between the wars.

Reference was made earlier to the fact that the outcome of economic policy decisions was as much a function of political pressures as of economic conditions. In reaffirming this point, it should be stressed that it would be mistaken to postulate a situation whereby the Treasury forced their view against Cabinet opposition. While certain politicians complained of the limitations placed upon policy by Treasury cautiousness, in general terms there was a coincidence of interests and views about the *essentials* of economic policy.

Treasury authority was also subject to certain additional constraints, the most important of which was that 'Treasury control had no basis save the authority in the Cabinet of the Chancellor of the Exchequer. If this authority is overborne, the Treasury must comply' (Jennings 1959, 163). The two main Chancellors of the period – Snowden (1929–31) and Chamberlain (1931–7) – were both politically strong figures, largely unchallenged within their Cabinets, the latter rising to Prime Minister (1937–40). Although criticized for excessive financial orthodoxy,[4] both by their colleagues and by wider political opinion, they were able to carry their Cabinets on all major policy issues. There was also the ultimate threat, that of resignation, which, with its serious repercussions both politically and on confidence, could be evoked in order to strengthen the Treasury's case. Such a threat was used by Chamberlain in 1935, both in order to prevent Lloyd George being admitted to the Cabinet and to limit the extent of any resumption of public works expenditures, a subject under review as a consequence of the political threat posed by Lloyd George's 'New Deal' (CP 1935a; Booth 1978).

Equanimity within Cabinet was not simply a reflection of the general consensus of opinion on financial issues, it was also a result of the way in which Treasury officials sought first to generate such a consensus at a departmental level. Whilst each department had a separate identity and outlook (Bridges 1950b, 15), there was also what might be termed a 'Whitehall view', a practical philosophy of government that transcended departmental boundaries.

Within the higher civil service there was 'a strong tendency to reach agreement and, where conflicts occur, to find as quickly as possible a generally agreed resolution', the objective being to obviate the need for ministerial intervention (Beer 1956, 112–13). This bureaucratic characteristic was reinforced during the interwar period by Fisher's resolve that relations between the departments be improved, 'that the administrative class of the Civil Service should be looked on as a single *corps d'élite*', and that policies should be co-ordinated through interdepartmental committees (Woods 1954, 376).

Apart from exclusively budgetary matters, questions of economic policy were frequently discussed by interdepartmental committees (at both official and Cabinet levels) representing the main economic departments.

As Chester (1951b, 14) has noted, this form of decision-making carried with it certain implications:

> The great value of the Whitehall process with its numerous interdepartmental committees and its stress on clearing matters at all levels with interested departments is that any course of action finally agreed upon is usually practicable, at least it is practicable in the eyes of Whitehall. Included in the term practicable is the acceptance of the policy by all the departments who will have some part in its administration. *The danger inherent in the process, indeed in any process in which a large number of interests and considerations have to be taken into account, is that the ideal course of action may be completely lost sight of in the discussion of departmental difficulties and objections.* [emphasis added]

It is contended that this style of decision-making invariably resulted in a bias against policies which, irrespective of their economic merits, posed considerable administrative difficulties. This, and the civil service's highly developed sense of caution, explains the poor response to the considerable administrative challenge posed by Britain's interwar economic difficulties.

The existence of policy views, widely shared and extending onto an interdepartmental level, also raises problems of a different order: those for the interpretation of the origins of policy and the channels whereby advice was transmitted to the Cabinet. First, such problems of exegesis derive from the fact that a departmental view was

> not something which ha[d] been imposed on a Department by any one individual . . . [but] in most cases [was] the result of nothing more startling than the slow accretion and accumulation of experience over the years. (Bridges 1950b, 15–16)

The manner in which a departmental view evolved is of especial relevance to any assessment of Treasury economic policy, and most particularly the 'Treasury view' on public works. From the way in which Hopkins (1930) gave evidence to the Macmillan Committee, it might be supposed that the 'Treasury view' originated from Hopkins, or alternatively from very senior Treasury officials. In fact, this was not the case. As will be shown in chapter 8, the opposition to large-scale public works was essentially a 'Whitehall view'. Whilst the theoretical, or strictly economic, constituent of this view was publicly articulated by the Treasury, the views so expressed reflected interdepartmental experience of administering public works schemes since the early 1920s.

In interpreting the basis of the 'Treasury view', indeed of a wide range of economic policy issues, the question arises as to whether the Treasury adhered to a formal and explicit theory of the economy's operation, and of the impact of their policies, or whether policy decisions and views were founded on a practical and administrative philosophy of government which owed little to such considerations. In resolving this question, it should be noted from the outset that the Treasury documents are not an entirely satisfactory source for this purpose. Both in its internal papers, and in public statements by Chancellors, the Treasury rarely expressed its *general* views about economic policy or theoretical issues. Almost without exception, statements were limited to an opinion about *specific* questions. Thus discretion needs to be exercised, and the records used assiduously, whenever conclusions of a general nature are drawn.[5]

Reference should also be made to a related difficulty: that many subjects are only infrequently mentioned in the records, even important issues such as the reasons for the continuing allegiance to balanced budgets. This seems to have been a result of certain characteristics of the Treasury as an organization, and of the personalities of the Treasury mandarins. These men undoubtedly 'shared a commonality of background, education and ideals that tended to produce homogeneity and conformity in [policy] advice and practice' (Newman 1972, 18). The result was a common ground in their approach towards specific issues, this based upon unstated assumptions which it was felt unnecessary to record in official memoranda.

Finally, the principal Treasury officials can now be introduced, beginning with Sir Richard Hopkins (affectionately known as Hoppy) who was undoubtedly the most important. Indeed, such was his influence as the principal financial policy adviser to successive Chancellors, that very likely he was 'more important in his own right than many cabinet ministers' (Beloff 1975, 213). Apart from Hopkins and Fisher, other Treasury officials of note were: Sir Frederick Phillips, Sir Frederick Leith-Ross, and Sir Ralph Hawtrey. (Details of their careers, and those of other contemporaries mentioned in this study, are given in appendix I.)

2 THE COURSE OF EXPENDITURE

The First World War resulted in an unprecedented expansion of the public sector, one manifest both in the extension of the range of economic activities subject to state control and in a near doubling of the ratio of public expenditure to GDP. Whilst in the years immediately preceding the war the expenditure ratio had followed an upward course, this increase (largely due to the Liberal welfare reforms) was to be completely overshadowed by developments occasioned by the war.

From 0.119 in 1913 the expenditure ratio rose to a peak of 0.436 in 1918. Following the end of the war expenditure was sharply curtailed, the expenditure ratio falling to 0.205 in 1920 (table 3.1), by which time nominal expenditure stood at over four times the 1913 level. While the intervening price inflation ensured that the real increase was much lower – at

Table 3.1 Public expenditure by economic category as % of GDP, selected years, 1913–37*

	Current goods and services	Gross capital formation	Subsidies and grants to private sector	Current grants paid abroad	Debt interest	Total
1913	8.1	1.2	0.9	–	1.7	11.9
1920	8.2	1.7	4.7	0.2	5.7	20.5
1924	9.0	2.2	4.3	0.2	7.9	23.6
1929	9.2	2.6	4.9	0.1	7.7	24.5
1932	10.1	2.8	7.2	0.1	7.8	27.9
1937	11.7	3.3	5.6	0.1	5.3	25.9

Source: Calculated from Feinstein (1972, tables 3, 14, 39).

Note:
* Public expenditure is here defined as current and capital expenditure by central and local government plus capital expenditure by the public corporations.

between 1.5 and 1.7 times, depending upon assumptions made about the price deflator – it was the nominal increase which none the less commanded public attention, strengthening the campaign for postwar retrenchment.

After 1920 further reductions in expenditure were hindered, first, by the conflicting nature of the government's social and fiscal policy objectives and, secondly, by the unfortunate concatenation of a change in economic conditions (1920–1) which was to make neither of these objectives attainable. On the one hand, the government's social policy, known popularly as a 'Land fit for Heroes', implied an increase in its expenditure commitments. On the other hand, since the Cunliffe Committee Interim Report of November 1918 (HMSO 1918) the prevailing economic view had been that expenditure must be drastically reduced, for only by this method could inflation be controlled and there eventually follow a reduction of taxation from wartime levels and a return to the gold standard at prewar parity (Morgan 1952).[6] In the debate that ensued within government, the latter group of objectives prevailed and budgetary policy was tightened considerably (on both the revenue and expenditure sides) during 1919–20. Thus, a combined public authorities budget deficit of 8.0 per cent of GDP in 1919 was transformed into near surplus (a deficit of 0.5 per cent) the following year (calculated from Feinstein 1972, tables 3, 14, 39), this a consequence of a tightening of fiscal stance rather than the effect of changes in the level of unemployment and economic activity (a distinction discussed fully in chapter 7). Of course, the irony was that the recession that followed (1920 II–1921 IV), a recession at least partially induced by deflationary fiscal operations (Howson 1974, 106; cf. Dowie 1975), was itself to frustrate temporarily further efforts to reduce expenditure.

The net effect of these developments was that the expenditure ratio continued to rise, by a further 5.1 percentage points of GDP over 1920–2. Expenditure, in nominal terms, had fallen (by 4.6 per cent), but the fall in GDP was very much greater (23.5 per cent). Thus at an early stage there appeared a problem that was to bedevil all interwar governments in their budgetary policies, the problem of the irreconcilability of the balanced budget rule with a budget structure, the characteristic of which was its sensitivity to cyclical fluctuations. In the prewar period, the interrelationship of the budget to the economy, and the implications of this for budgetary policy, was a problem that never raised itself to any important degree. The enlargement of the public sector brought about by the war, however, changed conditions fundamentally: public expenditure had reached such a proportion of GDP that this interrelationship could not be ignored. Indeed, in a sense, the history of subsequent developments revolves largely around the authorities' attempts to come to terms with this essential (Keynesian) economic truth. In addition, difficulties are also raised for any assessment of the impact of fiscal operations, a subject explored in chapter 7.

After further economies were made during 1922–3, the expenditure ratio then exhibited a slight upward trend for the remainder of the period under review, rising from 0.236 in 1924 to 0.259 in 1937. Around this upward trend the ratio fluctuated pro-cyclically: as with the fall-off in economic activity of 1920–1, the depression of 1929–32 was also accompanied by a sharp upward movement; this was followed by a fall in the middle 1930s as recovery progressed; and finally the later 1930s were to witness a resumption of the upward movement, this time mainly as a result of rearmament although the 1937–8 recession was also a contributory factor (see figure 3.1, p. 42).

From table 3.1 the enlargement of the public sector, as compared with prewar, can be seen to be the result of the greatly increased expenditures on debt interest and on subsidies and grants to the private sector. Both categories of expenditure constitute transfer payments, and as such do not represent direct claims upon resources (current expenditure on goods and services and public authorities' capital formation). Whilst transfer payments increased more than direct expenditures over 1913–20 (respectively from 2.6 to 10.4 per cent of GDP and from 9.3 to 9.9 per cent of GDP), over the subsequent period the trends were reversed: between 1924 and 1937 transfer payments fell from 12.2 to 10.9 per cent of GDP while direct expenditures rose from 11.2 to 15.0 per cent of GDP. Thus within the total of public expenditure, and in relation to GDP, the public sector's claim on resources was growing throughout the interwar period.[7]

A number of general factors underlay the upward trend of expenditure between the wars. These can be grouped under two headings: those that were largely exogenous or independent of policy, and those endogenous factors which in large measure were the consequences of policy and of the problems of the British economy.

Under the first heading, account should be taken of the various war-related expenditures, such as pensions and disability allowances, and of certain demographic changes which were to influence the pattern of expenditure. In particular, as was noted earlier (p. 13), the falling birth-rate resulted in a rising proportion both of the population who were economically active and of those of retirement age, the net effect being additional demands for pension support and, given excess supply in labour markets, for outlay on unemployment benefits.

With regard to the largely endogenous influences, of particular importance was the continuously high level of unemployment, which was to affect total expenditure both directly and indirectly. The direct influence operated through benefit payments and relief work expenditures for the unemployed; the indirect influence was broader in effect and of greater significance.

Whilst it might be supposed that the difficult economic conditions of the period would have served to frustrate demands for further social reforms, and therefore to have acted as a constraint to the continued growth of expenditure, in fact the opposite seems to have been the case. As was noted by contemporaries (see p. 90), and as has been confirmed in large measure by more recent experience, economic failures such as heavy unemployment or a deteriorating standard of living can be a potent force intensifying demands for increased social expenditures.

Accordingly, the upward trend of expenditure may be seen as another manifestation of the failure to resolve the unemployment problem. It should be noted, however, that the translation of these demands into increased expenditure was by no means automatically assured. It only resulted because there had occurred certain fundamental changes in political circumstances which were conducive to increased expenditure. The widening of the franchise and the emergence of the Labour Party, the two most conspicuous developments of the early twentieth century, were to create conditions of increased party rivalry and a political atmosphere whereby promises of increased expenditure were a powerful means of gaining electoral support.

The background to the interwar growth of the public sector has now been surveyed and the expenditure ratio used as an illustrative measure. Table 3.2 gives estimates of an alternative measure: the observed elasticity of expenditure growth relative to GDP growth. Estimates are presented for 1924–37 along with two sub-periods; for total public expenditure, for expenditure by central and local government; and for current,

Table 3.2 Observed elasticities of public expenditure growth relative to GDP growth (current prices) 1924–37

	Central government	Local government	Total public expenditure
(1924–9)			
Current	1.27	2.84	1.39
Capital	..	4.19	3.83
Total	1.24	3.14	1.61
(1929–37)			
Current	1.46	1.34	1.29
Capital	5.04	2.86	3.49
Total	1.52	1.71	1.53
(1924–37)			
Current	1.41	1.98	1.36
Capital	3.05	3.72	4.03
Total	1.45	2.38	1.60

Source: Calculated from Feinstein (1972, tables 3, 12–14, 34, 36, 39).

capital, and total expenditure. The results show that in each case the observed elasticity was greater than unity; that for total public expenditure the elasticity was historically high; that capital expenditure saw the most rapid expansion; and that it was local rather than central expenditures which were growing at the most rapid rate. The latter trend was of some importance and should now be discussed.

Central government

From tables 3.2 and 3.3 and figure 3.1 two general features can be established. First, that the cyclical timing of the central government expenditure ratio was similar to that for total expenditures, the major difference being that the amplitude of fluctuations was greater in the case of the latter. Secondly, on trend, central expenditures grew at a slower rate than total expenditure over the period as a whole, although in the 1930s the rates equalized as the pace of expansion quickened in the case of the former.

As was established above, the increased expenditure, as compared with prewar, was largely a function of greater outlays on debt interest and an extension of grants to the private sector. The significance of the greatly magnified debt burden is considered in chapter 5. As regards the other transfer payments, the most important were the national insurance benefits and other expenditures related to social objectives, and the

Table 3.3 Cyclical behaviour of expenditure ratios 1920–38

1 Total public expenditure

	1920–1	1921–5	1925–9	1929–31	1931–4	1934–8
expansion % points of GDP	5.3		0.9	3.7		3.0
contraction		2.2			3.2	

2 Central government

	1920–1	1921–5	1925–9	1929–32	1932–5	1935–8
expansion % points of GDP	3.0		0.6	3.0		2.1
contraction		2.1			2.3	

3 Local government

	1920–2	1922–3	1923–9	1929–31	1931–4	1934–8
expansion % points of GDP	3.0		1.3	1.3		0.5
contraction		0.5			1.0	

Source: Calculated from Feinstein (1972, tables 3, 12–14, 34, 36, 39).

grants to local authorities which were raised considerably after the 1929 local government reforms. The relative position of transfer payments was, however, to diminish as the period progressed – over 1924–37 current expenditure on goods and services and capital formation increased its share of total central expenditure from 25.5 to 35.1 per cent (Feinstein 1972, tables 3, 12, 39), the main explanation being the reduced debt burden resulting from the lower interest rates of the 1930s.

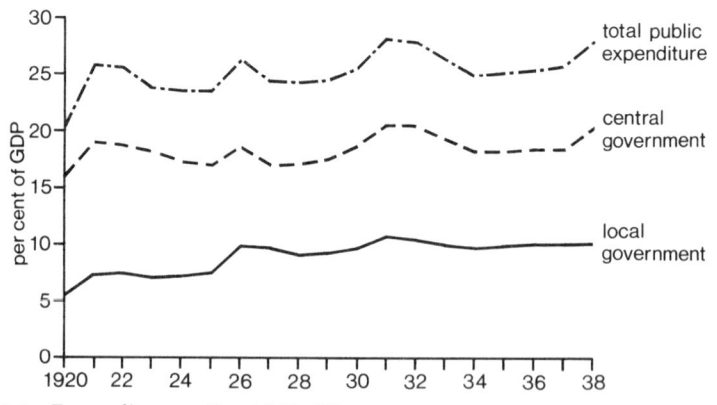

Figure 3.1 Expenditure ratios 1920–38
Source: Calculated from Feinstein (1972, tables 3, 12–14, 39).

The course of the expenditure ratio for central government suggests that this sector exercised a stabilizing influence on demand during the depressions of 1920–1, 1929–32 and 1937–8. This, however, needs to be qualified, for the ratio will show an upward movement not only if the numerator (expenditure) increases but if the denominator (GDP) falls. Such, in fact, was the case with the first two of these cyclical episodes, so that difficulties are raised in assessing the stabilizing nature of expenditure (see chapter 7). These can be illustrated with reference to the developments of the early 1920s.

Account should first be taken of the fact that, whilst the expenditure ratio rose by 3 percentage points of GDP between 1920–1 expenditure (expressed in nominal terms) only rose by 1.9 per cent, and whereas between 1921–2 the expenditure ratio only fell by 0.3 percentage points the fall in expenditure was much greater (12.0 per cent). The behaviour of GDP is thus crucial, but here there are also difficulties: at current prices GDP fell by 14.2 per cent over 1920–1 and by 10.8 per cent over 1921–2, but at constant prices GDP only fell by 5.8 per cent over the former period and rose by 3.5 per cent over the latter (Feinstein 1972, tables 3, 5, 12, 39).

The behaviour of prices, therefore, would also appear to be of some importance. Government expenditures, unlike revenue, were largely unresponsive to price changes, but as already noted they varied directly with the level of economic activity. Nevertheless, the behaviour of the expenditure ratio over 1920–3 was not solely a reflection of automatic changes such as fluctuations in GDP; at the same time, the authorities were attempting to make discretionary adjustments, both in total and in detail.

Mention should be made here of the campaign for retrenchment, ever active since the ending of the war, which intensified in 1921 as the recession adversely affected revenues, thereby threatening budgetary stability. The resulting government-appointed Geddes Committee[8] recommended economies (the 'Geddes axe') totalling £86 million, some 7.6 per cent of planned 1921/2 expenditures, with £46.5 million to come off Defence Votes and £18 million from the provision of education services. The turbulent political reaction to these reports, and the government's defensive response, were to be a portent for the second major attempt at economy nearly a decade later, that of the May report of 1931 (HMSO 1931b).

Whilst in 1922 a consensus undoubtedly existed that expenditure should be reduced, for this would permit the reduction of taxation required to stimulate economic recovery, predictably there was no such consensus about the form that the economies should assume. Consequently, there was a strong adverse reaction to these reports, even from within government (from the Admiralty), and there was thereafter a marked reluctance to make economy a live political issue. In these circumstances it is understandable that the further efforts made at economy, of 1926 and 1928, were limited in intent, and concentrated more on creating an atmosphere of parsimony which would constrain the further growth of expenditure than on making actual cuts in planned expenditures (for example, see PRO 1928).

In essence, these difficulties epitomized the political changes of the early twentieth century which had created such powerful forces for the growth of expenditure: the strengthening of vested interests, the changed nature of party rivalry, and the beginnings of the debate about the legitimate role of the state in economic affairs. This debate was undoubtedly of great significance, not only for the genesis of demand management, but also because a consensus had to be established on the criteria by which the growth of expenditure was to be evaluated. Without such a consensus, periodic crises, such as those of 1922 and 1931, were inevitable.

Local government

It remains to look at the local government sector, the expenditure of which, if not of equal weight to that of central government, was nevertheless of comparable importance. Indeed, as has been noted by Hicks (1938, 150), if transfer payments are discounted, then the direct command of resources by this sector actually exceeded that of central government. The weight of capital expenditures as between the two sectors was primarily responsible for this.

It should be noted, however, that the importance of local expenditure was diminishing in relation to total public expenditure when viewed from a rather longer historical perspective than that purely of the interwar period. The long-term growth of public expenditure (in relation to GDP) was accompanied, and in part caused, by a 'concentration' process, whereby there was an increased transference of responsibilities (and thereby expenditure) to the central authority (Peacock and Wiseman 1967, xxxiv–xxxv, 29–30). This process was, on the one hand, limited by the strength of local autonomy, and, on the other, fostered by 'economic development[s which] produce[d] changes in the technically efficient level of government, and also produce[d] demands for equality of treatment (e.g. in services such as education) over wider geographical areas' (Peacock and Wiseman 1967, xxxv). The strength of these opposing pressures is of some importance to the British case, and is considered later (pp. 51–4, 55, 56).

The estimates in table 3.2 showed that over 1924–37 the elasticity of expenditure growth relative to GDP growth was significantly higher for local than for central expenditures, and that the greatest difference between the respective elasticities was in the 1920s. We should therefore expect a rising ratio of local to total expenditures. However, at the same time, local government was also becoming increasingly dependent upon central grants, particularly after the reforms of 1929. Rates and other taxes on expenditure paid to local authorities, measured at current prices, increased by only 22.7 per cent over 1924–37 as against a rise of 39.1 per cent in local current expenditure. The shortfall was met by central grants, their volume rising steadily to over 30 per cent of local current expenditure by the later 1930s.

This situation was not of the local authorities' making. It followed from the technical deficiencies of rates as an income source, the erosion of the tax base by central government action – the 1929 de-rating of industry scheme – and the failure of the central government to countenance the devolution to local authorities of an additional revenue source, such as a local income tax which had long been under discussion (Middleton 1983). Thus local authorities were forced into a position of greater dependency upon central government, a dependency that was to have implications for economic management.

Public authorities' investment

For any comprehensive assessment of the stabilizing effects on demand of government policies the analysis should not be confined to the behaviour of expenditure but should encompass the complete range of policy instruments. Nevertheless, in the first instance, it is legitimate to consider separately the behaviour of public authorities' investment, for a successful stabilization policy requires not only the stabilization of total demand but also its constituent parts. The balance of supply and demand in capital goods markets is thus of some importance.

The first step in such an analysis requires details of the composition of gross domestic fixed capital formation (GDFCF) and the demand leverage exercised by the public sector. Table 3.4 shows, first, that the private sector's contribution to GDFCF was significantly greater during the interwar period than during the more recent period 1967–77. Thus, even given the absence of a commitment on the part of government to the countercyclical control of its investment, autonomous fluctuations in GDFCF (and thus GDP) were likely to be of greater amplitude than if the private sector had been of smaller dimension. The second feature of note is that the volume of capital investment undertaken directly by central government was small in relation to that of local government. For example, during the depression period 1929–32 an average of only 3.4 per cent of GDFCF was controlled by central government compared with 26.5 per cent by local government. In terms of demand leverage, this gives figures of roughly 0.4 and 2.7 per cent of GDP respectively, considerably less than that for the contemporary British economy.

Table 3.4 Gross domestic fixed capital formation by sector 1929–38

	Private	Public corporations	Central government	Local government	Total (%)	Total GDFCF as % of GDP
1929	72.2	0.5	3.4	24.0	100.0	10.4
1930	69.7	1.4	3.4	25.5	100.0	10.3
1931	65.2	2.5	3.4	28.9	100.0	10.5
1932	65.7	3.5	3.5	27.4	100.0	9.2
1933	73.7	2.8	2.8	20.7	100.0	9.5
1934	77.3	1.9	2.8	18.0	100.0	10.7
1935	74.8	1.5	3.1	20.6	100.0	10.9
1936	72.9	1.5	3.5	22.1	100.0	11.9
1937	69.7	1.6	4.0	24.7	100.0	12.2
1938	66.6	1.7	4.9	26.9	100.0	11.9
averages for periods:						
1924–9	70.0	—	3.8	26.2	100.0	10.1
1929–38	70.8	1.9	3.5	23.9	100.0	10.8
1967–77	57.4	18.1	5.6	18.9	100.0	19.0

Sources: 1924–38: Calculated from Feinstein (1972, tables 3, 39). 1967–77: Calculated from HMSO (1978, tables 1.1, 10.1, 10.3).

Two further points should also be made. First, while variations in public investment undoubtedly influenced GDFCF, it by no means follows that such investment could have been expanded sufficiently to fully compensate for autonomous fluctuations in private investment. Secondly, the fact that local authorities, rather than central government, largely controlled public investment had certain unfavourable results for economic management.

While table 3.4 brings out the weighting of the various sectors in GDFCF, the presentation in figure 3.2A better illustrates their cyclical and trend path.[9] Even this, however, is not completely adequate for our purposes: although the upward trend and cyclical fluctuations of GDFCF are clearly represented, the respective contributions of private and public investment are not immediately evident. Accordingly, the method adopted to assess the stabilizing effectiveness of public investment on GDFCF was to estimate the deviations (in volume terms) of public and private investment from their respective linear trends (at constant prices). The results are presented in figure 3.2B. For stabilization purposes, an optimal result would be for the deviations of the public sector to offset those of the private sector, so that the two summed to zero, and where the elasticity (or coefficient) of public sector deviations with respect to private is −1.[10]

THE TREASURY, ECONOMIC POLICY AND EXPENDITURE   47

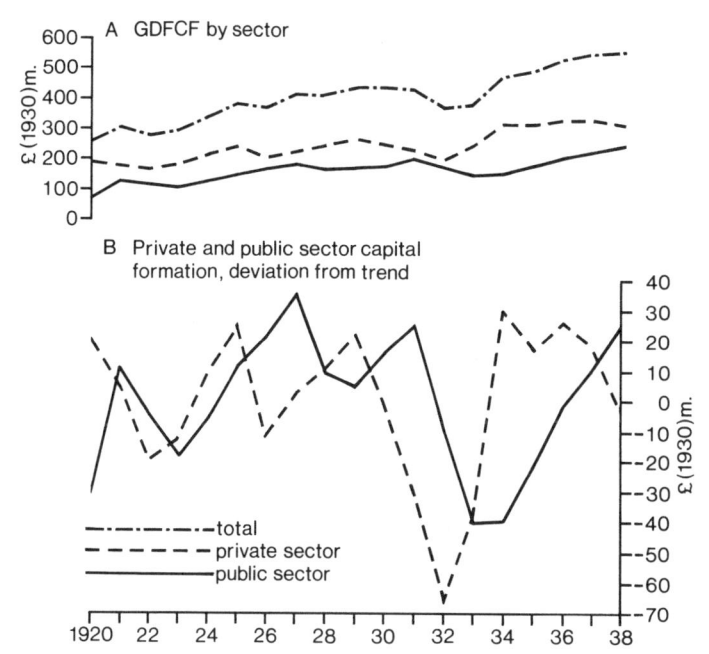

Figure 3.2 Fluctuations in gross domestic fixed capital formation 1920–38
Source: A: Feinstein (1965, table 3.34). B: ibid.; for method of calculation, see text.

For the data shown in figure 3.2B it proved impossible to obtain a statistically significant relationship. However, the introduction of a one-year lag, of public against private investment, did yield a statistically significant equation, with a coefficient of +1.4.[11] Thus, even when permitted a delay in responding to an autonomous fluctuation in private investment, the public authorities were destabilizing over the period as a whole.[12] Nevertheless, policy did respond correctly on occasions (1920–1, 1929–31, 1936–8) and was only seriously destabilizing on one occasion, 1931–2 (the trough of the depression). Furthermore, when judged against the destabilizing course of public investment in more recent periods (Price 1978, 124–6), the interwar period does not compare that unfavourably, although the amplitude of fluctuations was greater.[13] The question, which is explored in later chapters, is whether the stabilizing effectiveness of public investment would have been improved if there had been a commitment to a counter-cyclical policy or whether certain institutional factors would have militated against such an outcome.

3 THE TREASURY AND EXPENDITURE CONTROL

The Treasury's administrative responsibilities for financial control were both complex and of wide compass, permitting the Treasury to extend its authority from purely financial to policy questions. Treasury control, however, was far from complete, nor was it uniform as between the various spending agencies constituting the public sector. In particular, as will now be shown, the degree of control exercised over central and local expenditure varied considerably, and this was to have certain ramifications for economic management.

Central government

The 'saving of candle-ends' has been taken as the epitome of Treasury attitudes towards expenditure control. However, as Bridges (1950a, 6) complained, it was but

> a picturesque phrase . . . embodying the attitude of extreme frugality which has led to the reputation of cheese-paring or meanness that the Treasury has so long enjoyed (if that is the right term). It recalls at once the wish, believed by so many to be still endemic in Treasury Chambers, to refuse all proposals of expenditure however worthy the object.

In the following, it will be argued that this term is manifestly inappropriate to the reality of interwar expenditure control.

It has been traditionally maintained that expenditure control was excessively strict between the wars, both in total and in detail. For example, Roseveare (1969, 258) has argued that the period 'saw the painful and laboured reassertion by the Chancellors of both governing parties of the Gladstonian tradition of public finance, and they saw its ultimate eclipse'. Detailed scrutiny of the available evidence seriously weakens such arguments and finds the traditional interpretation largely wanting. First, reference has already been made to the fact that, when judged against a more recent period, the growth of expenditure was rapid between the wars. Secondly, the traditional view rests on a basic confusion between the Gladstonian administrative structure of expenditure control and the attitudes guiding that control. While the Gladstonian era may well have represented the apotheosis of economy in expenditure, it should be recognized that there occurred certain fundamental changes during the period of the Liberal administrations of 1906–14, and that these

> led to a much wider view of the proper objects and extent of Government expenditure in the modern State: and as a result Treasury Control became less concerned with the prevention of all public expenditure, and more concerned with ensuring the most prudent and economical spending of money on approved projects. (Bridges 1950a, 7)

Whilst it is indisputable 'that Gladstone contributed more to the development of the modern Treasury than any one man before or since', the legacy of the Gladstonian era was not an excessively severe attitude towards new expenditure, but the 'inheritance of . . . a unified system of efficient administration, spreading outwards from the Treasury to all parts of the Government machine, and a unified system of control of expenditure to match and support it' (Bridges 1966, 29).

This system of financial control, which after its long evolution was well-suited to normal peacetime conditions, was to be subject to severe strains during the First World War, for the war not only required expenditure on an unprecedented scale but also forced the abandonment of many traditional control mechanisms (Chubb 1952, 93–108). In the immediate postwar period, the Treasury naturally sought to reimpose these peacetime controls. They also attempted a more radical strengthening of expenditure control.

First, the position of Accounting Officer in each department was strengthened, the object being that policy and its financial consequences should not be treated separately but in conjunction with each other, a reform that 'did much to induce a greater sense of financial responsibility into Departments generally . . . [and] fostered an atmosphere of greater confidence between Departments and the Treasury' (Bridges 1950a, 11–12). Secondly, Treasury control was strengthened at Cabinet level with the resumption of the prewar arrangement whereby all schemes involving expenditure had first to be discussed with the Treasury. This was not an attempt to impose economy upon unwilling politicians. Rather, it was an important means whereby Treasury officials were able to relate possible expenditures to available resources, and to inform the Cabinet of the action that would be required were the proposal to receive approval (PRO 1923).

While there is little evidence to support the view that Treasury control of aggregate expenditure was unnecessarily constraining, given prevailing economic conditions and the unanimity of political opinion on the desirability of limiting expenditure growth, there is rather more substance in the charge that control was excessive in detail. The rearmament programme, undertaken from the mid-1930s, is a case in point; for officials, politicians, and outside observers all assigned to Treasury 'tight-fistedness' much of the blame for the programme's slow progress, its deficiencies, and the inadequate level of preparations at the outset of war (see Peden 1979b, 1–2 and references cited therein).

The point at issue is not whether Treasury control frustrated the defence departments in their efforts to expedite a rearmament programme *per se*, for this is admitted even by writers who have favourably judged the Treasury's stance on rearmament, but whether the way in which control was exercised operated to the actual detriment of Britain's preparedness – both military and economic – for 'total' war. The economic and budgetary problems posed by rearmament are discussed in chapter 6. It is sufficient to note here that the judgement of recent research has been that Treasury control, given the financial limits on expenditure, acted in a beneficial manner by enforcing priorities upon the defence departments and, by limiting the extent of disturbances to the civilian economy, preserved Britain's economic strength. Therefore, as Peden (1979b, 34) concluded:

> It would be rash to [argue] that laxer Treasury control before the war would have quickened the pace of essential parts of the rearmament programme, for the Treasury made every effort to see that essentials received due priority, and that less important proposals were not allowed to clog the programme.

The nature of Treasury control operated to put departments on the defensive, their expenditure plans being restrained by anticipation of Treasury criticism. Apart from the special difficulties raised by rearmament for Treasury control, it appears from the official papers that relations with the spending departments were generally harmonious and that Fisher had promoted 'team work throughout the Civil Service . . . with conspicuous success'.[14] Nevertheless, it would be quite wrong to suppose that conflicts never arose. Two examples, those concerning the Ministry of Labour Estimates for 1932/3 and 1933/4 and the expenditure of the Road Fund in 1935, are considered in later chapters (pp. 88, 101, 104).

Heclo and Wildavsky (1974, 47–9) have identified five maxims of modern-day Treasury control. These are equally applicable to the case of the interwar period.

1 The full implications of an expenditure proposal must be investigated in order to ensure that no large expenditure commitments are approved unknowingly because the expenditure seemed small in the early years.
2 There is the strongest possible bias against open-ended expenditure commitments.
3 There is the avoidance of precedent setting behaviour, the avoidance of settlements with one department which would have the effect of raising expenditures in another.
4 An antipathy towards disguised expenditure (such as subsidies and loans) which by being unidentified cannot be controlled.
5 A basic attitude of mind which sought to avoid risks in the planning of future expenditure commitments:

> The Treasury as an institution has never believed in the philosophy of economic growth. Its officials may not be against growth as such, but they are vehemently against committing resources on the basis of what one deputy secretary called a 'hoped-for, phony paper growth rate,

which only leads to false expectations, disappointments, cuts, and further disillusionment'. They want to see the colour of the money first and relish pointing out the risks of actions based on hypothetical increases in wealth. (Heclo and Wildavsky 1974, 48)

To conclude this part of the discussion, mention should be made of the general inflexibility of central expenditure control and planning systems. Space precludes a detailed discussion of the 'supply cycle', the term used to describe the compilation and eventual presentation to Parliament of the departmental estimates. The essential points for our purposes concern the chronology of events. First, consideration of the estimates began, as at present, in the early autumn and after discussions between the Treasury and the spending departments (and the Cabinet in respect of the defence estimates) they were presented to Parliament in the following February or March. Secondly, this chronology had certain important consequences, in particular that Parliament considered expenditure proposals prior to the budget, which was therefore only a tax budget. This state of affairs, of course, still prevails and has been the subject of recent criticism (see Armstrong Report 1980).

The supply procedures of the House of Commons were more rigid and inflexible than at present, and without modification would have been unsuitable for counter-cyclical purposes where the necessity would often arise for making adjustments in expenditure programmes at short notice. Once expenditure programmes had been settled, further supply would only be granted on application of a Supplementary Estimate. Whilst no major Supplementary was refused during the interwar period, they were used infrequently and with definite reluctance (Einzig 1959, 264, 275).

This general inflexibility in the setting of expenditure programmes was reinforced by the fact that central government had no specific powers to borrow funds without Parliamentary sanction (Hicks 1938, 223), and, as was noted above, the possibilities were severely limited for its stabilizing private investment by varying its own capital outlays.

Local government

Although economic policy was formulated at the centre, the British financial system had evolved in such a way as to limit the channels through which central government might operate its fiscal policies. Neither the Treasury nor Parliament directly controlled local expenditures, either on current or capital account, and despite the increasing importance of central grants, local authorities had not become simply the spending agencies of central government (Chester 1951a; Middleton 1983).

Local autonomy was strong, and seen as of some importance in British constitutional practice. Central control was limited to that granted by specific legislation. There were no general powers permitting central direction of the localities. In particular, central departments had no authority either to determine the level of rates which an authority might decide to levy or to prescribe directly how the funds so raised should be expended. In these circumstances, the degree of central influence on the economic activities of local authorities rested upon the effectiveness of persuasion, exhortation and financial inducement.

At the local level, the form of the prevailing administrative structure was less than propitious for direct central control. As Sykes (1939, 139) concluded, local authorities were 'not ordinarily the optimum economic spending units', there being no fewer than 25,340 separate units in 1927 having powers to enter into financial transactions, and even after the major reforms of 1929, this number was only reduced to 11,619. Moreover, there was a complete absence of any uniformity in their financial circumstances. The small size of many local authorities, combined with financial weakness due to depressed local economies, was in many instances to limit their ability to provide statutory social services, let alone works projects to mitigate unemployment (even with grant assistance). The classic example here is that of the south Wales mining communities, where the need for relief schemes was urgent but available financial resources were almost non-existent (HMSO 1934, 166–71).

A second major problem concerns the diffusion and fragmentation of central responsibility for local government. Control of the localities was dispersed across a wide range of departments, including the Treasury, the Ministries of Health and Transport, the Board of Education and the Scottish Office. None was charged with overall responsibility or a co-ordinating function, although the Ministry of Health (and, to a lesser extent, the Treasury) controlled loan sanctions and exercised general supervisory powers.

This state of affairs was part of a wider problem, much commented on at the time, that of the absence of effective co-ordination within central government. Thus C. G. Clark (1932, 263–4) argued that:

> unless we wish to see the existing responsibilities of the State diminished and discredited, we must think about creating some machinery which will weld into one policy, seriously thought out and properly planned in execution, these diverse activities of different departments. Without the creation of any important new powers, the coordinated direction of the existing powers of the State in the economic field would enable a Government really to have an economic policy, and to see the execution of this policy really bite upon the slippery and intractable economic situation.

Reference has already been made to the increasing importance of central grants to local authorities. The question should now be posed whether this growing formal dependence upon central government was of a form which permitted the centre to further its economic policy objectives. In particular, this question is of especial relevance to the ability of central government to stimulate local authority capital outlays as a means of stabilizing employment.

In approaching this question, it should first be stressed that grants were rarely designed to cover the full cost of a local service or capital project, so that it is necessary to take into account the form of the grant and the financial position of local authorities, both in general and those specifically seeking assistance. To local authorities, the attractiveness of a grant was dependent upon:

1 The likely increase in rates resulting from a decision to proceed with a service or project eligible for grant assistance.
2 The existing level of rates.

Local authorities between the wars were best spurred into action by specific grants, variable rather than fixed, and available for a limited period. Perhaps the most successful of such grants was the subsidy payable to local authorities under the Housing and Town Planning Act, 1919. Under this Act, local authorities received a subsidy equivalent to the difference between the capital cost of a house spread over a period of years and the amount of income the house earned – when let at rents that low-income families could afford – above the proceeds of an additional penny levied on the rates. The local authorities' liabilities were small and fixed and there was no obligation to economize on capital costs.

While, on the one hand, 'as a sheer creator of living accommodation', the Act was the 'most successful measure of its kind that Britain saw until after the Second World War', on the other, it forced up building costs, caused disruption in capital markets as local authorities took part in an 'uncoordinated scramble for house building money', and resulted in considerably greater expenditure than was felt to be necessary (Gilbert 1970, 144). Herein lay the root of the problem of central–local financial control, the conflict between the requirements of 'normal' expenditure control (equity, economy and ease of administration) and the objective of securing a large and immediate response from local authorities.

Four principal defects of the grant system can be identified. First, since the unemployment problem was ever present, if variable, to maintain the volume of local capital expenditures required ever increasing rates of grant as local authorities, after years of financing such programmes, became reluctant to incur further liabilities. By 1929–30, when a new public works effort was required, the situation had developed such that local authorities now sought near full reimbursement from the central government, a course the Treasury had long feared and the realization of which they were determined to prevent.

Secondly, for the greater part of the period, rates of grant were not discriminatory. They did not vary according to the financial resources of individual local authorities, but rather were determined by the types of projects being financed.

Thirdly, frequent changes in grants could cause difficulties at the local level (Chester 1951a, 200). For example, after the 1931 emergency budget measures, which resulted in many capital projects being suspended before their completion and in local authorities having to compensate their contractors, it is arguable that local authorities would have viewed with some suspicion a further general attempt to stimulate public works and that the results would have been disappointing.

Finally, there was a pronounced tendency for local authorities to delay submitting unemployment relief schemes to the central authority, even when urgently required to do so, if there was the possibility of obtaining more generous grants by so waiting (PRO 1930e, para. 3). In addition, local authorities also received grants-in-aid for work which would have been undertaken even in the absence of such grants. To the Treasury, this seriously questioned the validity of the assumptions underlying, and results of, Keynes's multiplier analysis as applied to local authorities' public works.[15]

These problems remained unresolved throughout the interwar period. Yet, as will be argued, the economic debate of the period should also have been accompanied by a far-reaching investigation of the suitability of existing methods of financial control.

Counter-cyclical expenditure control

Both the officials and economists responsible for the compilation of plans for postwar stabilization assigned considerable importance to the counter-cyclical variation of public expenditure (particularly capital expenditures). By contrast, public expenditure as a counterweight in balancing demand has actually held a subordinate position since 1945, and the volume and pattern of public expenditure have continued to be principally dependent upon a composite of the economic and social objectives associated with individual expenditure programmes (Dow 1964, chs VII–VIII; Price 1978). A case in point is that of public investment, where there was a growing appreciation of the resource costs associated with counter-cyclical regulation – the continual compromising of medium-term plans by destabilizing and disruptive short-term interventions – and the apparently insoluble problem of devising forms of expenditure control which both gave the requisite degree of flexibility and ensured the efficient allocation of resources (HMSO 1961).

The starting point for our discussion is that interwar public expenditure management should be viewed in relation to this postwar experience.

A distinction, however, should be drawn between the problems associated with increasing expenditure in a situation of chronic under-investment or prolonged cyclical depression, and the rather different problems posed by the mechanics of fine-tuning. In broad terms, the former might be taken as the case of the interwar period, and the latter as representative of the postwar period.

The higher average pressure of demand in the postwar period, as compared with the interwar period, and the fact that the trade cycle has been of shorter duration and lessened amplitude, has magnified the possibility that discretionary changes in public expenditure programmes might in fact be destabilizing. Such a situation was not a possibility of any importance during the interwar period. Consequently, the following comments about this period apply largely to the administrative, technical and political difficulties which would have arisen if it had been decided to stimulate public expenditure as a counterweight to a permanent, if variable, deficiency of demand.

At this stage of the argument, it is assumed that the balanced budget constraint (at both a central and local level) effectively precluded either counter-cyclical variation of current public expenditure or a significant increase in the overall demand leverage exercised by the public sector on current account, the latter option being discounted because of the requirement for additional revenue to finance the enlarged expenditures. The remaining option concerned an enlargement of public sector capital outlays, and it is on this that the following discussion concentrates.

The decision to adopt a public works programme of sufficient magnitude to exert a significant effect on aggregate demand would have required either a system of generous grants to local authorities, or a fundamental change in the financial relations of the centre to the localities, one that brought a greater volume of public investment under direct central control.

The first option involved a variety of dangers for normal expenditure control; the second was the subject of considerable political controversy and was implacably opposed by the Treasury, on grounds of both efficiency and the fact that it would threaten local autonomy.

Further considerations also need to be taken into account. First, while an immediate response from spending agencies has been an essential prerequisite of an effective stabilization policy in the postwar period – due to the fact that lags in implementing a policy could actually make it destabilizing – it is arguable that, although economic conditions were very different, this would also have been the case in the interwar period. The explanation, however, is rather different: assuming, for example, that the Treasury had become convinced by the case for large-scale loan-financed public works, and as is likely, that strong centres of opposition to such a policy still remained, then the policy would have been seen very much as an experiment, the validity of which would have been crucially dependent upon its *visible* results. There would undoubtedly have been the natural expectation that if a large programme was instituted, visible benefits would be both fairly immediate and of not inconsiderable magnitude. Were such expectations to be unrealized, it is not inconceivable that the reaction against the programme would have been sufficient to have threatened its continuance, and there might even have been a serious second order effect with adverse results for the level of economic activity. Thus, the question of timing is not one that can be dismissed.

Secondly, if the speed of a policy's implementation was of some importance, in particular in the case of an expansion of expenditures, it follows that a physical planning agency would have been necessary to prepare and co-ordinate the investment programmes of local authorities and public corporations, and that the form of central control over local borrowing might also be of some importance. Unfortunately, in both areas there were major deficiencies (Middleton 1983, 359–61).

Proposals for a National Investment Board, to assume such functions (Liberal Industrial Inquiry 1928, 111–15), were put on a number of occasions but were treated unenthusiastically by all interwar governments. Similarly, while the call for increased central control of public expenditure received widespread support from many quarters, outside of certain sections of the Labour and Liberal parties it was treated with disdain by the mass of politicians. The maintenance of local autonomy was an important political issue, a serious impediment to change. In addition, the fact that a major reform of central–local relations had already been undertaken with the Local Government Act, 1929, was to create the attitude that the new system should be tested for some years before further modifications were contemplated.

These administrative and political questions were rarely debated publicly, or indeed on any substantial level within government. Even when so debated, they were seen in some sense as separate from the issues raised by the economic debate of the period. More particularly, there was a failure on the part of economists to appreciate that major administrative reforms – increased centralization and greater flexibility in expenditure control – were a necessary concomitant to acceptance of the 'new' economics and its successful translation into practical economic management.[16] The unbalanced and one-sided nature of the policy debate that resulted from the divorce of economic from administrative and political issues has received almost no attention in the literature of the period. Yet, as is argued later, this omission is partially responsible for the confusion that still surrounds the interwar Treasury.

CHAPTER FOUR

THE REVENUE DEPARTMENTS, TAXATION AND POLICY

Studies of the interwar budgetary system have hitherto tended to focus on the expenditure side of the account; with few exceptions, taxation has been largely ignored.[1] The result of this somewhat narrow approach is that the role of taxation in the budgetary process remains largely unknown, while excessive attention has been paid to the determinants and course of expenditure. Accordingly, the purpose of the present chapter is to survey the revenue side of the account; to look at the revenue departments in the formulation of budgetary policy; the course and structure of receipts; revenue forecasting; and contemporary attitudes towards taxation and economic activity.

1 THE REVENUE DEPARTMENTS

By the interwar period the revenue departments had, like the Treasury, fully matured as departments of finance and, in large measure, had assumed the functions and responsibilities that they currently hold.[2] The Boards of Customs and Excise and Inland Revenue, together with their Secretaries' offices, constituted the central co-ordinating machinery of the two revenue departments. They were responsible not only for macro policy matters and for advising the Treasury, but also for the more detailed organization and administration of the tax laws. From this followed a certain duality in their position. While the Boards were responsible to the Chancellor, they also had a distinct constitutional existence of their own, the purpose of which was that the administration of the tax system be 'kept free from any suggestion that political influence might be exercised in relation to particular cases' (Johnston 1965, 21). In matters of taxation policy, however, the revenue departments were subordinate to the Treasury, both constitutionally and in practice.

There are few instances, at least recorded in the papers, in which the Treasury pursued a course of action in the face of strong objections from the revenue departments. When disagreements did arise, two general factors were primarily responsible. First, Treasury officials frequently voiced the concern that the revenue departments were too cautious, in particular with regard to the forecasting of tax receipts. Secondly, and of more importance, the Treasury as a department had to respond to much wider considerations than those confronting most other departments. In the field of taxation, the imperative of maintaining budgetary equilibrium (particularly in the early 1930s) often forced the adoption of tax changes and revenue devices which, in less difficult times, would have been considered totally unacceptable.

It should be stressed, however, that as with the Treasury's relations with the spending departments, disputes were rarely serious. In general, there was a coincidence of interests between the financial departments, one strengthened by the interchange of staff.[3]

This said, minor disagreements between the Treasury and the revenue departments were endemic. They normally assumed two standard forms, ones that mirrored the two general factors mentioned above.

1 As a counterweight to the inherent cautiousness of the revenue departments in forecasting tax yields, in almost all the years under review they were instructed to 'stretch' their estimates, thereby balancing the budget ('on paper') or reducing the extent of discretionary action required to ensure *ex ante* budgetary equilibrium. In general, this practice – part of a more general practice of creative accounting (see pp. 80–3) – was not pursued excessively although there were instances in which it was thought to be inadvisable (see CE 1929).
2 On occasion, Inland Revenue were instructed to vary the rate of collection of income and surtax, the objective being to transfer revenue between years according to the exigencies of the budgetary situation (see pp. 82–3). Recourse to this expedient was avoided if at all possible, for it carried with it the risk of adversely affecting the revenue of subsequent years (PRO 1930h).

Although disagreements rarely resulted over the advisability of a tax increase or modification of existing taxation arrangements, when they did occur the revenue departments did not easily succumb to Treasury persuasiveness and would fight the issue until overruled by the Chancellor. The revenue departments were thus far from passive in the budgetary process. Constitutionally they had to follow Treasury directives. Nevertheless, by virtue of their special expertise in taxation matters, they were able to exercise an important influence in budgetary deliberations, an influence much wider than that of specific taxation questions. This is clear from the advice they tendered during the 1931 financial crisis.

A fuller account of the 1931 financial crisis is provided in chapter 6. It is sufficient to note here that while discussions over the balancing of the budget during the crisis centred on the expenditure side of the account, there was also a debate about appropriate taxation measures. The May Committee in forecasting a prospective deficit of £120 million in 1932/3 had recommended economies of £96.5 million, leaving a residual of £23.5 million to be found from additional (but unspecified) taxation. The Labour Cabinet had failed to agree to such economies, while in addition the prospective deficit had risen to £170 million, so that a greater sum was required from additional taxation.

In these circumstances it might be supposed that the Cabinet would have given equal weight to the question of taxation in their discussions and actively considered the form of additional taxation. In fact, questions of taxation rarely feature in the Cabinet's discussions, and it fell largely to the revenue departments and the Treasury (including the Chancellor) to determine the form, though not the magnitude, of the additional revenue. As a result of the Cabinet's effective abnegation of much of its powers in the financial sphere, the financial departments were able, at a time of national political crisis, to assume responsibility for the taxation proposals. This in turn ensured that the form of fiscal adjustment proposed would proceed along conventional lines and that less orthodox solutions would be easily dismissed – for example, the Australian Premiers' Plan of 1931, which although 'unambiguously deflationary' in its effects was nevertheless 'widely applauded as an example of creative economic planning', there being a forced reduction of public and private interest rates as well as retrenchment and increased taxation (Schedvin 1970, 252; Shann and Copland 1931).

Apart from the amount of additional taxation to be imposed, discussions centred upon three interrelated questions.

1 The feasibility of a tax upon *rentier* incomes, there being a preoccupation with the increasing real burden of the national debt and a desire to tax those income groups which could be identified as having benefited from the falling price level.
2 The likely effects of an increase in income and surtax.
3 The way in which additional taxation should take a form compatible with the Cabinet's policy 'that the Budget must be balanced by the application of the principle of a common sacrifice and effort' (PRO 1931n). This principle was undoubtedly politically motivated, a disingenuous appeal to equity considerations which took account of neither the (admittedly rather thorny) problem of differing marginal

utility of incomes for taxpayers and benefit-recipients nor the minimum material needs of low-income groups.

The case for a tax upon *rentier* incomes differed somewhat from that of the capital levy proposed in the early 1920s (Hargreaves 1930, 263-90). Previously concern had centred on the debt's enlargement in nominal terms as a result of war expenditures; it now centred on the rising real burden of the debt resulting from the downward price trend. Within government, the proposal to tax the real gains of the *rentier* class had first been put by a Cabinet Committee in January 1931 (Howson 1975, 73). The proposal (in various terms) was renewed later that summer with the financial crisis, but was again rejected even though it commanded support from opinions as diverse as the TUC and certain elements within the Liberal Party. The attitude of the Inland Revenue was in part responsible for this.

The Inland Revenue favoured the principle of 'equality of sacrifice', but were concerned about adversely affecting the income tax's yield by additional taxation on higher-income cohorts, and more generally opposed a special tax on *rentier* incomes. Whilst this opposition was expressed in technical, rather than political, terms it seems that there was opposition to the use of taxation for redistributive purposes. Indeed, Sayers (1956, 97-8) reports that as late as 1942 the Inland Revenue were still strongly of the opinion that 'the purpose of the income tax is not the redistribution of income'.

When asked to report on the question in late August 1931 they pointed out, first, that the income tax system already strongly discriminated against investment incomes, and secondly, that few individuals had investment portfolios limited to fixed income securities. In fact, they contended that higher-income cohorts had suffered badly from the depression – for example, dividends had fallen by more than 20 per cent over 1929-31 – so that 'it is extremely doubtful whether the average investor had on balance gained in purchasing power over the last few years'. A universal tax on all investment incomes would pose serious administrative problems; a more preferable course would be a change in income tax allowances (PRO 1931q).

Apart from these technicalities, it was also felt that there were serious risks associated with further taxation of higher incomes, mention in particular being made of the stimulus this would give to tax avoidance and evasion (PRO 1931i). This problem, a relatively new one for Britain, was thus felt to constrain higher direct taxation – a view frequently expounded to the Treasury and one which they were forced to accept by early 1932. On these grounds, Inland Revenue argued against an increase in surtax rates. They expressed the fear that a further increase in income or surtax would have an adverse effect on the rate of collection of these taxes, thus deflating their yield (PRO 1931j), but conceded that it was possible

> that taxpayers would be willing to meet the extra demands upon them if the increased tax formed part of a scheme of equal sacrifice and they felt that they were not singled out to bear an undue share of the burden.
> (PRO 1931k)

On this basis, when the financial departments sent in their proposals for additional taxation of £37 million in 1931/2, the Inland Revenue's position clearly dominated their approach:

> we are not yet aware of the nature of the Government proposals in the sphere of economy and we wish to make it very clear that in our view the yields of direct taxation shown in this note will not be obtained unless the whole Government plan is received as a fair and just plan demanding equal sacrifices from all sections of the community.
> (PRO 1931m)

Thus not only was the Cabinet pressured externally to agree to acceptable economies (both in amount and in detail), it seems also that pressure was applied from within, from the bureaucracy. The document previously cited clearly hinted that unemployment benefits must be cut; other evidence suggests that Inland Revenue also stressed the urgency of immediate action, that the Finance Act must be passed quickly if direct taxes were to yield additional revenue because all income tax liabilities would have to be reassessed (PRO 1931k; r).

As had occurred previously, Inland Revenue objections to raising taxes on income were overruled: the September 1931 Budget saw an increase in the standard rate of income tax, a reduction of allowances and a surcharge on surtax. But the Treasury's victory was far from total, for certain concessions were made: the wear and tear allowances on plant and machinery were increased as a partial offset to the increased standard rate, while Hopkins had been forced to accede to the Inland Revenue's view that 'Direct taxation can no longer be relied upon as before' (PRO 1931i; l).

From this brief survey it can be seen that while the revenue departments were very definitely junior partners in the budgetary process, their role was not completely passive, and on occasion they could be an important influence on events. In the shaping of budgetary policy, Inland Revenue's contribution greatly surpassed that of Customs and Excise, whilst in addition, Customs and Excise were more frequently subject to Treasury directives about their estimates and were in a generally weaker position than Inland Revenue. The difference in influence exercised by the two departments is not easily explained, but it would seem to follow from the fact that the issues involved with taxes on expenditure were more straightforward (there being a narrow tax base of staple commodities, consumption trends of which were fairly predictable), and the relationship between these taxes and the level of economic activity better understood, than was the case with taxes on income where the issues were more open to debate and accurate revenue forecasting more problematic.

Finally, it should be stated that the key to understanding relations between the financial departments lies not in any conflict of interests between them but in the fact that there was a conflict of objectives as between the revenue departments and the Treasury. The Treasury's concerns were largely immediate and short-term: the balancing of the budget over a one-, or possibly two-year period. In the difficult conditions of the 1930s attainment of this objective often compelled the Treasury to overrule the revenue departments even though, had circumstances been more favourable, they would quite possibly have accepted their judgement. In this sense conflict was unavoidable. The revenue departments' concerns were less immediate; they operated over a much longer time horizon; and their concern was not solely with the yield of a tax, but also with its efficiency, equity and ease of administration.

2 THE COURSE AND STRUCTURE OF RECEIPTS

The course of expenditure was examined in some detail in chapter 3. We need not repeat this earlier exercise as fully in the case of revenue since both the expenditure and receipts ratios followed broadly similar paths. The latter is shown in table 4.1 for selected years 1913–37.

The ratio of public sector receipts to GDP almost doubled over the course of the war, from 0.113 in 1913 to 0.204 in 1919, largely as a result of

Table 4.1 Public sector receipts by economic category as % of GDP, selected years, 1913–37*

	Taxes on income	Taxes on expenditure	Taxes on capital	National insurance contributions	Property income	Current grants from abroad	Total
1913	1.8	6.9	..	0.8	1.8	—	11.3
1920	10.2	8.3	0.8	0.5	1.1	..	20.9
1924	7.9	10.1	1.4	1.4	2.3	0.2	23.3
1929	6.2	10.6	1.7	1.7	3.1	0.5	23.8
1932	8.2	12.1	1.7	2.1	3.3	..	27.4
1937	6.2	11.6	1.8	2.0	2.8	—	24.4

Source: Calculated from Feinstein (1972, tables 3, 14, 34).

Note:
* Public sector receipts are here defined as current and capital receipts by central and local government.

the increased yield of taxes on income. Whether this upward shift in the receipts ratio is comprehensible in terms of a 'displacement effect' or not, for Peacock and Wiseman's (1967) thesis has been subject recently to much criticism (see Recktenwald 1978), the point remains that over the course of the war the public's tolerance of higher tax rates undoubtedly increased. Thus, while public expenditure was rigorously curtailed in the immediate postwar period, no such development occurred on the taxation side of the account. Indeed, after a short interval, the receipts ratio continued to rise on trend, from 0.209 in 1920 to 0.244 in 1937.

This upward trend resulted from increased rates on existing taxes and some widening of the tax base. Over the course of the war taxes on expenditure had remained fairly stable, the aggregate average or effective rate of tax on consumers expenditure being about 5 per cent. Thereafter, as figure 4.1A shows, the effective rate exhibited a marked upward trend: from 7 per cent in 1920 to 10.7 per cent in 1937.

The most important development, however, concerned the income tax which 'changed out of all recognition' (Sabine 1966, 154). Between 1913/14 and 1918/19 the standard rate was increased from 6 to 30 per cent, the real yield from £47.3 million to an estimated £144.2 million. The standard rate was maintained at 30 per cent until 1922, when it was reduced to 25 per cent and a year later to $22\frac{1}{2}$ per cent. Thereafter, it fluctuated for the greater part of the period in the range 20–25 per cent, before being raised in the later 1930s with rearmament (to $27\frac{1}{2}$ per cent in 1938 and $37\frac{1}{2}$ per cent in September 1939). Details of rate changes and the various reliefs can be found in Mallet and George (1933, 561–3) and Sabine (1970, 304).

Further study of taxes on income is frustrated by the extreme paucity of quantitative information about the interwar British tax system. Nevertheless, from Feinstein's (1972) data for personal and corporate incomes, it is possible to calculate approximate values for effective rates of tax for the two sectors. These are shown as parts B and C respectively of figure 4.1.

The effective rate of tax on personal income was subject both to sharp fluctuations and to an upward trend, its course broadly reflecting changes in the standard rate of tax and the influence of rising incomes under a progressive rate structure. Before 1947 the taxation of corporate profits was integrated with the personal income tax, special taxes on profits only being levied as wartime measures to raise additional revenue. Thus there was no distinction between companies and individuals, income tax being levied at the standard rate on gross trading profits with little regard to the ownership or destination of the income. The estimates presented in figure 4.1C show that the effective rate of tax on corporate income, barring the disturbed conditions of the early 1920s, exceeded that for personal income, this largely because reliefs admissible against tax were much lower, there being few of the capital allowances, etc., which have so relieved the company sector since the Second World War.

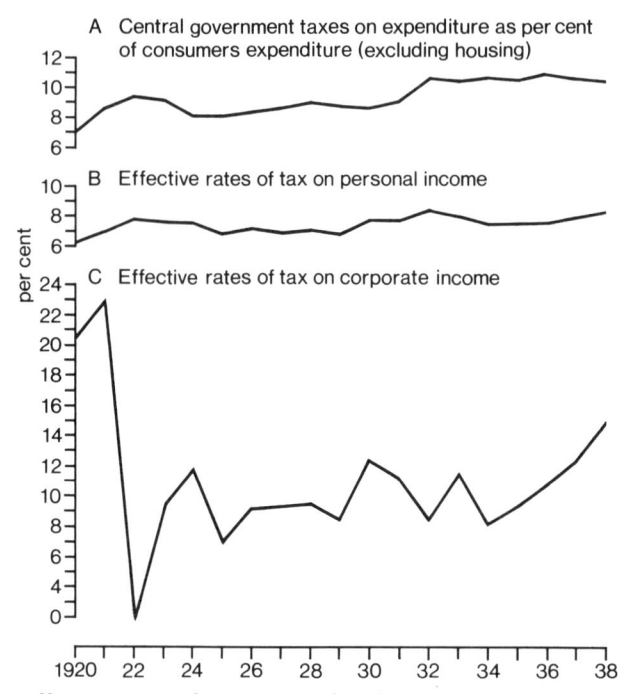

Figure 4.1 Effective rates of tax: personal and corporate income 1920-38
Source: Calculated from Feinstein (1972, tables 10, 12, 24, 32).
Notes:
A: Expenditure on housing is excluded from the tax base because it is liable to domestic rates. There is no data on the indirect allocation to consumption of taxes on industrial inputs and these have therefore not been excluded.
B: Taxes on income paid by the personal sector includes additions to reserves and national insurance contributions, while the tax base includes current grants from public authorities.
C: Corporate taxes are on an accruals basis (payment plus additions to reserves) with no account taken of overseas taxes because of data deficiencies. Corporate income, the tax base, is net of interest payments.

Looking now in more detail at the 1930s, and at central government, there were a number of important developments in the field of taxation. The base for taxes on expenditure was widened with the adoption of a protective tariff in 1931-2, and the reintroduction of the tea duty in 1932, while an additional tax on incomes, the National Defence Contribution, was inaugurated in 1937.

These changes were reflected in the structure of receipts (table 4.2). Taxes on expenditure increased from 7.3 per cent of GDP in 1929/30 to 9.3 per cent in 1933/4 and then remained fairly stable until 1936/7 before falling back to 8.1 per cent of GDP in 1939/40 as rising prices began to affect the specific duties. Taxes on income followed a similar course in the earlier period, rising to a peak of 9.5 per cent of GDP in 1931/2, but

Table 4.2 Central government revenue as % of GDP 1929/30–1939/40*

	1929/30	1930/1	1931/2	1932/3	1933/4	1934/5	1935/6	1936/7	1937/8	1938/9	1939/40
1 Taxes on income	7.0	7.9	9.5	8.3	7.4	7.0	6.9	7.0	7.5	8.3	8.6
2 Taxes on expenditure	7.3	7.4	8.1	9.2	9.3	8.9	8.8	8.9	8.5	8.1	8.1
3 Taxes on capital	1.9	2.0	1.7	2.0	2.2	2.0	2.1	2.0	1.9	1.5	1.4
4 National insurance contributions	1.9	1.9	2.2	2.3	2.4	2.3	2.3	2.4	2.3	2.2	1.9
5 Miscellaneous revenues	2.9	2.9	2.2	2.0	2.0	2.0	2.0	2.0	1.9	1.9	1.9
6 TOTAL (T)	21.1	22.1	23.6	23.9	23.2	22.2	22.1	22.3	22.0	22.0	21.9

Source: Appendix III.

Note:
* For the definition of receipts, see pp. 79–80.

thereafter fell significantly before resuming their upward trend in the later 1930s as rates were increased markedly, especially on income tax.

Taxes on capital exhibited a slight downward trend (varying between 1.4 and 2.2 per cent of GDP), while national insurance contributions rose to a peak of 2.4 per cent of GDP in 1936/7 and then fell back, again as a result of rising prices. Finally, mention should be made of the class of miscellaneous revenues, consisting of a variety of tax and non-tax receipts. These do not fit conveniently into a functional analysis of revenue and, for certain reasons, require separate treatment (see appendix II).

Changes in the structure of receipts reflected not only discretionary action on the part of the budgetary authorities, but also the effects of variations in economic activity on the main revenue classes. The characteristics of the fiscal system, and their relevance to budgetary policy, are considered more fully in chapter 7.

Before 1927 income and surtax were assessed on the average of the preceding three years' income; thereafter, income tax was levied one year and surtax two years in arrears (appendix III). There were two important consequences to this change in the method of assessment.

First, at the macro level, the income tax became more sensitive to cyclical variations, while increased progression in surtax also heightened its sensitivity (Bretherton 1937, 177–8; Hicks 1938, 300). Secondly, the lengthy delay between accruals of tax and tax payments affected the liquidity of the company sector, with fluctuations in tax payments frequently being in the opposite direction to those of profits and the lag being long enough to span the time between the upswing and downswing of the trade cycle, or vice versa. For example, profits earned in the peak of 1929 were paid in 1930/1 and 1931/2, years of worsening depression, while in the peak year of recovery, 1937/8, the taxes paid were levied on the profits of 1935 and 1936, the former a year of comparative depression.

This lag was sometimes of assistance to companies and sometimes not, its effect upon company liquidity being to accentuate the cyclical pattern of their investment expenditures. Thus, in 1933 and 1934, when there was a very pronounced recovery of fixed investment, financing problems were eased by the fact that the taxes due on the higher profits then being earned did not have to be paid immediately. Conversely, in 1930 and 1931, when profits were falling sharply, companies were forced to find the funds to discharge the high tax liabilities incurred in 1928–9, this acting to depress their investment expenditures. In the absence of detailed information about how the corporate sector between the wars made provision for discharging its tax liabilities, we cannot accurately measure the destabilizing effects of the system for taxing profits. If, as is likely, the provisions made were similar to those of the post-1945 period (Sayers 1967b), then the arrangements for taxing profits in the interwar period were destabilizing in like manner, though not necessarily to the same degree, as those of the more recent period (Hansen 1969, 406–7, 435, 446–7; Ward and Neild 1978, 23).

Income tax continued as the major tax on income. The importance of surtax diminished, despite higher tax rates. This was a source of some concern and, after 1931, the authorities were reluctant to impose additional burdens upon surtax payers. The final tax on incomes, the National Defence Contribution, remained relatively small (appendix III).

From 1932/3 to 1935/6 the relative weight of taxes on income fell as against taxes on expenditure, a result of the slow response of income and surtax to recovery, and the reduction in direct tax rates which was not matched by significant reductions in indirect taxes. After 1936/7 the process was reversed: both direct and indirect tax rates rose but taxes on income increased by 1.6 percentage points of GDP whereas taxes on expenditure were reduced by 0.8 percentage points of GDP. The reasons for this divergence become clearer as we examine taxes on expenditure.

Throughout the period there was a clear preference for taxes levied on a specific rather than an *ad valorem* basis, a reflection of the fact that the latter were more difficult to administer. Moreover, from the standpoint of the authorities' objective of maintaining a stable revenue in the face of fluctuations in economic activity, specific duties were preferable as they were less sensitive than those levied *ad valorem*. This followed from the fact that specific duties did not directly reflect changes in the price of the taxable commodity; rather, changes in the price level operated through the effective rate of duty which rose as prices fell, and vice versa.

In large measure, the behaviour of taxes on expenditure during this period was determined by the course of prices. For the specific duties, effective rates rose until the mid-1930s as prices fell; thereafter, prices rose and this was reflected in the diminishing importance of taxes on expenditure (from 8.9 per cent of GDP in 1936/7 to 8.1 per cent by 1939/40), the *ad valorem* duties being of insufficient weight to fully compensate for the erosion of revenue by rising prices.

Changes in the terms of trade were also of some importance. These improved by 24.2 per cent over 1929–33, but then deteriorated down to 1937 (by 12.1 per cent) before improving again by 7.6 per cent over 1937–9 (table 2.4, p. 25). Thus, during the periods when the budgetary authorities were most hard pressed, revenue from imports was being reduced (most import duties were *ad valorem*). At the same time, however, the improved terms of trade increased real incomes, with favourable effects upon consumers expenditure and domestic output – the deflationary Laursen and Metzler (1950) effect, whereby savings are a positive function of the terms of trade, being overridden by labour's real wage gains during the depression, the transfer of income from the unemployed to the employed and certain compositional effects (the consequences of cheaper food) which stimulated spending propensities (Richardson 1972).

A serious problem was that the base for taxes on expenditure was too narrow. The main commodity taxes were too selective to respond to a general movement in consumers expenditure, and, with the sole exception of the motor vehicle licence duties, there were no taxes which could pick up revenue from the increasing expenditure on consumer durable goods. Unfortunately, there are no estimates of the proportion of total consumers expenditure allocated to taxable goods. It may be conjectured, however, that this proportion was falling. An indication of this is given by the fact that over 1929–37 expenditure on durable household goods and transport and communications rose from 12.7 to 14.0 per cent of total consumers expenditure (Stone and Rowe 1966, table 71). Neither broad category of expenditure was subject to taxation of any importance.

The narrowness of the base for taxes on expenditure had a number of implications for budgetary policy. First, the limited range of commodities subject to tax was such that the yield of taxes on expenditure only just matched the growth of GDP (appendix III). Secondly, the 'wider the base of the tax – the larger the consumption taxed – the lower the rates needed to bring in a given revenue' (Hicks 1963, 80). Finally, there were considerable difficulties associated with any attempt to increase rates of duty on the main taxes. The system was inflexible; what was required was a form of sales tax. This came with the purchase tax, introduced in 1940.

When extra taxation was required, Customs and Excise feared the political repercussions of increasing the commodity taxes. For example, in 1938, when there was much public concern about the rising cost of living, they judged any increase in the tea and sugar duties politically inadvisable. Hydrocarbon oils, a product with a low price but high income elasticity of demand, were seen as the only item worth serious consideration, while tobacco, spirits and beer all carried the risk that an increased rate of duty might yield no additional revenue (CE 1938).

Nor did the import duties, greatly expanded in 1931–2, live up to expectations. The duties had two functions: first, the protection of the domestic market and encouragement of import substitution and reorganization of the staple industries; secondly, the raising of revenue. In terms of the authorities' expectations, the tariff was somewhat of a disappointment, proving to be more effective at protection than at revenue raising (PRO 1934b, 4).

Finally, despite these various difficulties, over the period 1929/30 to 1937/8 tax revenues expanded at a faster rate than GDP (at annual averages of 2.1 and 1.5 per cent respectively). Nevertheless, this was not solely a result of the automatic growth of revenue (with an aggregate tax elasticity of greater than unity); it was also a reflection of discretionary changes which increased the average tax burden (see Shirras and Rostas

1942, 15, 24–6; Barna 1945). As is shown in chapter 6, throughout the 1930s it was a source of considerable disquiet to the Treasury that the growth of expenditure constantly threatened to outpace that of revenue.

3 REVENUE FORECASTING

At a time when budgets were finely drawn, the importance of accurate revenue forecasting – a function performed by the revenue departments' Intelligence Branches – cannot be overstressed. Given prevailing circumstances, the record of revenue forecasting was in fact fairly impressive, with total receipts failing to meet the estimates during the depression phase (1929/30–1932/3) by an average of only 1.8 per cent, while over the recovery phase (1933/4–1937/8) receipts consistently exceeded the estimates, again by an average of 1.8 per cent.

The effective formulation of budgetary policy was nevertheless frustrated by the limited, and perforce rather crude, forecasting techniques available to the revenue departments. The revenue departments' documents abound with statements to this effect. For example, an Inland Revenue paper of October 1930 was forced to conclude:

> Any attempt to revise this [tax] forecast at the present date involves guess work as to the effect of the trade depression on the profits of the current year . . . and as to the length of time which must elapse before the depression passes away. (PRO 1930h, 3)

A detailed account of forecasting techniques is not possible here. Instead, the following discussion focuses on a number of general problems, the nature of which help to explain the cautiousness exhibited by these departments.

Although the determinants of individual tax yields were well understood, and rules of thumb applied with some precision as to likely yields, the number of variables involved and the possibility of unforeseen developments (such as forestalments – an increase in imports, unwarranted by current trade conditions, by traders anticipating duty increases) made forecasting problematical prior to the final quarter of the financial year. Indeed, it was not until the final month (March) that the revenue picture, for the year about to close, assumed any degree of certainty, and informed judgements could be made concerning the forthcoming year. As a result, the final stages of budgetary planning were invariably hurried: uncertainty left little time to consider new policy directions and tended to reinforce budgetary orthodoxy. Only once was a serious attempt made to forecast revenue over the medium term (see p. 104), thus permitting a rather longer time horizon for budgetary planning and consequently the possibility that a wider range of policy options might be considered.

Inadequate and incomplete statistical information lay at the root of the problem. National income data were not used in forecasting before 1941. The Inland Revenue (and other economic departments) had the expertise to compile national income accounts, indeed they did so in 1929 (Stone 1977), but the exercise was not repeated. Whether the potential applicability to taxation forecasting of national income accounts was perceived remains unknown.

More generally, the necessity of a strictly balanced budget placed impossible burdens upon the forecasters to produce accurate estimates. This made them extremely cautious and disposed towards risk aversion, the result being an in-built tendency to understate *ex ante* revenue. A further consequence was an attitude of secrecy on the part of the revenue departments which occasionally bordered on the extreme:

> This is another revised edition [of the tax forecast]. I think you had better keep this for yourself and the Deputy Chairman, and *not* send anything more to the Treasury unless they ask for it (and in *no* case send them the Table!). (CE 1934)

In these circumstances the countervailing Treasury pressures for the estimates to be stretched become rather more understandable. It seems also that, in this respect, there were certain impediments to Fisher's prospects for a complete moulding of the civil service into a single *corps d'élite*.

4 TAXATION AND ECONOMIC ACTIVITY

It remains to look briefly at the relation between taxation and economic activity, a theme that will be explored further in later chapters. The subject is of particular importance, for there were frequent complaints by the business community that excessive taxation was a primary cause of Britain's interwar economic difficulties.

Whether taxation levels were 'excessive', in any absolute sense, is impossible to determine. While the war resulted in a permanent upward shift in taxation levels – the per capita tax burden increasing nearly fivefold 1913–37 (Shirras and Rostas 1942, 15) – there are considerable difficulties involved in assessing the implications of this for economic activity. In particular, there is a dearth of objective yardsticks with which to make such an assessment and reliance usually has to be placed upon impressionistic evidence.

Sufficient data, however, are available with which to make international comparisons (see Ilersic 1955, table 13). From this it seems that the receipts ratio was high in Britain in comparison with other European countries (although less than half that of current levels); it seems also that there is a long lineage to the relative unimportance of indirect taxes in Britain.

The high level of taxation, vis-à-vis Britain's industrial competitors, was officially recognized, but the implications of this remained a subject of dispute. For example, the Colwyn report,[4] which might be expected to have considered this question in some detail, limited itself to the statement that the heavy tax burden had 'to some extent affected our industry ... although we regard it as of minor importance compared with more general difficulties affecting our foreign trade' (HMSO 1927a, para. 674).

Economic growth and full employment may be said to depend upon, *inter alia*, increased labour and capital inputs, increased productivity by those inputs, and the maintenance of a high pressure of aggregate demand. Since the early 1970s, and most particularly since the publication of Bacon and Eltis's (1976) influential study, it has become increasingly recognized that the achievement of these policy objectives may be constrained by the high level of taxation required to finance an enlarged public sector. In this view, high levels of taxation – or more correctly, high *marginal* rates of tax – may produce disincentive effects throughout the economy which both constrain the growth of output and make the economy uncompetitive. These disincentive effects can be considered at three levels.

1 At high levels of taxation the incentive to work may be reduced with consequent adverse effects on labour supply.
2 Investors may be discouraged from making new capital investments because high tax levels have reduced net of tax returns. It may also discourage risk taking.
3 High levels of taxation may discourage interregional and interoccupational mobility and retraining because the net returns to these investments in human capital are insufficient.

These issues were fully investigated by the Colwyn Committee, which reported in 1927, and in lesser detail by the Balfour Committee on Industry and Trade which issued reports between 1927 and 1929. With regard to individuals, it was concluded that the income tax 'had no important effect on their work and enterprise', although for higher-income cohorts the adverse effect on savings was 'quite considerable' (HMSO 1927a, paras 350, 377). The former conclusion is reflected in modern studies of taxation and labour supply (for example, Godfrey 1975); the latter is more problematic. The empirical evidence on taxation and savings is very ambiguous (Atkinson and Stiglitz 1980, 90–4), and is of little assistance in assessing the validity of the significant and positive interest elasticity of savings postulated by the Colwyn Committee.

Turning next to profits, the committee investigated the thorny problem of the burden of the income tax: whether, as business representatives maintained (for example, the London Chamber of Commerce 1925, 516–33), there was a divergence between the formal and the effective incidence of the tax, for if there was shifting from producers to consumers then the income tax was 'responsible for raising prices, and [was] therefore a potent factor in depressing trade' (HMSO 1927a, para. 293). Following the evidence of economists such as Pigou (1924b, 41, 47–9), who presented a Marshallian partial equilibrium analysis of taxation as falling upon pure profit, the committee rejected the business view. Instead, they concluded that 'prices [were] determined by considerations into which the Income Tax [did] not directly enter', this being true 'over practically the whole field and for practically the whole of the time, any exception being local or temporary and insufficient to invalidate it' (HMSO 1927a, paras 308, 324).

This conclusion, one that was accepted by the Treasury and Inland Revenue and thus guided policy, is open to doubt. Nevertheless, there is little to be gained from subjecting it to extensive scrutiny. As with the issue of taxation and savings, there is little agreement in the modern public finance literature about the effective incidence of a corporate profits tax. Ultimately, the question is an empirical one, resolution of which requires a satisfactory general equilibrium model of the operation of the interwar British economy, together with information, *inter alia*, about firm behaviour and the competitive nature of markets. We do not have such a model or the requisite information.

While economists between the wars continued to doubt the existence of a large-scale shifting of tax incidence (for example, Silverman 1931, chs VII–VIII; Hicks 1938, ch. XV), the business community also remained committed to their view. Whether the business view was simply self-serving or founded upon a view of macroeconomic relations may well have determined the extent to which there was a consequent adverse effect upon their expenditure behaviour. Although somewhat ambiguous, there is evidence to suggest the likelihood of such an effect (see pp. 94, 159–60). Whatever, this cleavage between business and official opinion suggests that the task facing the interwar budgetary authorities was not solely one of acknowledging the necessity for Keynesian demand management, but that there was also a need for a more intelligent appreciation of distributional questions. The papers of the Treasury and Inland Revenue reveal their extreme amateurism in this latter respect. Moreover, a comprehensive assessment of the burden of taxation also requires that account be taken of the benefits to industry of the government expenditures financed by the higher level of taxation. These were invariably left out of account in contemporary debate.

For the Colwyn Committee, the principal problem confronting British industry was not high taxation but the reduced purchasing power of our overseas markets and excessive domestic costs of production, the latter – as previously established – being largely independent of the income tax (HMSO 1927a, para. 451). Thus, a lower standard rate of tax might improve corporate liquidity, but it would not promote a more general business expansion.

As was noted earlier, the business community neither concurred with this view or the assumptions underlying it. Thus throughout the interwar period organized business pressed the contrary view: that high rates of taxation depressed business confidence and, while other market forces contributed to the difficulties of British industries (particularly in export markets), a reduction of the income tax was the primary means whereby government could assist economic recovery.

The opinions of organized business on taxation questions can be illustrated further by reference to the papers of the Federation of British Industries (FBI), the largest and most influential of the employers' organizations (Finer 1956). Throughout the period the FBI pressed, both publicly and in representations to the Treasury, for a reduction of income tax; this to be financed by further economies in expenditure.

The FBI's attitude on this question was well expressed by its President, Sir James Lithgow, at a meeting of its taxation committee in March 1931. Lithgow 'emphasised the fact that, in the past, increases in public expenditure had gone hand in hand with increased industrial prosperity, which alone rendered the country able to bear the burdens', but that since the war public expenditure and national income had not grown in line, thereby 'directly depriv[ing] industrialists both of the capital and of the psychological incentive which was essential to real development' (FBI 1931a).

In part, the FBI's views on taxation followed from their conception of the role of government in economic affairs, so that the question of high taxation was not a purely economic one. For example, shortly after the 1931 crisis, the following policy statement was approved for publication:

> Heavy expenditure on social services and on general administration and the crushing load of direct taxation has undoubtedly seriously accentuated the difficulties inevitably imposed upon the country by the world crisis. In the opinion of the Federation the country has been attempting to work an economic system based on private enterprise under circumstances which made the successful conduct of such a system impossible. Private enterprise can only function efficiently and afford good employment and a good standard of living for the people if it is allowed to operate with reasonable freedom from Governmental restraints and is given the essential conditions for success. The most essential of these conditions is a plentiful and cheap supply of capital. Great Britain must therefore again become a country in which it is easy to accumulate capital and attractive to invest it. Heavy direct taxation, especially of the present type, e.g. Income Tax, Super Tax [sic], and Death Duties, all at high rates, is peculiarly inimical to the accumulation

of capital and a serious deterrent to its investment. It is also psychologically a serious discouragement to the enterprise and initiative which is essential to the wellbeing of an industrial and trading nation.

(FBI 1931b)

Rarely did the FBI voice its opinions so strongly. Nevertheless, the passage clearly illustrates the strength of feeling against prevailing tax rates and the antipathy towards public expenditure upon which it was founded.

Within the business community, and in its discussions with government, debate focused not only on the rate of income tax but also on the question of allowances for business undertakings. A limited measure of financial relief had been granted in 1929 with the de-rating scheme, whereby rates were reduced on property used for productive industry or freight transport, the central government reimbursing to local authorities a sum equal to the estimated loss of revenue from these sources.

Following the Report of the Royal Commission on the Income Tax (HMSO 1920), depreciation allowances had been granted in respect of wear and tear on plant and machinery,[5] a further (obsolescence) allowance also being paid if a capital asset was replaced. The Royal Commission had further recommended that the obsolescence allowance be granted irrespective of whether the capital asset was replaced or not. This proposal had not been accepted, but was seen by the business community as an important means whereby the income tax could be used to promote industrial rationalization.

The implication of this proposal was that firms which sought to scrap excess capacity were offered no incentive to do so by the taxation system, whereas firms which both scrapped and reinvested enjoyed a relative tax advantage. Had the proposal been adopted retained earnings and trading performance would have improved in the former group, there also being the possibility of a second-order effect if the additional resources now available after capital destruction were reinvested in expanding, profitable sectors. However, the proposal raised an important question of equity: with no tax on capital gains then being levied, would not an allowance for capital losses breach the neutrality requirement of a good tax system? Moreover, the positive second order effect was not automatically assured. In any case, when judged against the conventional criterion for investment incentives – the unit investment gain per unit of revenue foregone – the proposed instrument was actually an inefficient means of securing its stated purpose.

If the government had sought to promote the scrapping of excess physical capital through the tax system a more effective course would have been a cut in the standard rate or accelerated depreciation, the latter reducing the effective rate of tax by postponing the due date of tax liabilities.

However, here also there was a difficulty, for many of the firms in the industries requiring rationalization were tax-exhaustive (a situation of zero tax liabilities as a result of low or negative profitability) or nearly so. Thus, to make assistance effective, current allowances would have had to be converted into direct Exchequer grants (see HMSO 1982, ch. 15). It is difficult to imagine that such a tax instrument would have been acceptable between the wars when the basic tenet of government industrial policy was that the private sector, not the public, bear the responsibility for, and costs of, industrial rationalization. This said, such an instrument would have provided an important means for assisting the staple industries, one moreover that could also have lessened the regional problem if a requirement for receipt of these capital allowances had been that reinvestment be within the depressed areas.

To return now to the proposal as put, rather than the hypothetical alternatives, certain of these issues were considered in some detail by Inland Revenue and the Treasury in 1930. The objections raised by the two departments against capital allowances have a wider applicability, to the general question of using taxation to stimulate economic activity.

First, Inland Revenue maintained that since the real difficulty was in obtaining capital to finance rationalization schemes, rather than in entrepreneurs being 'deterred from [so doing] because they [did] not get obsolescence allowances', such allowances would do little to generate *additional* investment. Therefore, 'as a subsidy given from the Revenue to industry for the purpose of fostering rationalisation . . . the price would prove to be altogether out of proportion to the results' (PRO 1930c, 3–4). While such an argument was far from decisive, it was overshadowed by other, more weighty, objections: the schemes' cost was difficult to estimate – both departments were always reluctant to enter into open-ended commitments; and it threatened certain basic canons of the income tax code – therefore carrying with it the risk that it would be used as a precedent by other groups and would eventually result in a marked diminution of the tax base (PRO 1930g).

Capital allowances were firmly opposed throughout the rest of the 1930s. Indeed, all but very limited financial concessions to industry remained an anathema within Whitehall. Nowhere is this more clearly evident than in the very strong reaction of the authorities to the third report of the Special Areas Commissioner for England and Wales. The Commissioner, Sir P. M. Stewart, had not only made the radical suggestion that the further growth of industry in London should be controlled, but had also suggested a package of financial measures to induce new firms to locate in the Special Areas. Of these, the most controversial was the proposal to relieve from income tax profits not distributed but put to reserve, and exempt from income tax profits not exceeding £500 (HMSO 1936, para. 30).

Inland Revenue, believing 'that the trouble of the depressed areas [was] high cost[s] of production and [that] the taxation of the profit margin cannot lower the cost[s] of production', dismissed the proposal as of little financial significance to firms in these areas (PRO 1936f). Moreover, there were grave dangers associated with such a proposal: it was quite indefensible to give preferential treatment to new industry over existing industry in the Special Areas and, in the case of large companies, impossible to differentiate which of their factories made what profit; in the case of factory extensions it would be impossible to tell the extra profits due to the extension; concentration on profits gave no help to firms making losses; the Special Areas were not the only areas having depressed industries; and finally, tax reliefs could never be temporary. Accordingly, the memorandum concluded:

> that if the State is to embark upon the policy of holding out financial inducement for the development of enterprise in the Special Areas the true course is to determine the subsidy in a form that is available irrespective of the profits that may result from the enterprise and is directed to reducing any handicap that these areas suffer from. To attempt it through the Income Tax queers the Income Tax pitch and produces a capricious form of relief that does nothing effective to assist the Special Areas. (PRO 1936g)

The Treasury shared these objections to the proposal.[6] More generally, they placed special emphasis upon the fact that subsidies (either as negative or positive expenditures), by virtue of the fact that they were not selective, were financially expensive in terms of the results achieved, and raised administrative and political questions much wider than the specific issue of financial assistance to the Special Areas (PRO 1936h).

Financial assistance on any substantial scale to the business sector was seen as the first step in an irreversible process which would steadily erode the revenue base, and therefore threaten budgetary stability. It would also open up a Pandora's box of administrative difficulties with profound political implications for the role of the state in the economic–political life of the country. Experience since 1945 lends support to the existence of these difficulties, the legitimacy of which is largely a matter of political choice rather than economic debate. There was a definite reluctance to use the taxation system as a vehicle to aid industrial recovery; in addition, as is well established, interwar governments generally avoided intervention wherever possible. Where intervention proved unavoidable, as increasingly became the case in the 1930s (e.g. shipping), intervention was *ad hoc*, was directed to the industry as a whole, and most importantly did not operate through the taxation system.

Finally, a few preliminary conclusions may be drawn. Whilst there was a reluctance to use the tax system in a discriminatory manner, it was firmly accepted within the financial departments that taxation was a potentially important instrument of economic management, and that in particular a cut in income tax (which would affect both corporate and personal incomes) could have beneficial effects in promoting recovery. It was also recognized that in a depression increased taxation could exacerbate deflationary forces. Thus the foundations for modern economic management were already in existence; but it was the continued adherence to the balanced budget rule which prevented the effective translation of these attitudes into practical demand management. The reasons for the maintenance of budgetary orthodoxy must now be examined.

CHAPTER FIVE

THE BUDGET AND BUDGETARY POLICY: INTRODUCTION

Limited in its scope and objectives, seriously destabilizing in its operation. Such have been the judgements passed upon interwar fiscal policy (for example, Richardson 1967, 211–12; Pollard 1973, 209–10). These questions are explored in this and the two following chapters. First a satisfactory definition of the budget is obtained, and then the main issues involved in evaluating interwar budgetary policy are introduced. In chapter 6 the budgetary history of the period 1929–39 is chronicled; and, finally, in chapter 7 constant employment budget balance estimates are employed as a measure of changes in fiscal stance.

1 BUDGET DEFINITIONS

A necessary starting point in any discussion of interwar budgetary policy is the budget definition employed by the authorities. Hitherto, in discussing policy and its effects data have been presented for the combined public sector and its constituent parts. Hereafter, the figures used in this study relate to central government plus the social insurance funds. For the interwar period, when there were no nationalized industries and only a few public corporations, the principal omission is local government. Our objective is to embrace within our definition of the budget that sector of the economy over which the Treasury had effective control and through which it therefore exercised its fiscal policies. Since local government was largely independent of central control, its omission is therefore permissible. This does not, however, preclude consideration of the expenditures of local authorities and public corporations where appropriate; for example, when assessing the total effects of fiscal operations in chapter 7.

The interwar financial statistics for central government present a number of difficulties.

1. The budget, as conventionally defined at the time (identity (5.1) below), was not based on a coherent concept, nor did its definition remain constant. The exact components of the two sides of the account in any year were 'to some extent at least a matter of chance and partly even of choice' (Hicks 1938, 279).
2. The accounts were not only an amalgam of current and capital receipts and outlays, the composition of which varied from year to year, but in addition the budget did not cover the whole of central government activities; in particular, it excluded the social insurance funds (although the central government contribution to these funds was included in 'Ordinary Expenditure').
3. Expenditure as conventionally defined (G_c in identity (5.1) below) also omitted expenditure financed by borrowing under specific Acts of Parliament, while debt redemption was included in general expenditure. Revenue (T_c in identity (5.1) below), on the other hand, covered not only current tax and non-tax revenue but also included non-recurrent transfers as devices to aid the balancing of the budget.

Account of these factors was taken when redefining the budget on an unchanging and unambiguous basis. The starting point was the conventionally defined budget.

$$B_c \equiv T_c - G_c \tag{5.1}$$

where B_c was the budget balance; T_c 'Ordinary and Self-Balancing Revenue' which included the major tax receipts, the proceeds of sales of state property, repayment of loans granted to foreign governments, interest payments, shares in profits, receipts from special funds and the revenue from the Post Office; and G_c 'Ordinary and Self-Balancing Expenditure' which covered debt interest and sinking fund payments, expenditure on the armed forces and civil departments, capital expenditure (except certain items voted outside the budget by specific Acts relating mainly to outlay by the Post Office and, in the later 1930s, to defence expenditure), and the current account expenditure of the Post Office.

Thus defined, B_c was the balance used by the authorities and economic commentators in presenting and assessing policy. A balanced budget therefore meant that G_c should not exceed T_c.

The definition of the budget used in this study is:

$$B \equiv T - G \qquad (5.2)$$

where B is the budget balance and

$$T \equiv T_c - NRT + SIFPC \qquad (5.3)$$
$$G \equiv G_c + (CE + OB + DB - SF) + (SIFB - SIFGC) \qquad (5.4)$$

where T_c and G_c are as before, and

NRT = non-recurrent revenue included in T_c
SIFPC = private sector contributions to the social insurance funds
CE = capital expenditure financed by borrowing
OB = other expenditure financed by borrowing
DB = defence expenditure financed by borrowing
SF = sinking fund payments included in G_c
SIFB = total benefits paid by the social insurance funds
SIFGC = central government contributions to the social insurance funds included in G_c.

These adjustments serve two purposes. First, they revise the coverage of the central government accounts so that they conform more closely to those now currently in use. Secondly, they remove the effects of fiscal window-dressing: that is, the exclusion of non-recurrent receipts and the inclusion of various items of expenditure financed by borrowing nullifies the accounting devices employed by the Treasury to aid the achievement of a target balance B_c.

2 FISCAL WINDOW-DRESSING

Table 5.1 records the conventionally defined budget balance (B_c) and the adjustments made to expenditure and revenue as part of the procedure for obtaining an unchanging, and economically more significant, definition of the budget (B). As above, these adjustments can be considered in two stages.

The exclusion of sinking fund payments and extension of the budget definition to incorporate fully the social insurance funds requires little comment. Its effects are clear: the budget balance is improved in the case of the former; whereas, in the case of the latter, the balance of the social insurance funds could, at certain times (for example, 1929–31 when unemployment was rising rapidly), have important consequences for budgetary stability.

Prior to 1937 fiscal window-dressing on both sides of the budget accounts was small in magnitude at less than 1 per cent of GDP. Thereafter the difference between the conventionally defined and interim budget balances (cols 1 and 4) widened appreciably as fiscal window-dressing

Table 5.1 Central government budget balance: conventional and adjusted definitions 1929/30–1939/40 (£m.)

	Conventionally defined budget balance (B_c)	Fiscal window-dressing receipts	Fiscal window-dressing expenditure	Interim balance	Sinking fund	Social insurance	Adjusted budget balance (B)
	(1)	(2)	(3)	(4)	(5)	(6)	(7)
1929/30	−14.5	−3.5	−15.3	−33.3	+47.7	+3.0	+17.4
1930/1	−23.2	−23.2	−11.0	−57.4	+66.8	−33.6	−24.2
1931/2	+0.4	−20.9	−18.1	−38.6	+32.5	−39.6	−45.7
1932/3	−32.3	−11.9	−33.4	−77.6	+26.3	+1.1	−50.2
1933/4	+31.2	−10.0	−6.5	+14.7	+7.7	+10.9	+33.3
1934/5	+7.5	—	−7.5	0.0	+12.3	+13.5	+25.8
1935/6	+3.0	−8.0	−10.5	−15.5	+12.5	+19.0	+16.0
1936/7	−5.6	−11.8	−13.5	−30.9	+13.1	+32.5	+14.7
1937/8	+28.8	−5.1	−81.9	−58.2	+10.5	+32.0	−15.7
1938/9	−12.7	−1.5	−150.7	−164.9	+13.2	+14.5	−137.2
1939/40	−276.0	−1.4	−513.8	−791.2	+7.2	+34.8	−749.2

Source: Appendices II and III.

altered in form. The expenditure element increased markedly as defence expenditure (only part of which was included in G_c) came to dominate the course of budgetary policy, while on the revenue side fiscal window-dressing became insignificant, the scope for such transactions being greatly reduced as potential sources of revenue were exhausted.

Whilst for the greater part of the period the total magnitude of fiscal window-dressing was not large, such practices were central to budgetary planning. Consequently, an appreciation of them is crucial in understanding budgetary policy during this period, for fiscal window-dressing acted to conceal deficits and thus provided, within certain limits, a means of avoiding discretionary action and its consequent adverse effect on demand, if a target balance (B_c) was to be attained.

Fiscal window-dressing on the expenditure side took the form of excluding various categories of expenditure financed by borrowing – for capital purposes, defence and miscellaneous items – which more correctly should have been assigned to the budget. Although in one sense these items were visible, even if only to a few financial experts, and the veil over the authorities' activities was transparent, in general the authorities were successful in obscuring the true expenditure position and conveying the impression of adherence to orthodox financial principles.

Similarly, on the revenue side, non-recurrent items were brought in which should have been excluded according to the accounting practices ostensibly in use. These receipts were varied from year to year, according to the exigencies of the budgetary situation, as the Treasury sought to maintain the illusion of a balanced budget throughout the greater part of the 1930s. While the sums involved in this sphere of fiscal window-dressing were generally smaller than on the expenditure side, the operations were more intricate, largely invisible and involved a more complicated subterfuge.

The ability to indulge in this type of fiscal window-dressing or cosmetic action primarily stemmed from the absence of a rigorous statutory definition of the budget. By the interwar years, as Chancellors were forced to try and accommodate demands for greater social expenditure within the dictates of budgetary orthodoxy, the budget identity had become an amorphous hybrid, an amalgam of current and capital accounts, devoid of any internal consistency or tangible economic significance. There is no evidence in the Treasury papers that budgetary reform was seriously considered. Primarily because few were really aware of the extent to which such devices were employed in budgetary policy, there was no real pressure for reform. As Phillips argued:

> there is no great technical difficulty in producing for a series of years budgets which are balanced at the end of the year to the nearest penny. ... Perhaps half a dozen financial writers in the country would understand from published accounts what was happening, but I doubt if any one of the half dozen is capable of making the position clear to the public. (PRO 1936i)

There were, however, limits to the Treasury's activities in this field. Under Churchill's stewardship of the national finances (1924–9) 'devices of unprecedented ingenuity for balancing the budget' had been employed which deeply offended conservative financial interests (Hicks 1938, 7, 11). In the 1930s the Treasury was careful not to run the risk of having its activities exposed. Hence the use of such expedients in any one year was limited; for example, in April 1933 (when the Treasury had already decided to appropriate £10 million from the War Loan Depreciation Fund), Phillips suggested that in addition £3.8 million could be obtained by taking two years' surplus from the Savings Banks in one year. Hopkins, however, firmly opposed such a course: 'in my view one big sin like the Depreciation Fund is all right, but one big one and one little one side by side sounds too unorthodox and I shouldn't do it' (PRO 1933i).

While non-recurrent receipts paid into revenue (T_c) were postponed or accelerated according to 'necessity',[1] in addition, during discussions preceding the presentation of the budget, the Treasury would manipulate the revenue and expenditure estimates so that a potential deficit 'would then be covered on paper' (PRO 1935b). As was shown in the previous chapter, the Inland Revenue would occasionally relax pressure for the collection of income and surtax in the final quarter of the financial year if it was anticipated that the estimate would be exceeded and the financial position was likely to be more serious the following year. The sums not collected would then be taken as arrears the following year. In normal circumstances the Treasury avoided recourse to the device of underestimating expenditure and inflating the revenue estimates, for in the first case they ran the risk of having to introduce a Supplementary later in the year, while the second course entailed the danger that their activities would be exposed (PRO 1934c; 1935c). Moreover, a budget that was so tightly planned would not contain a 'hidden reserve' which was seen as necessary to meet unforeseen contingencies (PRO 1932l). Nevertheless, the serious budgetary difficulties of the early 1930s meant that such devices were employed; in particular, the estimates for expenditure on unemployment were reduced in 1932 and 1933 below the figures recommended by the Ministry of Labour as part of the Treasury's attempts to avoid raising taxation further and thus retard the nascent recovery (p. 101).

In the circumstances of the 1930s where the existence of mass unemployment made it politically difficult to achieve the tightening required to balance the budget in the face of autonomous fluctuations in activity, fiscal window-dressing and related practices served the essential function of allowing the Treasury apparently to adhere to orthodox financial principles whilst simultaneously limiting the extent of fiscal tightening required in a depression to maintain a balanced budget (B_c).

The existence of such budgetary practices would support the rather cynical view, expressed in a more recent budget debate, that 'all Budgets are to some extent mythical creatures comprising a considerable admixture of illusions' (*Hansard* 1979). It also suggests some scope for revision of the traditional interpretation of the authorities' belief in balanced budgets, in that adherence to budgetary orthodoxy would appear to owe something to political expediency as well as 'sound' economic principles.

3 BUDGETARY ORTHODOXY

We consider first the principles underlying nineteenth-century public finance: for it was the supposed adherence of interwar governments and their officials to these principles that underlay the 'new' economics' critique of fiscal policy.

In general terms these principles can be summarized in a set of propositions which hinged on the balanced budget convention (or rule), that the minimum objective of government in the financial sphere was to cover its expenditure with its receipts. Two exceptions, or relaxations of this rule, were permitted: the one, in wartime, when the exigencies of the situation allowed *limited* recourse to borrowing; the other, capital projects, which if shown to be remunerative in an accepted accounting sense could be financed by borrowing.

A number of related propositions followed from the balanced budget convention and the view of the limited functions of the state from which it, in turn, derived.

1 Since taxes were a burden on productive enterprise, and expenditure should be limited to those functions of government considered absolutely necessary, the size of the budget (in relation to GDP) should be kept small, and the aim of budgetary policy should be an *ex post* surplus to permit debt redemption and/or remission of taxation.
2 The balanced budget convention was further reinforced by the antipathy towards deficit-finance, a process which was viewed as withdrawing funds from productive employment.

An appreciation, however, is essential of the historical setting in which these principles evolved: first, in understanding their strength and diuturnity; and secondly, why they ceased to be appropriate in the changed economic and political conditions of the twentieth century.

When Adam Smith propounded the maxim in *The Wealth of Nations* (1776), which underlay the balanced budget convention, that 'what is prudence in the conduct of every private family, can scarce be folly in that of a great Kingdom', the target for attack was the then prevailing mercantilist doctrines. It was not intended as an absolute rule, immutable, and applicable to all historical situations. Rather, it derived from Smith's conviction (which was shared by the later 'classical' economists) that the state was an inefficient form of organization for wealth creation, because it rested on a pattern of special trading privileges, grants of monopoly and tariffs; and that governments, unless constrained by a balanced budget rule, would retard capital formation if they were permitted to borrow funds since these would otherwise be productively invested. Thus the classical case for balanced budgets rested on a series of interrelated propositions, of both an economic and political nature, which reflected attitudes towards the role of the state, the responsibilities of government, and the belief that the unconstrained operation of market forces would ensure full employment equilibrium (Burkhead 1954, 193, 215).

Similarly, the preoccupation of contemporary economists and financiers with redeeming the national debt reflected prevailing conditions, notably that control over the rate of interest or the domestic price level was not within the power of the authorities, and thus the debt could become an important restrictive element in the economy whilst, in addition, frustrating operations calculated to reduce the burden of the debt (Hicks 1953, 26).

A number of other factors were also important. In the conditions of primitive accounting control which held prior to Gladstone's reforms of the 1860s, a balanced budget was used as a means of assessing the efficiency of financial management. More generally, the budget was a political event, a means of discussing and criticizing the economic policy of a government (Hicks 1963, 144–5). As has recently been shown, the balanced budget convention, the cornerstone of the nineteenth-century 'fiscal constitution', was not 'some unthinking Victorian moral code which had nothing whatsoever to do with the rational conduct of government affairs'; on the contrary, it 'played a crucial role in . . . constraining the otherwise inherent biases of that system to over-expenditure and deficit-finance' (Buchanan *et al.* 1978, 46–7). These biases or weaknesses in the fiscal constitution centred on fears of profligacy of politicians in a democratic political setting, the weak position of Parliament in the financial control it exercised over the executive, and the leverage exerted by the service departments, with their incessant demands for increased expenditure, within the executive.

As Hicks (1953, 28) has argued, adherence to balanced budgets in the nineteenth century was 'a sound economic instinct' given the backcloth of rapidly expanding population and growing prosperity. Moreover, the evidence suggests that towards the close of the century there occurred 'a not insignificant change of heart, at least in the sense of reluctance to increase tax rates substantially in bad times', while the balanced budget convention

> became increasingly embarrassing, and indeed economically inappropriate, as the strong expansionary phase of the British economy died away. It seems that a sort of horse-sense prevented the later Victorians from following too faithfully an inappropriate fiscal policy. The attempt to return to the pure milk of Gladstonian finance in the next Great Depression (particularly in the second budget of 1931 . . .) finally demonstrated that the old medicine was no longer safe, unadulterated, for internal use.

Returning now to the interwar years, we may summarize as follows the traditional interpretation of the allegiance to budgetary orthodoxy:

1 Many have argued that the Treasury, consciously or unconsciously, adhered to some sort of belief, stemming from classical economics,

> that all factors of production are normally and inevitably utilized by private business, [and that] it follows that the State can obtain the use of such factors only by preventing private business from using them. . . . From this it follows that the first principle of 'sound' Public Finance is that the budget should be balanced.
> (Schumacher 1944, 86)

2 Unbalanced budgets were counterproductive because they would have an adverse effect on business confidence, especially if they resulted

from unremunerative public works. As Arndt (1944, 55) put it, 'what was gained on the swings of public investment was, therefore, liable to be lost in part on the roundabouts of private investment'.
3 Within this schema it was further contended that unbalanced budgets were inflationary.
4 An increase in the size of the deadweight national debt was seen as highly undesirable for the increased debt charge would place additional burdens on productive enterprise.

Against these supposed tenets of orthodox thought Keynes and other advocates of a more active and interventionalist policy argued that in the circumstances of the 1930s it was absurd to hold that a budget deficit would 'crowd-out' private sector demand or that an increase in the money stock would be inflationary. The fact that the financing of the deficit would have monetary consequences, in the sense that the government's debt operations acted on the credit base, was not a matter of contention. Rather, the area of dispute was whether inflation was automatic and not instead dependent on the pressure of demand in the labour market. This issue, a central theme of the interwar policy debate, is considered in greater depth in the following section and in chapter 8.

The automatic association of budget deficits with inflation stemmed principally from a misinterpretation of the causes of inflation, this in turn resulting from the fact that classical economic theory drew an artificial distinction between real and monetary forces (Winch 1972, 97–8). In addition, there had developed a strong and apparently irrational fear of inflation – for the course of the price level was downwards over 1920–34 – by those who had witnessed the continental inflations of the 1920s (see pp. 91–2). This was to influence many of the policy decisions of the period, in particular, the return to the gold standard in 1925 and the heroic attempts made to remain on gold in 1931.

It is usually argued that the preoccupation with the national debt stemmed from a fundamental confusion between the position of a private business or individual and that of the state, for it ignored the fact that whereas the former must default unless able to meet expenditure out of income, the latter's debt was not a burden in the same sense since the state represents the community as a whole and holds its debt with the same body it represents. In fact, the authorities' fears were not as irrational as one would suppose. As has been shown, the interwar years were characterized by a falling price level, fears about future population trends, and a greatly enlarged debt charge caused by the First World War. The latter was to reinforce the already existing deflationary bias in budgetary policy, while the greatly increased transfer payments within the economy acted, given the generally regressive nature of the tax system, to depress the overall propensity to consume and thus aggregate demand.

The question whether the direct demand effects of an unbalanced budget would be counteracted by an adverse effect on business confidence and therefore private sector demand, through the effect either on the rate of interest or more generally on business expectations, was central to the economic policy debate of the 1930s. Moreover, it is still pertinent today, for to a large extent the success of fiscal operations in a capitalist society depends on their being favourably received by financial markets.

On strictly economic issues the Treasury's position has been misunderstood. On the question whether unbalanced budgets automatically resulted in inflation, the Treasury, in the early 1930s, held the following position:

> it would be an entire mistake to suppose that an unbalanced Budget means immediate or rapid inflation. In the case of a financially strong country the process from Budget deficits to inflation is a long drawn out agony. . . . So long as the Government can borrow from the public to cover the deficit there is no inflation . . . the crash will only come, if it does come, at long last when the public is completely discouraged and will lend the Government no more money. Till that moment arrives there will be no inflation. (PRO 1933c, 1–2)

This document suggests that the balanced budget convention in addition to having an economic rationale also derived from political and psychological origins.

While maintenance of balanced budgets was publicly expressed in terms of adherence to certain economic principles, in fact within government it was political considerations that were paramount. On this point it is worth citing at length a Treasury document – a comment on Keynes's *Means to Prosperity* (1933) – which articulates these political considerations and puts the policy prescriptions of the 'new' economics within a political, as well as economic, context:

> Keynes and Co., whilst agreeing that normal Budgets must be balanced to prevent disaster, say that this is the one psychological year when a concatenation of circumstances has arisen to justify deliberately unbalancing the Budget. But can anyone suppose that, once a precedent of this kind was set, people would remember the special arguments adduced to justify it? Whatever may be thought by people outside, members of the House of Commons will realise how impossible it would be once we had abandoned the principle of paying our way to stop a rising tide of expenditure. Within a year or two (i.e. very near the next General Election) there would be the sort of situation we had in 1931, i.e. the need for new cuts and new taxes.

From this a very important conclusion followed: remission of taxation only had a favourable psychological effect when occasioned by a previous budget surplus:

> Would there be the same psychological effect when the remission was only given by unbalancing the Budget and when it would be followed immediately by clamant demands for new expenditure, every demand justified on the same grounds as had led to the original unbalancing of the Budget and the beginning of borrowing. Would not the ordinary taxpayer and the business man very soon begin to have a feeling of uneasiness and apprehension? After all people will realise that the bill must be paid if not this year next year or the year after. Uncertainty and apprehension as to the future would very quickly cancel out any immediate psychological benefit which the reduction of taxation by unbalancing the Budget would promote. (PRO 1933j, 1–2)[2]

Thus the precept of the balanced budget acted as the ultimate constraint on the growth of expenditure, since it moderated and tempered the natural demands of politicians and sectional interests for new expenditure, and provided a 'neutral' framework within which competing demands were reconciled.

This conclusion relates to recent literature in 'public choice' economics, in particular the new critique of Keynesian economics developed by Buchanan and Wagner (1977) and Buchanan et al. (1978). This is concerned less with the fundamental accuracy of the Keynesian diagnosis of inherent instability and potential for under-employment equilibrium in market economies, and more with the realism of the political philosophy underlying the 'new' economics. This critique rests on two premises.

1 The instrument Keynes introduced to ensure full employment – budget deficits – removed completely the institutional constraint to the growth of expenditure.
2 Keynes's assumptions about political behaviour – described by his biographer as the 'presuppositions of Harvey Road' (Harrod 1951, 183, 192–3) – were naïve and had dangerous implications for political–economic stability. Thus, serious doubts have been cast upon Keynes's presupposition that the small élite responsible for formulating economic policy would, even in the face of historical evidence to the contrary, always act in accordance with the public interest and not succumb to political or other pressures.

It is contended that such a view, combined with the additional instrument of economic policy provided by the 'new' economics, was both unrealistic and totally unsuitable for the conditions of a representative democracy, for the abandonment of the balanced budget constraint permitted politicians to engage in operations against the long-term public interest by serving their short-term political and electoral advantage.

The foregoing analysis suggests that the Treasury held a similar position, although it was never articulated in such a systematic and precise form. Instead, it derived from an intuitive conviction that, whilst Keynes and other advocates of an active fiscal policy essentially desired long-term balanced budgets,[3] such a policy of 'functional finance' was politically unrealistic and even naïve, for political pressures would vitiate the imperative of raising taxation (to create the surplus) as boom developed.

Even in the 1944 *Employment Policy* White Paper, the so-called 'formal recognition of the principles of the Keynesian Revolution in Britain' (Winch 1972, 279), there was a definite unwillingness to countenance unbalanced budgets as a long-term policy. Thus Beveridge (1944, 264) accused the Treasury of being 'still far too inhibited in regard to central finance, too fearful of increasing the national debt'. Correct as this accusation was, the Treasury's continuing doubts about deficit-finance owed little to theoretical considerations and instead reflected the fear, widely voiced in Whitehall, that the complete removal of the balanced budget rule (either over one year or the course of a trade cycle) would lead to an explosion of expenditure and the assumption of greatly increased state powers in the postwar period.

It is also interesting to note that in the formative period of the monetarist counter-revolution of the 1960s, an integral part of the attack on the efficacy of fiscal policy centred on an appreciation of the political factors involved in formulating budgetary policy and the way in which discretionary action could in practice be destabilizing. Admittedly, the main thrust of attack centred on theoretical issues, in particular whether changes in the money stock had an indirect effect on aggregate demand as a result of wealth effects, but as Friedman (1968, 3) says:

> In the United States, the revival of belief in the potency of monetary policy was strengthened also by increasing disillusionment with fiscal policy, not so much with its potential to affect aggregate demand as with the practical and political feasibility of so using it.

In the following chapters it will be shown that while on economic grounds alone the Treasury remained sceptical throughout the 1930s of the efficacy of the policy prescriptions of the 'new' economics, on strictly political grounds monetary policy remained a more acceptable instrument of stabilization policy for in a sense it was politically neutral. Thus Phillips, when asked to compare the respective merits of fiscal and monetary policy, concluded that while both sets of instruments could be used to promote recovery, monetary policy was preferable, deficit-finance 'being a useless complication and a very dangerous one because it

[was] difficult to reverse and [could get] completely out of control' (PRO 1933c, 2–3).

For the budgetary authorities, gravely concerned as they were about current expenditure levels, deficit-financing was thus unacceptable because it would have strengthened the already powerful forces making for expenditure growth. These forces were described by the May Committee in the following terms:[4]

> After the heavy sacrifices of the war large sections of the nation looked to the post-war period with the natural expectation of a general improvement in the old conditions of life. The disappointment of many hopes in the economic sphere seemed to intensify demands for improvements from political action and all parties have felt the insistent pressure for promises of 'reforms' as the price of support. . . . At election times those desiring increased expenditure on particular objects are usually far better organized, far more active and vocal than those who favour the vague and uninspiring course of strict economy; and as a result candidates not infrequently find themselves returned to Parliament committed, on a one-sided presentation of a case, to a course which on fuller knowledge they see to be opposed to the national interests. (HMSO 1931b, 12–13)

What exactly should be understood by political neutrality, in the context of the choice of monetary or fiscal policy? Political neutrality can be considered at two levels. First, the belief in the *laissez-faire* ideal that market forces, unencumbered by government interference, would ensure the attainment of full employment equilibrium and the optimal allocation of productive resources. Secondly, the fear, in some Hayekian sense (Hayek 1944; 1979), that since political parties and pressure groups always violate general economic rules, acceptance of the policy prescripts of the 'new' economics would create the opportunity for politicians to interfere with the operation of market forces for the benefit of particular groups, this development culminating in the situation in which politicians, for electoral purposes, would be forced to pursue policies against the long-term public interest.

The Keynesian revolution as applied to public finance overthrew the balanced budget convention but failed to substitute an alternative set of guidelines calculated to constrain the natural profligacy of politicians in a democratic political setting. Thus was created the possibility of political–business cycles.

While such cycles were not possible in the interwar period, the influence of political factors cannot be completely discounted. Accusations were made against Churchill's 1929 budget (delivered only some six weeks before a general election), which had remitted taxes across the board, that it was a blatant act of electioneering. Similar comments were evoked by the change in the government's unemployment policy in 1935, the liberalization in attitudes towards public works reflecting the political threat posed by Lloyd George's 'New Deal'. Finally, there is no doubt that Chamberlain's budgetary strategy of 1932-5 was also strongly influenced by political considerations.

The importance of political neutrality as a guideline for policy may be illustrated by reference to two important episodes during the interwar period: the adoption of tariffs in 1931-2, and the motives for the return to the gold standard in 1925.[5]

At first sight the adoption of tariffs would seem to conflict with the view that, in general, the economic policies adopted during these years attempted to solve economic problems without creating a series of vested interests which would endanger long-run economic and political stability. But, in the eyes of the authorities, such a situation was guarded against by the creation of the Import Duties Advisory Committee which, rather than the Board of Trade, was charged with overseeing the operation of the tariff and considering applications from specific groups for further tariff protection, thus appearing to take tariff questions 'out of politics'. This objective is visible from the very earliest stages of planning the tariff. Indeed, the correct functioning of this committee was seen as the most important issue in framing the tariff (Conservative Party 1931, para. 33).

In a rather different sense the idea of political neutrality has an applicability to the motives underlying the return to gold, for in its most extreme theoretical form the gold standard can be viewed as the very embodiment of the *laissez-faire* ideal in that the adjustment mechanism would be entirely automatic, thus precluding state intervention or management. For example, at the famous dinner party in March 1925 when Churchill assembled together Keynes, McKenna, Niemeyer and Bradbury to discuss the merits of return, Grigg (1948, 183) – the only source for this episode – relates that Bradbury 'made a great point of the fact that the Gold Standard was knave-proof. It could not be rigged for political or even more unworthy reasons.'

This raises the interesting question of why the economic authorities, indeed informed opinion generally, were unwilling to trust politicians with economic management. A form of self-denying ordinance undoubtedly prevailed in the 1920s, one in part stemming from an innate fatalism about governmental impotence in the economic sphere, but more importantly deriving from a deeply rooted fear of political abuse of economic instruments. The former influence was not a serious impediment as such, for success with active economic management would soon overcome this inhibition, as indeed it did in the 1930s. The latter fear, however, posed a greater constraint as it

> derived partly from the experience of inflation during and after the

war, which was put down to political chicanery rather than to the war. Out of it arose the moral denunciation of the 'managed currency' of 1914–25, and the dangerous myth that a gold standard like the one of 1925–31 was automatic, and not (as it in fact was) also 'managed'.

(Pollard 1970, 18)

In the creation of this 'myth' the example of the continental inflations of the early 1920s was undoubtedly influential. Whilst we can see *ex post facto* that this fear of inflation stemmed from a misunderstanding of cause and effect in inflationary processes, we can also appreciate the profound impact on those responsible for formulating economic policy in Britain of the impoverishment and destitution of much of the German middle class and the subsequent growth of extremist politics. Nor should the British inflation of 1919–20 be forgotten: this was to have a lasting impression upon policy-makers and, very likely, was to prejudice the case against deficit-finance in the very different circumstances of the 1930s.

The balanced budget convention and belief in the automatic operation of the gold standard were thus in a sense analogous, in that they were perceived as a means of controlling political action which could be disadvantageous to the long-term public interest, and had developed as responses to the dangers inherent in a democratic, pluralistic society. It is within this framework of analysis, rather than one which views adherence to balanced budgets exclusively in terms of an economic rationale, that we can now proceed to survey the budgetary history of the 1930s. Before doing so, however, the crowding-out issue is further considered.

4 CROWDING-OUT

In this final section we introduce more fully the crowding-out debate, its relevance to the issue as to whether budget deficits and public works could be employed as policy instruments to stabilize demand, and the reasons why the business community might react adversely to particular economic policies. A detailed analysis of the 'Treasury view' is deferred until chapter 8.

In discussing the crowding-out issue it is necessary first to distinguish between real productive resources and financial resources, a distinction not always made evident in the literature (Kahn 1978, 545). Our concern here is with the latter, although as is shown in chapter 8 the Ministry of Labour's objections to the 1929 Liberal public works programme centred upon real factors, in the form of labour supply.

Financial crowding-out may be described in the following manner: with a given money stock, an increase in bond sales (to finance a budget deficit and/or public works programme) would have little or no impact on aggregate demand because the rise in interest rates required to sell the additional bonds would crowd-out an equivalent volume of other expenditures (private investment and consumption, in so far as they are sensitive to interest rates). In its most extreme form, therefore, it would be held that fiscal operations could not affect the level of aggregate demand, their influence being limited to determining the allocation of expenditure between different purposes.[6]

Unfortunately, the use of such arguments during the interwar period was characteristized by a failure to specify clearly what factors were operating to raise interest rates and the channels through which they operated. Two main alternatives suggest themselves.

1 That with a fixed money stock and at a position of full employment, the financing of a deficit purely by bond sales crowds-out private expenditure because extra transaction balances are required for a higher level of incomes and these will be released from asset balances only as interest rates rise.
2 Also with a fixed money stock but at a position of less than full employment (or, indeed, irrespective of the state of demand in labour markets), a deficit financed by bond sales would crowd-out private expenditure if there was sufficient opposition to, and apprehension about, the government's policy that there was an increased demand for cash balances (a change in liquidity preference) which prevented idle balances from taking up the additional bonds without raising interest rates.

The first case represents what is commonly termed crowding-out; the second may be viewed as a form of psychological crowding-out. It is of especial relevance to the interwar policy debate where the attitude of financial markets could effectively neutralize fiscal operations. In both cases, *ceteris paribus*, an accommodating monetary policy – financing the deficit or increased public works expenditures by new money rather than by bond sales – could have prevented crowding-out. But here also, there was scope for adverse confidence effects; that is, such a monetary policy might be viewed as irresponsible, thus reducing private sector investment via an adverse change in business confidence (Nevin 1955, 63).

The first form of crowding-out also represents the supposed position of the Treasury during the interwar period. Thus Stein (1969, 138–9 and n. 17) (in common with other economists) has described the 'Treasury view', as expressed in the infamous *Memoranda on Certain Proposals Relating to Unemployment* (HMSO 1929), as

> the position that the amount of savings available at any time was given and in use, so that an increase in government borrowing to pay for public works would only displace private investment and would not add to total employment.... [This view was] a particular application of

'Say's Law', an old economic principle which says that supply creates its own demand and that there cannot be a general deficiency of demand. This is the same as saying that all income that is saved is automatically invested and constitutes a demand for goods.

However, references by the Treasury to a crowding-out mechanism were not of this first type, but rather of the second (see pp. 153–5, 161–3). Accordingly, the determinants of confidence amongst the business and financial communities – as understood by the Treasury – require consideration.

Why were these groups in general assumed to be so opposed to a counter-cyclical fiscal policy that the effectiveness of such a policy would be constrained by a rise in interest rates resulting from an adverse change in liquidity preference when the bonds to finance such a policy were marketed? A number of explanations may be suggested.

1 The business community had a very low level of trade cycle consciousness (i.e. a limited perception of the trade cycle) and tended, in times of depression, to attribute their difficulties 'to particular factors which affect the particular business or at best the particular industry, such as the activities of competitors at home and abroad, a shift in the direction of demand, and so on', rather than to a general deficiency of demand (Bretherton et al. 1941, 32).
2 On political grounds the business community might view as undesirable an increase in government expenditure because it would – especially in the case of public works – be accompanied by increased state interference in industry.
3 More generally, if it was believed on economic grounds that fiscal operations were incapable of permanently raising the level of employment – because they did little to improve the economy's productive base – such a policy would flounder on the fears that the increased debt charge would eventually have to be covered from higher taxation. The *prospect* of such an increase in taxation might anyway itself ensure the failure of such a policy as a result of disincentive effects on investment.

Similar considerations applied to the state of confidence in financial markets, although special factors, stemming from London's pre-eminent position as an international financial centre, should also be taken into account. In particular, apprehensiveness (no doubt made legitimate by the 1931 crisis) that the government's financial policy would be viewed abroad as 'unsound', with the risk of an outflow of sterling (with consequences for the domestic credit base) and upward pressure on short-term interest rates, imposed an 'external constraint' on policy-making.

The strict standards required to act as a leading financial centre imbued economic policy with a moral dimension which, by the interwar years, acted to Britain's disadvantage because it made imperative more exacting standards of financial conduct than those adhered to by other countries. When, as occurred in 1931, Britain was deemed to have failed to meet these standards, the consequences were severe. Moreover, the reluctance to balance the budget strictly, characteristic of other countries during periods of depression, was an important means of avoiding the deflationary demand effects of adherence to budgetary orthodoxy in the face of severe autonomous fluctuations in activity. British policy-makers considered this course of action to be unavailable, although fiscal window-dressing was to serve the same objective, albeit with a large element of deception.

It is contended that, in the past, arguments which rely on business psychology as an explanation of opposition to the policy prescriptions of the 'new' economics have been too easily dismissed by holding that such opposition was irrational and/or unascertainable (for example Winch 1972, 218–19). By virtue of its intangibility confidence cannot be accurately specified or measured; that fact, however, hardly questions its existence or potency. Moreover, this dismissive viewpoint has resulted from an approach which is too narrow in its perspective, in that it has focused on what would appear to be the purely economic interests of the business and financial communities and has ignored the political and indirect economic dimensions of the question.

Unfortunately, the business community rarely expressed the grounds for their opposition to unbalanced budgets and large-scale public works programmes as remedies for unemployment.[7] Nevertheless, from such evidence as is available (for example FBI 1930), it is clear that, for organized business, the preferred remedy for high unemployment, low demand and low profitability was remission of taxation, a remedy based on an implicit belief in the potency of market forces and, as already noted, the view that income tax entered into costs.

Given the balanced budget constraint, continued 'unproductive' expenditure on public works inhibited such a remission of taxation. Moreover, in so far as businesses viewed the demand for their products in narrow terms (part of the aforementioned low level of trade cycle consciousness), it was difficult for them to perceive that expenditure on public works was more effective in inducing recovery than a reduction in costs and stimulus to investment afforded by a reduction in direct taxation.

In these circumstances, opposition to unbalanced budgets and public works programmes becomes rather more cogent. While on strictly economic grounds this viewpoint might be suspect, because in general the multiplier effects of an increase in expenditure can be expected to exceed those of a cut in taxation, in formulating this policy preference attention was not exclusively confined to the direct economic issues. Therefore, assumptions about the state of confidence must once again be accorded a significant role in any explanation of the continuance of financial orthodoxy by governments during the interwar period.

CHAPTER SIX

BUDGETARY POLICY 1929-39

The 1930s witnessed important changes in the nature and functions of budgetary policy, such that by the eve of the Second World War fiscal instruments had assumed a central role in macroeconomic management, the latter itself a new activity for government. The objectives of this chapter are twofold: to survey the budgetary history of the 1930s; and to illustrate the practical operation of budgetary orthodoxy, together with the changes in policy occasioned by rearmament, so as to provide a backcloth for our later discussion of the 'Treasury view'. The chapter divides into three parts: first, an outline budgetary history; second, a discussion of the principal developments in budgetary policy; and third, some preliminary conclusions about the progress made towards the managed economy by 1939. An evaluation of changes in fiscal stance, and the influence of the characteristics of the fiscal system upon such changes, is deferred until the following chapter.

1 BUDGETARY HISTORY

The overall budgetary position is summarized in table 6.1. Tables 6.2, 6.5 and 6.7 are budget summaries, showing the main details of the annual budgets for each of the three cyclical episodes under review.[1]

Depression 1929–33

The depression had an immediate and marked effect on the budget balance which moved into deficit as a result of the automatic response of receipts and expenditures to a cyclical downturn, not because of discretionary action for stabilization purposes. As table 6.1 shows, between

Table 6.1 Central government receipts, expenditure and budget balance: conventional and adjusted definitions 1929/30–1939/40*

(% of GDP)	(T_c/Y)	(G_c/Y)	(B_c/Y)	(T/Y)	(G/Y)	(B/Y)
1929/30	19.2	19.5	−0.3	21.1	20.7	+0.4
1930/1	20.7	21.2	−0.6	22.1	22.7	−0.6
1931/2	22.0	22.0	0.0	23.6	24.8	−1.2
1932/3	21.9	22.7	−0.9	23.9	25.2	−1.3
1933/4	21.1	20.3	+0.8	23.2	22.3	+0.9
1934/5	19.8	19.7	+0.2	22.2	21.6	+0.6
1935/6	19.9	19.9	+0.1	22.1	21.7	+0.4
1936/7	20.2	20.3	−0.1	22.3	22.0	+0.3
1937/8	19.9	19.3	+0.6	22.0	22.3	−0.3
1938/9	19.9	20.1	−0.3	22.0	24.7	−2.7
1939/40	20.0	24.8	−4.9	21.9	35.1	−13.2

(£m.)	(T_c)	(G_c)	(B_c)	(T)	(G)	(B)
1929/30	815.0	829.5	−14.5	893.9	876.5	+17.4
1930/1	857.8	881.0	−23.2	915.1	939.3	−24.2
1931/2	851.5	851.1	+0.4	914.5	960.2	−45.7
1932/3	827.0	859.3	−32.3	903.9	954.1	−50.2
1933/4	809.4	778.2	+31.2	890.0	856.7	+33.3
1934/5	804.6	797.1	+7.5	899.3	873.5	+25.8
1935/6	844.8	841.8	+3.0	935.7	919.7	+16.0
1936/7	896.6	902.2	−5.6	990.0	975.3	+14.7
1937/8	948.7	919.9	+28.8	1,051.5	1,067.2	−15.7
1938/9	1,006.2	1,018.9	−12.7	1,114.1	1,251.3	−137.2
1939/40	1,132.2	1,408.2	−276.0	1,241.0	1,990.2	−749.2

Sources: The actual figures are drawn from *Financial Accounts of the United Kingdom*, 1929/30–1939/40, House of Commons paper, annual (hereafter *Financial Accounts*) and the working notes to Feinstein (1972); the GDP figures from table 7.1.

Notes:
* See pp. 79–80 for the budget definitions.

1929/30 and 1932/3 the budget balance (B/Y) deteriorated by 1.7 percentage points of GDP (or £67.6 million). The deterioration of the conventionally defined balance (B_c/Y), however, was smaller (0.6 percentage points of GDP, or £17.8 million) and followed a somewhat different course, reflecting the authorities' attempts to minimize by fiscal window-dressing the published deficit.

Tables 6.1 and 6.2 record the authorities' efforts to restore budgetary equilibrium in the face of deepening depression; they indicate that before September 1931 these centred on raising additional taxation. The emphasis in the 1930 budget was almost exclusively on direct taxation,

Table 6.2 Budget summary 1929/30–1932/3: published forecasts and results (£m.)

	1929/30	1930/1	1931/2 (April)	1931/2 (Sept.)	1932/3
1 Budget balance (B_c) of previous year	+18.4	−14.5	−23.2	..	+0.4
2 Budget on existing basis					
Revenue (T_c)	834.7	823.6	847.6	825.8††	846.4
Expenditure (G_c)	822.7	870.9	889.9	900.5‡‡	848.1
Balance (B_c)	+12.0	−47.3	−37.4†	−74.7	−1.7
3 Discretionary changes					
(i) Taxation					
first year					
– direct	—	+31.5	+10.0‡	+29.0	—
– indirect	−7.9	+2.3	+7.5	+11.5	+2.5
full year					
– direct	—	+43.5	—	+57.5	—
– indirect	−8.0	+2.4	+8.0	+24.0	+3.0
(ii) Economies	—	—	—	+35.7***	—
(iii) Miscellaneous	—	+16.0*	+20.0**	—	—
4 Budget Estimates					
Revenue (T_c)	826.8	873.3	885.1	866.3	848.9
Expenditure (G_c)	822.7	871.0	884.9	864.8	848.1
Balance (B_c)	+4.1	+2.2	+0.1	+1.5	+0.8
5 Budget outturn					
Revenue (T_c)	815.0	857.8	—	851.5	827.0
Expenditure (G_c)	829.5	881.0	—	851.1	859.3
Balance (B_c)	−14.5	−23.2	—	+0.4	−32.3

Sources: *Financial Accounts*; *Financial Statements*, House of Commons paper, annual (hereafter *Financial Statements*); appendix II.

Notes:
* Transfer from Rating Relief Suspense Account.
† Deficit reduced from £42.3m. to £37.4m. by a transfer from the above account.
‡ This gain derived from a rescheduling of income tax payments, the benefit to the Exchequer only applying for one year.
** Planned transfer from Old Exchange Account.
†† Since the April budget the revenue estimates had been reduced by £59.3m., this composed of an Inland Revenue shortfall of £25m., Customs and Excise £4m., and the result of the Hoover moratorium £30.3m.
‡‡ The £15.6m. net increase in expenditure since the April budget consisted of the following changes in estimates: Hoover moratorium (−£13.6m.), debt interest and sinking fund (−£4.8m.), cessation of borrowing for the Unemployment Fund (+£25m.) and the Road Fund (+£9m.).
*** Comprising economies of £22m. and a reduction in planned sinking fund payments of £13.7m.

while in the 1931 budgets direct taxation was raised by approximately twice as much as indirect.

This strategy followed from two factors:

1 On grounds of equity, and under the influence of electoral pressures, the Labour Government attempted to minimize the increase in indirect taxes because of their regressive incidence.
2 In the early stages of a depression indirect taxes were more sensitive to income changes whereas (because of the lag between earnings and assessment) income and surtax maintained their yield.

By early 1931 serious concern was being expressed about the expenditure side of the account (see Hopkins 1931), the deepening depression having resulted in a marked deterioration of the Unemployment Fund's finances (table 6.3).[2] Since the fund was not fully consolidated into the conventionally defined budget accounts, not all of the increased outlay on benefits revealed itself in the published budget balance (B_c). This source of relief, however, was to be short-lived as the fund's borrowings became the focus for comment and criticism of budgetary policy generally.

Table 6.3 Outlay on unemployment benefits 1929/30–1931/2 (£m.)

	Exchequer contributions to unemployment insurance and transitional benefits	Balance of income and expenditure of Unemployment Fund for the period	Status of the Unemployment Fund at the end of the period	Total outlay on unemployment benefits
1929/30	20.4	−3.0	−39.0	59.7
1930/1	36.8	−36.4	−75.4	103.5
1931/2	57.9	−39.6	−115.0	125.1

Sources: Working notes to Feinstein (1972); HMSO (1932b, 157–61).

The question of economy in the wider sense was, of course, to culminate in the May Committee report, published on 1 August 1931. This, in effect a second 'Geddes axe', was to recommend economies of £96.5 million (some £66.5 million to come from unemployment insurance alone) and new, unspecified taxation of £23.5 million to meet the £120 million deficit forecast for 1932/3 (in all equivalent to a fiscal adjustment of some 3 per cent of 1931/2 GDP). The role of this report in exacerbating the financial crisis, the failure of the Labour Government to agree on the required economies, and the subsequent formation of the National Government, are well known.[3] Here we merely note that the final magnitude and form of fiscal adjustment implemented in the September 1931 emergency budget was not substantially different from that which had been agreed by the Labour Government (see Skidelsky 1967, 379), but which was deemed unacceptable by the financial community for the purpose of restoring confidence and securing the necessary credits for defending the exchange rate.

While the issue is complicated by the fact that within a week of the May report's publication the prospective deficit for 1932/3 had been revised upwards to £170 million, the only substantial difference between the Labour and National Government budgetary packages was that the latter incorporated a 10 per cent cut – not 20 per cent as recommended by the May Committee – in unemployment benefits. Thus, Labour had agreed to economies of £56.4 million (with £22 million off unemployment) and taxation of £88.5 million, a total of £144.9 million; while the programme implemented consisted of economies of £70 million (£34 million off unemployment) and taxation of £81.5 million, a total of £151.5 million, the £18.5 million residual being met by a reduction in sinking fund payments. Without seeking to revive the rather tired arguments about the existence of a bankers' ramp, the suspicion remains that the financial community treated Labour less leniently than a National Government. The adjustments required were marginal relative to the total budget, but were invested with great significance in the fraught atmosphere of the time; the ratio between economies and increased taxation bore no resemblance to that recommended by the May Committee; while the fact that a reduction in sinking fund payments did eventually prove permissible lies uneasily with the following statement made by Snowden to the Labour Cabinet shortly before its collapse:

> the Leaders of the Conservative Party, and also the Representatives of the Bankers, had stated that any attempt of this kind to camouflage the true position would be at once detected, and that it was of paramount importance that the Budget should be balanced in an honest fashion.
>
> (PRO 1931p)

Details of the September 1931 budget measures are given in outline in table 6.2. The form of the cuts in expenditure are particularly interesting since they differ in an important respect from those instituted during similar episodes in the postwar period. The major economies comprised expenditure on goods and services and transfer payments to the unemployed; the only capital item curtailed was road expenditure at £7.9 million (HMSO 1931c). By contrast, postwar governments – with the exception of the Thatcher administrations beginning in 1979 – when faced with the necessity of cutting expenditure, principally during sterling crises, have been able to take the politically more palatable and less disadvantageous course of concentrating their cuts on capital items (Price 1978, 113–16), for the composition of expenditure has changed markedly over the intervening period, the proportion of capital expenditure to total expenditure having increased significantly.

The financial crisis was far from being ended by the emergency budget. Such was the uneasiness of international financial markets and the speculative pressures against sterling that the budget proved insufficient to prevent Britain's abandonment of the gold standard shortly afterwards, on 21 September (the growing balance of payments deficit on current account would eventually have compelled this course anyway – see Moggridge 1970; cf. Cairncross and Eichengreen 1983, 72–83). Thereafter, the authorities conducted a managed float of sterling (Howson 1980), this at least lessening the previous exchange rate constraint upon domestic policy. However, the budgetary crisis continued.

As tables 6.1 and 6.2 show, 1931/2 closed with a small surplus (B_c, not B where the deficit in fact widened), while 1932/3, although planned to balance, actually realized a deficit. The period covered by these two budgets was perhaps the most fraught of the 1930s, for the Treasury could not admit to their difficulties, nor risk the deflationary consequences of further taxation, lest such statements or actions threatened business confidence, upon which all their hopes for recovery were necessarily founded. Thus, in framing the 1932/3 budget, their only possible recourse was to fiscal window-dressing and to the inflation of the revenue estimates, creative accounting which on this occasion taxed their ingenuity to its limits.

Since even these actions were insufficient for the pretence of *ex ante* balance, the expenditure estimates had also to be manipulated, a risky enterprise which says much about the primacy of expediency over strict budgetary orthodoxy. Here the burden of adjustment fell upon the Ministry of Labour who – at a time when the unemployment position was most uncertain – were compelled to trim nearly 10 per cent from their 1932/3 estimate (PRO 1932b; c; h; 1933a). Moreover, such was the tightness of the budgetary situation that this expedient was also adopted the following year, this despite the fact that the Ministry did overspend in 1932/3 and a politically embarrassing Supplementary Estimate was required.

With such a small margin for manoeuvre, given the policy constraint of a balanced budget, remissions of taxation or restoration of the expenditure cuts were unachievable. Thus the crisis measures were maintained during 1931–3, the clear expectation being that there would be a limited recovery in the following year which would permit a loosening of fiscal stance. The 1932/3 budget was thus clearly based upon an 'act of faith'. An impasse had been reached: the Treasury awaited a recovery of the real economy, unable to directly promote this by fiscal means, or to contemplate a further tightening of fiscal stance, the public mood having changed in 1932–3 towards demands for a more active recovery policy rather than an intensification of retrenchment (see, for example, *The Economist*, 1 April 1933, 680).

At this juncture, a relaxation of monetary policy intervened to offer the prospect of relief, less so immediately than in setting the scene for the subsequent recovery phase 1933–7. Here mention should be made of the War Loan conversion operation, for the course of budgetary policy in the early recovery period was primarily determined by the easing of monetary conditions that resulted from the successful conversion of the 5 per cent War Loan to a 3½ per cent basis (Howson 1975, 76, 86–9; Sayers 1976, II, 430–47). Undertaken between June and December 1932, some 92 per cent of the £2,085 million (outstanding at 31 March 1932) 5 per cent stock was converted, resulting both in lower interest rates and a significant easing of the burden of debt payments on the budget. Cheap money had long been a Treasury objective, a means of promoting industrial recovery and of relieving budgetary pressures; and once instituted, it was to become (with tariffs) the centrepiece of domestic recovery policy. From table 6.4 is can be seen that the advent of cheap money afforded little or no benefit to the 1932/3 budget; the benefits were not manifest until 1933/4, the first budget of the recovery phase.

Table 6.4 Expenditure on debt service 1929/30–1939/40 (£m.)

	Interest	Management and expenses	US war debt	Sinking fund	Total* £m.	as % of GDP
1929/30	277.5	2.3	27.5	47.7	355.0	8.4
1930/1	264.6	1.3	27.3	66.8	360.0	8.7
1931/2	274.0	1.9	13.6	32.5	322.0	8.3
1932/3	260.2	2.1	19.9	26.3	308.5	8.2
1933/4	211.9	1.1	3.3	7.7	224.0	5.8
1934/5	210.7	1.0	—	12.3	224.0	5.5
1935/6	210.5	1.0	—	12.5	224.0	5.3
1936/7	209.8	1.1	—	13.1	224.0	5.0
1937/8	215.3	1.0	—	10.5	226.8	4.7
1938/9	215.7	1.1	—	13.2	230.0	4.5
1939/40	221.8	1.0	—	7.2	230.0	4.1

Sources: Financial Accounts; GDP data from table 7.1.
Notes:
* Total payments equal Fixed Debt Charge.

Recovery 1933–7

The main details of the budgets over the recovery phase are summarized in table 6.5 which should also be examined in conjunction with table 6.1 above.[4]

Chamberlain, Chancellor from November 1931 to May 1937, sought to maintain the impression that the budgetary crisis never subsided. Thus, during the recovery period the policy pursued was presented as an orthodox and cautious one of maintaining the national finances in an unassailable position so as to permit a progressive loosening of fiscal stance in line with the recovery of the real economy (see PRO 1933l).

Table 6.5 Budget summary 1933/4–1936/7: published forecasts and results (£m.)

	1933/4	1934/5	1935/6	1936/7
1 Budget balance (B_c) of previous year	−32.3	+31.2	+7.5	+3.0
2 Budget on existing basis				
Revenue (T_c)	795.2	814.0	826.1	872.4
Expenditure (G_c)	781.0	784.9	820.5	893.7
Balance (B_c)*	+14.3	+29.1	+5.6	−21.3
3 Discretionary changes				
(i) Taxation				
first year				
– direct	−11.5†	−20.5	−4.5	+12.0
– indirect	−11.5	−0.2	−1.1	+4.5
full year				
– direct	+0.9	−24.0	−10.0	+16.5
– indirect	−13.4	—	−1.3	+4.7
(ii) Economies	—	−7.6	−4.0	—
(iii) Miscellaneous	+10.0‡	—	+4.5**	+5.3**
4 Budget estimates				
Revenue (T_c)	782.3	791.2	824.8	894.2
Expenditure (G_c)	781.0	790.4	824.3	893.7
Balance (B_c)*	+1.3	+0.8	+0.5	+0.5
5 Budget outturn				
Revenue (T_c)	809.4	804.6	844.8	896.6
Expenditure (G_c)	778.2	797.1	841.8	902.2
Balance (B_c)	+31.2	+7.5	+3.0	−5.6

Sources: Financial Accounts; Financial Statements; appendix II.

Notes:
* In contrast to previous years no sum was specifically allocated for debt redemption, nor was provision made for US war debt payments.
† Includes a one-year-only transaction of £12m. remitted when restoring payment dates for income tax to their original basis.
‡ Transfer from War Loan Depreciation Fund.
** Transfer from Road Fund.

As will be shown, while the presentation of this policy was to infuriate many contemporaries, it was also to provide an excellent shield for his less orthodox actions.

Shortly after assuming office he initiated a completely new departure in forward budgetary planning: an exercise, known as 'Old Moore's Almanack', involving the Treasury and the revenue departments in a detailed estimation of the scope for fiscal relaxation over 1932–5.[5] The assumptions made about the economy's recovery and thus the tax bases – assumptions which, barring the unemployment forecast (1.2 million by 1935), were to be broadly realized – were based upon a 'middle course between optimistic and pessimistic prophecies' (PRO 1933d; f). Yet the results were extremely disappointing, the scope for reduced taxation and restoration of the economy cuts being limited to the 'mournfully small' sum of £80 million by 1935 (PRO 1932j), equivalent to about one-half of the 1931 emergency budget measures.

Fortunately, this rather bleak outlook was tempered by the reduction in debt charge resulting from the War Loan conversion and low Treasury Bill rates (see table 6.4). Nevertheless, the Treasury were still forced to resort to the now established practices of fiscal window-dressing, the stretching of revenue estimates and the creation of an atmosphere of parsimony as a means of at least partially containing the onward march of expenditure. Such were their difficulties, that in the months immediately preceding the budgets, more attention seems to have been given to the intricacies of fiscal window-dressing, than to the issues we would more conventionally associate with budgetary deliberations. Moreover, in 1935, the pressures were such that Chamberlain was compelled to raid the Road Fund. For the first time, therefore, fiscal window-dressing involved incurring the opposition of a colleague, the Minister of Transport arguing that such an action questioned the five-year road programme then being considered as an unemployment measure (PRO 1935d; g).

We noted earlier that there was a change in the public mood between 1932–3, demands for a more active recovery policy and a relaxation of the fiscal stance becoming more insistent. Beginning in the summer of 1932 an influential group of economists became increasingly vocal in their opinion that the budget strategy was doomed to failure because of the absence of effective measures to induce recovery (a concern in part shared by the Treasury – see PRO 1932o).[6] By early 1933 a full-scale campaign for fiscal relaxation was in progress – an alliance of *The Times*, MPs of all parties and a number of leading economists (Winch 1972, 217). What distinguished this from the earlier pressures, however, was Keynes's intervention, in the form of his now famous pamphlet *The Means to Prosperity*. This sought to advance both the theoretical basis of the expansionist case, now much strengthened after Kahn's (1931) formulation of the multiplier, and to propose a package of fiscal measures (public works and income tax cuts totalling £110 million, or approximately 2½ per cent of GDP) which by stimulating recovery would strengthen the budgetary position and thus allow further fiscal relaxation.

The scope for fiscal relaxation in 1933 was extremely limited (table 6.5), and the campaign did not persuade Chamberlain of the case for deficit-finance. That said, he was to deviate from the strict path of orthodoxy in his debt management policy, with a consequent lessening of the deflationary fiscal stance (see pp. 137, 139). Pressures for reflation did not abate in the two following years. Indeed, they were intensified in January 1935 when Lloyd George launched his 'New Deal', a £250 million two-year programme centring upon public works and deficit-finance (Lloyd George 1935). Furthermore, attention was already being given to the timing of the next general election (CP 1934a; b; 1935b; c) and a popular pre-election budget was imperative in order to counter a successful attack by the Opposition parties on the government's recovery policy. On economic grounds, it had also been noticed that there had occurred a slackening in the pace of recovery in the second half of 1934 (PRO 1935f), and a further fiscal stimulus was obviously desirable.

The question of fiscal relaxation was first discussed at Cabinet in December 1933, when it was unanimously agreed that the benefits from the improved budgetary position should be distributed to those who had suffered the economy cuts as well as to those who had borne the additional taxation (PRO 1933m). The restoration of the cuts in unemployment benefit and public employees' salaries in the budgets of 1934 and 1935 served a clear social and political purpose. The remission of taxation, however, was directed towards additional ends, Chamberlain having decided in 1934 that the form of tax cuts should be determined by economic considerations, a reduction in the standard rate of income tax being adopted rather than increased allowances (both having been altered in 1931) because it would have 'the greatest psychological effect' as well as 'impart[ing] the most immediate and vigorous stimulus to the expansion of trade and employment' (*Hansard* 1934, cols 925–6). Only in 1935 did Chamberlain increase the personal allowances, to give assistance to low-income groups.

The 1935 budget was the last of the decade to remit taxes, in effect the final peacetime budget for thereafter the course of budgetary policy was dominated by the needs of rearmament. The September 1931 crisis budget had imposed additional taxation calculated to yield £81.5 million in a full year, while the three budgets 1933/4–1935/6 had only remitted taxation totalling £60.2 million (*ex ante*, full year effects). Therefore, although exact comparison is precluded by forecasting errors and by changes in the tax bases resulting from fluctuations in the level of economic activity, it does seem that the 1932 predictions of 'Old Moore's Almanack' were not unduly pessimistic. The surplus available by 1935

Table 6.6 The financing of defence expenditure 1935/6–1939/40 (£m.)

	Defence expenditure			Change in defence expenditure financed from revenue since previous year	Change in all other items of expenditure since previous year	Total change in expenditure since previous year	Total central government expenditure (G_c)	Revenue			Budget balance (B_c)
	Financed from		Total					Change in total revenue since previous year	Resulting from		Total central government revenue (T_c)	
	Revenue	Defence Loans Acts, 1937 and 1939							Automatic growth‡	Discretionary changes in taxation		
1935/6	136.9	—	136.9		+21.7	+44.7	841.8	+40.2	+45.8	−5.6	844.8	+3.0
1936/7	186.2	—	186.2	+49.3	+11.1	+60.4	902.2	+51.8	+35.3	+16.5	896.6	−5.6
1937/8	200.3	64.9	265.2	+14.1	+3.6	+17.7	919.9	+52.1	+36.9	+15.2	948.7	+28.8
1938/9	272.1	128.1	400.2	+71.8	+27.2	+99.0	1018.9	+57.5	+27.1	+30.4	1006.2	−12.7
1939/40												
(April)*	247.8	380.0†	628.8	−24.3	+18.0	+6.9	1025.8	+19.8	−4.5	+24.3	1026.0	+0.2
(Sept.)*	..	502.4†	1249†	..	..	+488.5	1514.3	+52.7	−54.3	+107.0	1078.7	−435.6
(outturn)	242	491.7**	1142†	−30.1	..	−106.1	1408.2	+126.0	..	..	1132.2	−276.0

Sources: Financial Accounts; Financial Statements; PRO (1940).

Notes:
* Budget estimates.
† Approximate figure.
‡ Automatic growth in revenue plus fiscal window-dressing (which more correctly is a discretionary item).
** In addition, £408.5m. of the September 1939 Vote of Credit was taken.

for remission of taxation was, as Hopkins had warned, 'mournfully small'.

The authorities' principal difficulty was that expenditure, which was beginning to become influenced by rearmament, was outstripping the growth of revenue, itself slow to respond to recovery. As a consequence the 1936 budget marked not just a halt to further tax remissions, but the beginnings of increased taxation (in this case a $2\frac{1}{2}$ points rise in the standard rate of income tax). The (apparent) tightening of fiscal stance does not seem to have had markedly adverse effects, for the pace of recovery accelerated during 1936–7 as the economy moved towards a position of 'cyclical' full employment (pp. 26, 29).

Rearmament and recession 1937–9

The final phase of budgetary policy was dominated by the needs of rearmament: total military outlays rose from £265.2 million in 1937/8 to £1,142 million in 1939/40, an increase of 330.6 per cent, while total central government expenditure (G) only increased by 86.5 per cent over the same period. Table 6.6 records this increase in expenditure and the way in which it was financed, while table 6.7 summarizes the main details of the budgets over this period.

While peacetime finance effectively ended with the 1935 budget, the 1937 budget was of greater significance for this marked the beginnings of deficit-finance. Borrowing for rearmament had been agreed in principle in December 1935, but was not undertaken until 1937/8 because it was first judged necessary to reach a position whereby at least £170 million of defence expenditure was financed from revenue, this figure being the estimated annual debt charge once the rearmament programme was completed. The defence loan was viewed from two different, although interrelated, perspectives:

1 That it would permit the execution of a larger rearmament programme than that possible under the constraint of a balanced budget.
2 By reducing the additional taxation required to finance a programme of a given size, it would minimize the electoral disadvantages of rearmament, an important consideration in its initial stages when the Cabinet were by no means convinced that a full-scale rearmament programme would be politically acceptable (Middlemas and Barnes 1969, 797, 912–13).

Budgetary policy in the 1930s was essentially incremental in character; never more so than after 1937 as the authorities sought to navigate the uncharted waters of peacetime deficit-finance. A rearmament programme totalling £1,500 million for the quinquennium 1937/8–1941/2 had been agreed by early 1937. The amount to be borrowed was initially

Table 6.7 Budget summary 1937/8–1939/40: published forecasts and results (£m.)

	1937/8	1938/9	1939/40 (April)	1939/40 (Sept.)
1 Budget balance (B_c) of previous year	−5.6	+28.8	−12.7	..
2 Budget on existing basis				
Revenue (T_c)	923.1	994.8	1001.7	971.7
Expenditure (G_c)	938.0	1024.8	1025.8	1514.3
Balance (B_c)*	−14.9	−30.0	−24.1	−542.6
3 Discretionary changes				
(i) Taxation				
first year				
– direct	+15.2	+22.3	+13.3	+76.5
– indirect	—	+8.1	+11.0	+30.5
full year				
– direct	+36.0–41.0†	+26.5	+21.5	+160.0
– indirect	—	+9.0	+12.4	+66.5
(ii) Economies	—	—	—	—
(iii) Miscellaneous	—	—	—	—
4 Budget Estimates				
Revenue (T_c)	938.3	1025.2	1026.0	1078.7
Expenditure (G_c)	938.0	1024.8	1025.8	1514.3
Balance (B_c)*	+0.3	+0.4	+0.2	−435.6
5 Budget outturn				
Revenue (T_c)	948.7	1006.2	—	1132.2
Expenditure (G_c)	919.9	1018.9	—	1408.2
Balance (B_c)	+28.8	−12.7	—	−276.0
6 Planned defence borrowing	80.0	90.0	380.0‡	500.0

Sources: Financial Accounts; Financial Statements.

Notes:
* As for the period 1933/4–1936/7 no special sum was allocated to debt redemption.
† Full-year yield of National Defence Contribution uncertain, but estimated at £20–25m.
‡ The Estimates in February 1939 had provided for borrowing of £342.5m., but in the budget it was announced that owing to defence acceleration and expansion the figure might be expected to rise to £380m.

set at £400 million (an additional £400 million was agreed in February 1939). Hereafter, budgetary policy centred upon the proper balance between tax- and deficit-finance. While the latter increased the authorities' room for manoeuvre, it was also attended by certain difficulties. As Hopkins had argued during the discussions preceding the decision to allow defence borrowing, there were considerable dangers 'if the country began to think of a Defence Loan as a comfortable Lloyd Georgian device for securing not only larger forces but also lower estimates, Budget surpluses and diminishing taxation' (PRO 1935h, 1–2).

Hopkins's cautionary advice was to prove prophetic. By late 1937 the Treasury were deeply concerned that their control of the defence departments was but tenuous, while the onward march of civil expenditure seemed relentless. Increased taxation was thus a necessity, not just to secure an appropriate balance between tax- and deficit-finance, but as a means of disciplining the spending departments (PRO 1938b). Budgets became as much directed towards influencing the spending propensities of Whitehall as of those of the private sector.

The budgetary problem was further complicated by the economy's move into recession 1937–8, this depressing the tax bases. At a time when the authorities were anxious to avoid anything which might impair confidence or unsettle the financial markets – upon which the success of deficit-finance ultimately depended – such a situation could have been expected to result in substantially increased taxation. Taxation was increased, especially upon incomes (table 6.7), and evoked much adverse comment, but the proportion of defence expenditure financed from revenue fell substantially: from 75.5 per cent in 1937/8 to 21.2 per cent in 1939/40. The Treasury were, as one contemporary put it, 'contriv[ing] to combine extensive borrowing with an impression of draconian orthodoxy' (*The Economist*, 18 June 1938, 665). The background to this deliberate policy, and it implications, are discussed in the following section.

2 THE TRANSITION OF BUDGETARY POLICY

With our outline budgetary history now complete, we can turn our attention to the changing attitudes and forces which guided budgetary policy over this period.

The May Committee and the pursuit of orthodoxy

A natural starting point is with the May report, the discussions that it engendered illustrating much of interest about contemporary attitudes, especially during a period of crisis when the pursuit of orthodoxy assumed a less flexible form than was the case in more settled times.

Operating from the premise that 'the country must face the disagreeable fact that its public expenditure . . . is too high and that it must be brought down to a lower level' three general principles guided their recommendations:

> (i) that the rise in the value of money in recent years provides a strong prima facie case for the revision of money obligations fixed under other considerations. . . .
>
> (ii) that existing financial difficulties make it necessary for the nation like the private individual to consider seriously what it can afford and not merely what is desirable. Reviewed from this standpoint much expenditure is unwarrantable at the present time, which, under more favourable conditions, we should deem justifiable and even a wise investment of the national resources.
>
> (iii) that only by the strictest regard to economy and efficiency over a long period can the trade of the country be restored to its pre-war prosperity and any substantial number of the unemployed be re-absorbed into industry. (HMSO 1931b, 16, 220)

The principle of a balanced budget, even in time of depression, was not questioned, not even by the minority report signed by the committee's two Labour members. Dissent was limited to the way in which the economies were to be achieved. In the case of the minority report, it was decided that the principle of 'equality of sacrifice' should be adopted, and that this could best be attained by imposing a surcharge on *rentier* incomes. Nevertheless, even with these reservations, the task of balancing the budget was pursued with doctrinaire purposefulness, as evidenced by the demand that cuts in expenditure, rather than increased taxation, must make the major contribution towards the restoration of budgetary equilibrium (HMSO 1931b, 221).

The major emphasis within the proposed economies was on the necessity for cutting outlay on unemployment benefits. Whilst this was the most rapidly growing item of expenditure – because of its cyclical sensitivity (see p. 132) – cuts in unemployment benefits also assumed a symbolic importance. As one contemporary later put it:

> The recent 10 per cent. cut is not important because of the relief it gives to our national expenditure. The cut is important because the dole is a support and a symbol of our lack of flexibility and our blind *resistance* to change. (Benham 1932, 23)

The majority and minority reports' diagnosis of the causes of budgetary disequilibrium differed fundamentally. The majority report (and later Cabinet discussions) justified the cuts in pay and benefits on the grounds that the declining price level had increased the real burden of these outlays (HMSO 1931b, 220; PRO 1931o), while the minority report used the same reasoning to press for higher taxation of *rentier* incomes. While the majority report saw the budgetary difficulties as stemming from the unceasing growth of social expenditure, itself determined by the weakness of politicians who succumbed to electoral pressures, the minority report maintained that such services were 'essential to modern large-scale industry', and that the real villain of the piece was the increasing real burden of the debt charge. They contended that it was here that remedial action was required (HMSO 1931b, 13, 229).[7]

A reasoned and informed debate about the May report's criteria for budgetary equilibrium was frustrated by the crisis atmosphere engendered by the report. With policy enslaved to considerations of confidence or symbols such as unemployment benefits, two critical questions were evaded: that of the British budgetary position *vis-à-vis* other countries; and that of the likely employment effects of balancing the budget in the manner recommended by the May report.

Table 6.8 gives the budget accounts, on roughly comparable bases, for the four principal industrial nations of the time. While these data do not

Table 6.8 Central government budget accounts: Great Britain, France, Germany and United States 1929/30–1932/3

		Receipts	Expenditure	Balance	Debt payments included in expenditure
Great Britain	1929/30	815.0	829.5	−14.5	47.7
(£m.)	1930/1	857.8	881.0	−23.2	66.8
	1931/2	851.5	851.1	+0.4	32.5
	1932/3	827.0	859.3	−32.3	26.3
France	1929/30	64,268.0	58,849.0	+5,419.0	—
(francs m.)	1930/1	53,094.0	53,265.0	−171.0	—
	1931/2	50,977.0	53,362.0	−2,385.0	—
	1932	38,069.0	42,991.0	−4,922.0	—
Germany	1929/30	7,509.8	8,186.6	−676.8	—
(Reichmarks m.)	1930/1	7,784.2	8,391.8	−607.6	—
	1931/2	6,812.4	6,994.9	−182.5	—
	1932/3	5,821.6	5,964.7	−143.1	—
United States	1929/30	4,044.6	3,854.2	+190.4	553.9
($m.)	1930/1	3,191.6	4,127.5	−935.9	440.1
	1931/2	2,003.9	4,865.3	−2,861.4	412.7
	1932/3	2,083.7	3,873.4	−1,789.7	471.6

Sources: League of Nations (1936, V, table IIa; 1937, XI, table IIa; XII, table II; XXXIV, table II).

allow us to make judgements about the stance of fiscal policy in the four countries, it is clear that the balance of the budget in 1930/1 and 1931/2 was closer to equilibrium in Britain than elsewhere (see also PRO 1931g): evidence which further supports our earlier conclusion that Britain's special position dictated that it adhere more strictly to orthodox financial principles than were considered to be necessary in other countries.

The effects on employment, incomes and output of the adoption of the proposed measures also received scant attention. At the official level, the question was in one sense irrelevant (since the restoration of budgetary equilibrium was paramount), but it was of importance with regard to forecasting *ex ante* what the *ex post* effect of the measures would be on endogenous budget items. Keynes, however, did give the matter some thought. First, in a letter to the Prime Minister he condemned the economies as not only deflationary but unnecessary, for he believed the overvalued exchange rate and speculative pressures would soon force Britain off the gold standard anyway. This would remove one of the basic constraints on domestic policy, permitting the eventual pursuit of a reflationary monetary and fiscal policy (KP 1931b).

In a *New Statesman* article Keynes advanced the argument one step further by presenting estimates of the macroeconomic effects of balancing the budget, the first time that such an approach had been used in the interwar policy debate. Concerned that the May Committee 'show[ed] no evidence of having given a moment's thought to the possible repercussions of their programme, either on the volume of unemployment or on the receipts of taxation', Keynes pointed to the symmetry of fiscal action: 'the immediate consequences of the government reducing its deficit are the exact inverse of the consequences of its financing additional capital works out of loans.' A £100 million reduction in expenditure, Keynes calculated, would only reduce the budget deficit by £50 million because of the adverse effect on employment and incomes of reduced government demand. Accordingly, he concluded:

> At the present time, all governments have large deficits. For government borrowing of one kind or another is nature's remedy, so to speak, for preventing business losses from being, in so severe a slump as the present one, so great as to bring production altogether to a standstill. It is much better in every way that the borrowing should be for the purpose of financing capital works, if these works are any use at all, than for the purpose of paying doles. . . . But so long as the slump lasts on the present scale this is the only effective choice which we possess, and government borrowing for the one purpose or the other (or a diminished Sinking Fund, which has the same effect) is practically inevitable. (Keynes 1931)

These arguments, which were in effect the first clear statement of automatic stabilizers made between the wars, went unheard. This was also true of critical voices within Whitehall. For example, both Hopkins and Henderson had argued that the May report's criteria for a balanced budget were excessively strict (PRO 1931f; g). While the government was not immune to the logic of these dissentient voices, such was the state of domestic politics and international opinion that deflation remained the only course available if the crisis was to be overcome. Thus the real failure of government lay not so much in the course of action eventually taken, but in the government's conduct during the crisis, its seemingly helpless passivity making that course inevitable. With more imaginative statesmanship it might have been possible for the Labour Government to establish the terms upon which the budgetary debate was conducted, rather than the May Committee. One such episode should have been a sufficient object lesson for the Labour Party; yet a similar judgement can be applied to Labour's conduct during the public expenditure–balance of payments crisis of 1976.

The retreat from orthodoxy

The demise of the second Labour Government and the emergency September 1931 budget marked the zenith of fiscal orthodoxy, the triumph of political and economic conservatism. With the passing of the crisis atmosphere, however, reflationary pressures were renewed and the wider fiscal policy debate resumed. There resulted a progressive, but ultimately limited, retreat from the orthodoxy exhibited in 1931, with fiscal policy acquiring a flexibility reminiscent of Winston Churchill's tenure at the Exchequer.

The change in policy was at first subtle, largely invisible to those outside the Treasury and Cabinet. Parliamentary pressures for further retrenchment had been maintained during the year following the financial crisis.[8] The budgetary position remained highly difficult. Nevertheless, Treasury officials were firmly of the opinion that the only scope for further economies was as part of another comprehensive programme of budgetary adjustments, and that this was most undesirable on political and economic grounds (PRO 1932n; q). Chamberlain's previous enthusiasm for strict economy, that held during the 1931 crisis when it served political as well as economic ends, had also waned considerably now that the political objective of ousting Labour had been achieved (see Hansard 1932a, cols 2345–7).

The continued increase in unemployment lends further support to this view, that by mid-1932 the Cabinet had tacitly agreed that economic and political considerations now made a further tightening of fiscal stance impracticable. Indeed, not only had they to accept the inevitability of a Ministry of Labour Supplementary Estimate to finance the increased unemployment, but they willingly deferred to Treasury advice (PRO 1932p) that everything possible should be done to dispel the current mood of pessimism which was threatening to retard recovery. In effect, therefore, budgetary policy had changed since the 1931 crisis, though obviously this change could not be communicated to the public.[9]

A further important change occurred in 1933, that of a major alteration to debt management policy. With the conversion operation, cheap money and the suspension of US war debt payments the annual debt charge was reduced by £60–70 million, itself a significant sum. Yet further relief to the budget – say £25–50 million per annum – was gained by the decision to abandon any provision for debt redemption, powers even being taken to borrow for the statutory sinking funds. Although not really appreciated at the time, this practice – which was continued throughout the remainder of the 1930s – did constitute a radical shift in policy. Relative to the strict standards of debt management policy of the 1920s, the sinking fund was suspended after 1933, thus easing the burden of budgetary difficulties and lessening the deflationary impact of fiscal operations.

Cheap money, however, was not without its costs. While recent research has reaffirmed the traditional view that cheap money underlay the strong recovery of 1932–7 (Howson 1975, ch. 5; Dimsdale 1981, 338–40; cf. Aldcroft 1970b, 53–64), it was also to inhibit the adoption of other, less orthodox policy instruments. In particular, the authorities' fear that cheap money would be threatened – via adverse confidence effects – by a policy of deficit-finance and/or resumption of large-scale public works programmes acted to reinforce the commitment to an orthodox budgetary policy. Thus a trade-off existed, that between an active monetary policy and an expansionist fiscal policy (*Hansard* 1933d, col. 61).

The budgetary relief afforded by cheap money completely failed to satisfy those who had campaigned in 1933 for a relaxation of budgetary policy sufficient to directly stimulate demand. Chamberlain was not indifferent to these pressures: political wisdom dictated that the Treasury mind be engaged to construct an acceptable defence for his orthodoxy in face of the challenge posed by Keynes's *The Means to Prosperity* (Howson and Winch 1977, 128–30), but by temperament and economic conviction he was as wedded to orthodoxy as Snowden, his predecessor. His adherence to balanced budgets may be said to derive from two interconnected influences, first that economic policy was a quasi-moral issue, secondly that unbalanced budgets were ineffective in inducing recovery.

The former, a means of deflecting criticism by appeal to a supposed moral dimension of policy, was well expressed in his dismissal of Keynes's pamphlet:

> I can assure the Committee that I am not dismissing this idea [of an unbalanced budget] merely because it is unorthodox. On the other hand, I am not impressed by the suggestion that its acceptance would

be a proof of courage on my part. Courage does not always lie in taking the easiest and most popular course. (*Hansard* 1933d, col. 58)

This hairshirt philosophy of economic policy is discussed further in chapter 9. As regards his more technical objections to deficit-finance, here Chamberlain employed another familiar tactic – that of crude empiricism:

> Of all the countries passing through these difficult times the one that has stood the test with the greatest measure of success is the United Kingdom. . . . By following a sound financial policy we have been enabled to secure low interest rates for industry and it would be the height of folly to throw away that advantage. If we were to reverse our policy, just at the very moment when other Governments are striving to follow our example and to balance their Budgets, after experience of the policy which we are now asked to adopt, we would stultify ourselves in the eyes of the world and forfeit in a moment the respect with which we are regarded to-day. (*Hansard* 1933d, cols 60–1)

Budgetary policy during the recovery phase clearly owed little to the influence of the 'new' economics. The Treasury cannot, however, be accused of financial orthodoxy in any nineteenth-century sense. The period 1932–6 saw a number of major departures from orthodoxy: the virtual abandonment of sinking fund payments and the use of fiscal window-dressing to conceal deficits. This said, in a wider sense the influence of the nineteenth-century fiscal constitution on policy formulation is clearly discernible, in the refusal to countenance deliberately unbalanced budgets and in the reliance on 'normal' channels to promote trade recovery (see *Hansard* 1935, col. 1637). It was only with the advent of rearmament that the Treasury were to have recourse to deficit-finance, and even then they laboured long and hard to preserve traditional expenditure controls and at least some vestige of sound finance.

Rearmament as a budgetary problem

It is now commonplace that deficit-finance not only permitted the pursuit of a larger rearmament programme than that considered possible under tax-finance, but that it also stimulated the real economy, thereby assisting rearmament indirectly through the provision of additional real and financial resources. Such a favourable outturn, however, was by no means assured at the time: the Treasury were entering uncharted territory with the decision to borrow, spurred on by the sheer necessity of reconciling the needs of rearmament with the requirements of budgetary stability, ever vigilant of the risks that this course entailed. This said, compared to the earlier efforts made to justify balanced budgets, the decision to borrow was taken with surprising ease (Shay 1977, 144-7; Peden 1979b, 71-9). Once more, therefore, strict budgetary orthodoxy became subordinate to economic and political expediency.

The needs of the situation probably also explain why little attention was given at this stage to technical issues such as the implications for monetary policy of deficit-finance or of possible resource costs for the private sector. These only received attention later, once borrowing was actually underway. Meanwhile, the Treasury were more concerned that the decision to borrow should not intensify demands for expenditure by the military and civil departments now that the traditional constraint of a balanced budget was in abeyance.

Treasury control of the rearmament programme sought to achieve a 'balance of risks between military and economic weakness . . . in face of an uncertain and unpredictable future'. As a result:

> The balance between military and economic priorities moved from a position in 1932, when defence expenditure was entirely subordinated to the economic situation, to the summer of 1939, when priority for defence was such that the Treasury had to advise the Government that quasi-wartime controls over the economy would be required to maintain current defence expenditure after the autumn of that year.
>
> (Peden 1979b, 67)

The financial and economic determinants of this 'balance of risks' received detailed consideration in Inskip's December 1937 interim report to the Cabinet on the status of the defence programmes. This report was not only to guide policy thereafter, but was also important as a more general statement of Treasury economic thinking. For example, it clearly shows that the 'Treasury view' was not narrowly confined to financial resources, but also embraced real resources: labour supply, industrial capacity and the balance of trade. The latter, in particular, was seen as of central importance, for any weakening of the external account would threaten financial confidence and thus the whole strategy of deficit-finance.

Finally, the report closed with a classic statement of finance as the 'fourth arm in defence'. Defence strategy assumed that any future war would be a prolonged conflict, victory only being secured once all resources had been mobilized. Therefore, the most effective deterrent was not simply adequate military preparation but also economic strength, 'a fourth arm in defence, alongside the three Defence services, without which purely military effort would be of no avail' (PRO 1937f).

This report puts into proper perspective the Treasury's refusal to accommodate the defence departments' insistent demands for greater expenditure. Furthermore, it shows as misfounded the accusation, made at the beginning of the war and repeatedly thereafter, that Treasury control of expenditure had dangerously prejudiced military preparations for war.

For analytical purposes we may separate the motives for controlling rearmament expenditure into three classes.

1 Economic: rearmament was constrained by the availability of financial and real resources. Throughout the period 1937–9 the authorities attempted to strike a balance between increased taxation and borrowing, the former being increased to that level which was considered just compatible with a continuance of trade recovery, the latter being determined by the twin objectives of preventing inflation or a hardening of interest rates. The constraints imposed by the availability of real resources were considered to be of equal importance: aggregate government expenditure, and its components, was planned with the specific intention of preventing an exacerbation of the already existing supply constraints, in particular the shortages of skilled labour and productive capacity in the capital goods industries (see Hornby 1958; Parker 1981). A connected problem was the deteriorating current account of the balance of payments, a problem first brought to the Cabinet's attention in late 1936; and one which was a partial reflection of the adverse effects of rearmament: either directly, by the redirection of exports to the home market and the high import content of rearmament expenditures, or indirectly, by the increase in export prices.[10]
2 Political: in essence the question here was to make decisions about the relative magnitudes of the military and civil components of total government expenditure, a decision to increase military outlays meaning that either total expenditure had to be raised or civil outlays constrained. Such a choice had a political dimension.
3 Strategic: the control of expenditure assumed a strategic dimension by virtue of the fact that with limited total resources available, the object of control was to ensure that essential programmes 'received due priority, and . . . less important proposals were not allowed to clog the programme' (Peden 1979b, 34). The problem facing the Treasury was its 'increasing inability to challenge the programs of the services on technical grounds, because of the escalating technological expertise required to evaluate those programmes, and the services' monopoly of that expertise' (Shay 1977, 186). Accordingly various schemes of rationing were employed to ensure that rearmament expenditure did not grow more than was compatible with the achievement of the government's other objectives.

Rearmament and demand management

Since the onset of defence borrowing there had been much criticism in the financial press that no statement had been issued outlining the criteria used for deciding upon the balance between additional taxation and borrowing (see, for example, *The Economist*, 29 April 1939, 237). Thus the 1938 and April 1939 budgets, by increasing taxation and appearing to control expenditure growth, were first directed towards reassuring the financial markets. A second objective was to minimize any direct deflation of demand or microeconomic adjustments which might impair the civilian economy. This, in turn, was linked to the rearmament programme: the active management of demand being adopted of necessity to ensure the uninterrupted acceleration of the programme after the *Anschluss* and Munich crisis.

This development owed much to Phillips's influence upon the Treasury's internal budget discussions of December 1938. It was then estimated that the 1939/40 budget would provide £230 million out of revenue for defence, while the annual maintenance costs of the services would be approximately £300 million once the rearmament programme was completed. Additional taxation of £70 million was thus required if the Treasury were to remain true to the principles of rearmament finance established in 1935–6. That they did not is largely explained by the decisive influence of the following arguments put by Phillips:

> I can see no prospect of obtaining any such sum except by further very heavy taxation of profits and by the imposition of a substantial turnover tax. The effect of such additional taxation on the scale required would be to depress general trade and in particular to reduce the yield of the income tax and surtax. Nor is it quite the type of taxation which is suitable in present circumstances.
>
> At this point it would be well to consider what are the dangers we are running from our policy, now to be extended, of borrowing large sums for defence. It is commonly said that this means all round inflation and imperils the exchange value of the pound. The second of these statements is true but not the first. *There is not in fact grave danger of inflation until we shall be much nearer than at present to a state of full employment. Inflation is a thing which is inconsistent with the existence of 1,800,000 unemployed.*
>
> But the danger to the pound is real. We are borrowing great sums and shall borrow more, to be spent largely on wage payments and increased profits to people who make munitions and aeroplanes. If the sums so disbursed are spent [on domestically produced output] . . . no great harm is done to the £. But we know that a substantial part will on the contrary be spent on increased imports, largely of a luxury type, . . . and that is where the danger lies.   (PRO 1938e; emphasis added)

Accordingly, Phillips recommended that additional taxation be limited to a token £20 million, and that this be directed towards managing the composition of consumers expenditure and to a strengthening of the external position.

From these tentative suggestions were to follow the first attempts to actively manage demand – in a Keynesian sense – using the budget as an instrument of economic policy. By the time of the April 1939 budget the Treasury were awaiting the achievement of full employment – induced by the greatly expanded military outlays – for only then could taxation be significantly increased. Full employment, with its accompanying higher level of savings, would also permit greater borrowings from the non-banking sector. These were important changes in fiscal policy. They were, however, partially (and deliberately) obscured from public view as the Treasury sought to maintain the appearance of orthodoxy. As with earlier periods, the objective at this time was to maintain confidence. The Treasury felt that the size of borrowing in 1939/40 was such that it could only be financed, without inflation, by raising aggregate demand. While defence expenditure would, *ceteris paribus*, ensure this end, a collapse of confidence with its consequent adverse effect on private sector demand would jeopardize this increase and therefore the increase in current savings felt to be necessary. The question of confidence thus assumed a new meaning.[11]

Phillips's views were not immediately accepted. Indeed, Fisher pressed for very heavy increases in taxation, though more for political than for economic reasons (PRO 1939a). Hopkins and Simon, however, sided with Phillips and it was agreed that additional taxation was to be 'in the nature of a gesture rather than a substantial contribution to fill the gap' (PRO 1939b).[12] With the defence estimates at £630 million, and available revenue at £223.5 million, it was agreed that borrowing should be set at £380 million (compared with £128.1 million in 1938/9) and that an additional £24.3 million should be raised from taxation. This increase in taxation was less than in the previous year, while the amount provided for defence out of revenue was also lower (see table 6.6, p. 106).

It would seem, therefore, that in the circumstances of the time the Treasury were rather appreciative of the freedom provided by deficit-finance: for under the guise of rearmament they could also avoid actions which would have intensified recession in the civilian economy.

The Treasury's difficulties of 1938–9, those posed by the twilight between peace and war finance, were political as well as economic in character. The management of the proto-war economy, in particular the suppression of the inflationary pressures generated by the rearmament programme, ultimately could only be exercised with the full range of controls available, and politically acceptable, in wartime. Thus certain constraints were placed upon fiscal policy before the outbreak of war. Nevertheless, policy was not unsuccessful in this final phase. On the one hand, the Treasury recognized that since the effects of the rearmament programme on domestic demand were slow to appear, heavy increases in direct taxation were to be avoided in the initial stages of the programme; on the other hand, that confidence had to be maintained and the policy of extensive borrowing should, to some extent, be masked by the appearance of financial orthodoxy.

Finally, the Treasury had gained much needed expertise and self-confidence from their experience of managing the proto-war economy:

> once full employment has been reached, the country can very well stand increased financial pressure *without* going back to a state of unemployment, and there will be no reversion to deflation unless the monetary authorities are ignorant of their job. (PRO 1939d)

The extent of their intellectual conversion to peacetime demand management by fiscal means, however, remains to be established.

3 CONCLUSIONS

A few preliminary conclusions can now be drawn. A more complete analysis must await discussions of the effects of fiscal operations and the public works issue; these are considered in the two following chapters.

We have seen that from 1937 onwards rearmament necessitated large-scale borrowing and a relaxation of the strict tenets of financial control; that the Treasury recognized that rearmament orders were stimulating employment; and that the budget was being used as an instrument to manage both total demand and its components by the eve of the Second World War. Thus in the 1938 and April 1939 budgets borrowing expanded more rapidly than taxation as the Treasury sought a recovery of demand. In addition, the increase in tobacco and motor vehicle duties in April 1939 marked an attempt to redirect demand, improve the balance of payments and release industrial capacity for rearmament orders. Moreover, the Treasury records, especially those for the later 1930s, corroborate Bridges' (1950a, 9) statement 'that from the 1920s onwards, the Treasury staff began to think of expenditure rather less in terms of the prospect of the spending of so much public money and rather more in terms of the employment of resources'.

That there were changes in budgetary policy over this period is not a matter of dispute (Howson 1975, 126). The question at issue is the form of these changes and the underlying principles which guided them. In chapter 8 it is shown that the Treasury's moves towards conscious economic management were less the result of deep-seated changes in its theoretical thinking, and rather more a pragmatic response to the political and economic problems generated by rearmament.

Furthermore, the rearmament phase saw but a temporary lapse from orthodoxy. The partial financing of rearmament by borrowing after 1937 was accompanied by an intensification of demands for greater expenditure (of both a military and civil nature). As had been predicted in the 1933 policy debate over unbalanced budgets, the relaxation of the balanced budget rule considerably weakened Treasury expenditure control. The rearmament phase also suggested two further lessons for the authorities.

1 The experience of under-spending in the programme's initial stages reinforced the already existing belief that the rapid execution of a large public expenditure programme presented major technical difficulties.
2 The significant lag experienced before rearmament orders had beneficial effects on employment, and the narrowness of these effects in terms of the range of industries affected by rearmament, must also have strengthened the authorities' reluctance to embark, in the future, upon a large public works programme as an employment measure.

Finally, the Treasury remained committed to a return to balanced budgets from 1942/3, when the rearmament programme was completed and borrowing powers terminated.

Despite the absurdity by 1939 of the system of budget accounts ostensibly in force there were still no moves towards reform. Nor had the Treasury begun to contemplate the necessary changes in the characteristics of the fiscal system which would have made the maintenance of balanced budgets less problematical in face of severe autonomous fluctuations in economic activity. While it was recognized that rearmament expenditures were directly stimulating employment,[13] this as such did not give validity to the policy prescriptions of the 'new' economics. Rather, it highlighted and reinforced what the Treasury had always maintained: that public expenditure could only be used, and would only be effective, as an employment measure in special circumstances, these dependent upon a favourable concatenation of political, economic and psychological factors.

CHAPTER SEVEN

AN ASSESSMENT OF CHANGES IN FISCAL STANCE 1929–39

Having completed our survey of 1930s budgetary history we can now proceed to more detailed issues: first, the summary measure of fiscal influence employed in this study (the constant employment budget balance); secondly, the characteristics of the fiscal system and their influence on the course of policy; and thirdly, the application of the constant employment budget balance estimates to an evaluation of changes in the authorities' fiscal stance.[1]

1 THE MEASUREMENT OF FISCAL INFLUENCE

It is now well established in fiscal policy studies that the actual *ex post* budget balance is an inadequate and misleading indicator of fiscal stance since it is subject to

> the well-known difficulty that it does not distinguish changes in the budget balance caused by variations in tax rates or expenditure programmes from changes caused by movements in income and expenditure associated, for example, with autonomous variations in investment or exports. (Ward and Neild 1978, 2)

The resulting inadequacy of movements in actual budget balances as a measure of changes in fiscal stance was particularly acute in the 1930s, when there were marked cyclical variations in unemployment rates. As soon as the dependence of tax receipts and endogenous expenditures on the level of aggregate income is acknowledged, it follows that variations in economic activity, unless the authorities take countervailing action, will automatically act on the budget balance. A fall in income, therefore, will cause the budget balance to deteriorate even when fiscal policy is contractionary, and vice versa (Blinder and Solow 1974, 13-14).

Thus the inadequacy of the *ex post* budget balance as a measure of fiscal stance stems from its failure to separate the effects of discretionary action from those of autonomous changes in economic activity; to distinguish the budget's influence on the economy from the economy's influence on the budget. To remedy this central defect, the concept of the full (or constant) employment budget balance was developed.[2] This is defined as the budget balance that would result (with the same nominal tax rates and public spending plans) if private sector demand was just sufficient continuously to maintain activity at a constant rate of unemployment. It is thus a measure of the budget balance which would have occurred had there been no deviation of economic activity from its trend path. Since such a measure will not be 'affected by fluctuations in economic activity that shrink or swell the revenue base relative to that associated with the path of potential growth', it consequently provides a means 'to focus on the policy actions that determine expenditure programs and tax rates, and to separate them from a consideration of the autonomous strength of private demand and of the posture of monetary policy' (Okun and Teeters 1970, 78). While this is the most appropriate measure for our purposes, before proceeding further with our analysis we ought to briefly consider alternative measures (see Lotz 1971; Chand 1977 and Shaw 1979 for a fuller discussion).

The selection of any summary measure of fiscal influence requires that abstractions be made concerning the structure of the economy and the channels through which the budget interacts with the economy. As Chand (1977, 406) says:

> It is, therefore, possible to construct a wide variety of summary measures, depending on the underlying assumptions made regarding the dominant objectives of fiscal policy (whether the control of unemployment, inflation, or some other variable); the nature of the economy (whether industrial or developing); the theory chosen to explain the macroeconomy (whether Keynesian, monetarist, or some other); and diverse other reasons such as the availability and use of data or the mode of analysis.

The choice of measure was first dictated by the 'diverse other reasons' referred to by Chand, in particular that the quantity and quality of interwar budgetary data are seriously deficient. This must frustrate any attempt to apply complex measures of fiscal influence developed for postwar economies to the interwar case. Moreover, with only one published modern econometric model available for the interwar period (T. Thomas 1976; 1981), our econometric understanding of the key macroeconomic relationships is very slight.

The estimation of the constant employment budget balance does not require complex modelling of either the fiscal system or the macroeconomy. Other summary measures of fiscal influence have such requirements. For example, Broadberry (1984) has suggested a fiscal leverage measure as more appropriate to the interwar case. This measure requires that a model be employed to describe both total variations in GDP and those which would have taken place in the absence of a government sector, the residual being the deduced impact of fiscal operations.[3] Such a measure is also normally demand weighted, to take account of the differential demand effects of the various endogenous budget items (the balanced budget multiplier, whereby changes in government outlays supposedly have a greater impact upon final demand than comparable adjustments to taxation or transfer payments).

The fiscal leverage measure produces markedly different results from those of the unweighted constant employment budget balance. For example, since the budget deficit widened during the early depression phase (1929–31) as a consequence of expenditure growth outpacing the yield of additional taxation, the former measure yields a more favourable assessment of the impact of fiscal policy than the latter (Broadberry 1984, 96–8). This is unacceptable for a number of reasons. First, the fiscal leverage measure, which was first formulated by Musgrave (1964), treats taxation and government expenditure as autonomous. The measure is clearly inappropriate when one of the objectives of this study is to show the endogeneity of the budget, and the implications of this for policy. Secondly, at present too many conceptual and empirical problems remain unresolved for satisfactory use of a weighted measure of fiscal influence. In particular, without firm econometric evidence of the values for the expenditure and tax multipliers in the 1930s it cannot be presumed that the balanced budget multiplier exceeded unity. That its value does not invariably approximate to unity has long been demonstrated (Baumol and Peston 1955); that in practice it is actually less than unity would seem to be the current interpretation of both modern public finance literature and contemporary 'Keynesian' models of the macroeconomy (Cook and Jackson 1979, 9).

2 THE CONSTANT EMPLOYMENT BUDGET BALANCE

The following identity is used for the constant employment budget balance, or fiscal stance:

$$\frac{B^*}{Y^*} \equiv \frac{t \cdot Y^* - G^*}{Y^*} \tag{7.1}$$

where B^* is the budget balance at constant employment, t the overall tax rate, Y^* the constant employment level of GDP (i.e. the estimated value of what GDP at actual prices would have been if the percentage rate of unemployment had remained constant at the figure chosen for the exercise), and G^* the value of central government expenditure at the constant employment level of incomes. (Hereafter, the superscript* denotes the constant employment value of an item.)

A change in B^*/Y^* between two periods indicates a discretionary change in fiscal policy (the fiscal stance); a higher constant employment balance denoting a more restrictive policy, and vice versa.[4] The automatic stabilizing properties of the fiscal system are measured by the change in B (the actual budget balance) in relation to the change in Y (the actual level of GDP) when Y deviates from Y^*.

We should note at this point the sense in which the terms discretionary and automatic change are here being used. Discretionary changes have usually been defined as those resulting from a change in tax rates or expenditure programmes, while automatic changes are those resulting from variations in economic activity. Such a definition, however, gives rise to the problem that with a progressive tax structure there is an automatic tendency for tax revenue to rise with the growth of income, and if that is not off-set by reducing nominal tax rates and/or increasing public expenditure, the fiscal stance will tighten. Hence, changes in nominal tax rates or expenditure programmes cannot be taken as evidence of a change in fiscal stance unless income is unchanged. Consequently, the more appropriate definition would seem to be that discretionary action is 'any act which causes a change in fiscal stance, regardless of whether this is associated with changes in *nominal* rates of taxation or benefit' (Ward and Neild 1978, 3).

3 CONSTANT EMPLOYMENT GDP

The rate of unemployment selected for the computation of Y^*, the constant employment level of GDP for any year, will affect the value of B^*/Y^*, the constant employment budget balance, but will have a minimal influence on the changes exhibited year to year in the value of B^*/Y^*. Thus the value assigned to Y^* is of secondary concern, since the major focus for study is the yearly changes in B^*/Y^*.[5]

The series for Y^* were calculated as follows: two base years, 1929/30 and 1937/8, were selected when unemployment rates were approximately similar, at 10.8 and 11.1 per cent respectively of the insured workforce, while they also represented peaks in economic activity. Following the method established by E. C. Brown (1956, 869) in his study of fiscal policy in the US in the 1930s, the actual series for GDP at constant factor cost were interpolated between the two base years assuming that the growth of Y^* was the same as that of Y between the two base years. GDP at constant factor cost grew by 19.6 per cent between our two base years, equivalent to an annual rate of growth of 2.25 per cent. An index was calculated of Y^* at constant factor cost using this annual growth rate (table 7.1 col. 2) from which the deviations of Y from Y^*, termed the ratio (col. 3), were obtained for each year. The series of money Y was then adjusted by the ratio to obtain a series for Y^* at current prices (col. 5).

Table 7.1 Actual and constant employment GDP 1929/30–1939/40

	GDP (constant factor cost)			GDP (current prices £m.)	
	Actual	Constant employment	Ratio	Actual	Constant employment
	(Y)	(Y^*)	(Y^*/Y)	(Y)	(Y^*)
	(1)	(2)	(3)	(4)	(5)
1929/30	100.0	100.0	1.000	4245	4245
1930/1	98.0	102.3	1.044	4146	4328
1931/2	95.5	104.6	1.095	3872	4240
1932/3	96.6	106.9	1.107	3783	4188
1933/4	101.0	109.4	1.083	3831	4149
1934/5	106.2	111.8	1.053	4054	4269
1935/6	111.2	114.4	1.029	4236	4359
1936/7	116.7	116.9	1.003	4438	4459
1937/8	119.6	119.6	1.000	4777	4777
1938/9	118.8	122.3	1.030	5068	5220
1939/40	122.7	125.1	1.020	5668	5781

Source: Calculated from Feinstein (1972, tables 3, 6, 8). The standard method was used for adjusting calendar year data on to a financial year basis.

It is well established that in the short run unemployment varies less than output and with a time lag (Neild 1963; Godley and Shepherd 1964). Moreover, there are grounds for supposing that in a prolonged depression labour exhibits a tendency to transfer into the low wage, low productivity service sector. A substantial movement of this type appears to have occurred during 1929–32,[6] and given the lower productivity growth of this sector relative to the industrial sector (Aldcroft 1970a, 117–20), there are some grounds for stating that GDP in 1937/8 would have been somewhat higher if constant employment had been *continuously* achieved during the 1930s, and therefore that the trend rate of growth interpolated between the two base years understates the constant employment trend rate of growth.

Whether this higher productivity trend should have been taken into account or not depends on the hypothesis that is made regarding the duration of the constant employment level of activity. If it were assumed that we were measuring the level of activity and the budget balance if constant employment had been continuously maintained throughout the period, then the higher productivity trend is a relevant consideration. A full counterfactual history, however, is not being postulated; instead, we are measuring the level of income and the budget balance if, immediately within a year, or from one year to the next, the economy had shifted from the actual to the constant employment position. In these circumstances, it is appropriate to use the actual productivity trend since it is valid to assume that, in the short run, labour is slow to transfer between sectors and the effect on productivity is delayed.

In calculating the constant employment level of GDP no adjustment was made to the composition of GDP between the broad categories of income that comprise the main tax bases (consumers expenditure, income from employment and profits) since the elasticity of the major component of taxes on expenditure, Customs and Excise receipts (other than import duties), with respect to GDP (0.96–1.30) was of the same order of magnitude as the overall elasticity of receipts with respect to GDP (1.02–1.22). Hence, the effect of changes in the share of consumers expenditure in GDP, within the range of variations observed in the 1930s, was found to be relatively unimportant, and other compositional effects were ignored.

4 THE CHARACTERISTICS OF THE FISCAL SYSTEM

Summary measures of the response of the budget to income variations can be used to indicate the changing characteristics of a fiscal system over time. For this purpose macro-marginal budget rates have been used, defined as the ratio of a change in receipts and endogenous expenditures to a change in income.[7] The advantage of macro-marginal budget rates over tax elasticities is that they incorporate the tax elasticity and also take account of the response of endogenous expenditures to income variations and the size of the budget in relation to GDP.

The response of the budget balance to income variations depends on the form the variation takes.

1 The growth of real GDP over time, at constant employment, resulting from productivity growth and the increase in the labour force.
2 Cyclical changes in real GDP.
3 Changes in the price level.

Changes in the price level are not explicitly considered since the composition of the budget was such that these effects were relatively unimportant.[8] Prices fell for the greater part of the period but had insignificant effects on public expenditure, since only some public sector employees'

Table 7.2 Response of central government receipts to trend growth in real GDP 1929/30–1939/40*

	1929/30	1930/1	1931/2	1932/3	1933/4	1934/5	1935/6	1936/7	1937/8	1938/9	1939/40
Trend macro-marginal budget rate $\left[\dfrac{\Delta T^*}{\Delta Y^*}\right]$	0.215	0.231	0.278	0.299	0.295	0.282	0.272	0.272	0.270	0.269	0.272
Tax elasticity $\left[\dfrac{\Delta T^*}{T^*} \Big/ \dfrac{\Delta Y^*}{Y^*}\right]$	1.02	1.06	1.17	1.22	1.23	1.22	1.20	1.20	1.21	1.22	1.21
Ratio of receipts to GDP $\left[\dfrac{T^*}{Y^*}\right]$	0.211	0.218	0.238	0.245	0.240	0.231	0.227	0.227	0.223	0.221	0.225

Sources: Data taken from *Financial Accounts* and adjusted on to a constant employment basis using the estimation procedures outlined in appendix III.

Notes:
* Estimates are shown on a receipts basis, although they incorporate income and surtax estimated on an accruals basis to take account of the lag between earnings and assessment. Stamp and estate duties are excluded, their trend growth being negligible.

wages and salaries were index-linked. The major influence came on taxes on expenditure, the yield of *ad valorem* duties falling relative to those duties levied on a specific basis.

Two macro-marginal budget rates, corresponding to (1) and (2) above, were calculated.

$$b_t = \frac{\Delta B^*}{\Delta Y^*} = \frac{\Delta T^*}{\Delta Y^*} \tag{7.2}$$

where b_t is the macro-marginal budget rate with respect to trend growth.[9] Since, on trend, all expenditures are by definition autonomous, this is identical to the macro-marginal tax rate, and measures the growth of central government receipts at the trend rate of growth of real GDP on the basis of nominal tax rates prevailing in each year.

$$b_y = \frac{(B^* - B)}{(Y^* - Y)} \tag{7.3}$$

where b_y is the macro-marginal budget rate with respect to cyclical variations in real GDP and is a measure of the automatic stabilizing properties of the fiscal system.

Macro-marginal budget rates and aggregate tax elasticities with respect to the trend rate of growth of real GDP at constant employment are given in table 7.2. The trend macro-marginal rate rose markedly between 1929/30 and 1932/3, reflecting a rise in the aggregate tax elasticity and a significant increase in the average tax burden as the authorities attempted to achieve a target *ex post* budget balance in the face of a cyclical downturn. Thereafter the macro-marginal rates fell to 1935/6 as taxes were cut, and then remained fairly stable until the end of the period. Tax rates were raised yearly from 1936/7 (although the fiscal stance continued to loosen as expenditure outstripped the growth of revenue), but the macro-marginal rate failed to rise while the ratio of receipts to GDP remained below its peak level of the early 1930s. During the later 1930s a number of influences seem to have been operating.

1 The failure of the aggregate tax elasticity to rise, as had occurred with the tightening of 1929/30 to 1933/4, is probably explicable in terms of (a) a reduction in the elasticity of taxes on income consequent upon a rise in the average effective rate of tax on personal and corporate incomes from 1936/7 (see figure 4.1, p. 64); and (b) discretionary increases in taxes on expenditure, especially in 1939/40, centred on those duties with a low elasticity with respect to GDP compared with the aggregate tax elasticity.

2 Simultaneously, the rise in the general price level (by 10 per cent over 1936–9) resulted in the yield of taxes levied on a specific basis (which comprised the bulk of taxes on expenditure) falling relative to those levied on an *ad valorem* basis.

Table 7.3 Response of budget balance to cyclical variations in real GDP (selected years) and autonomous expenditure 1929/30–1939/40*

	1929/30	1930/1	1931/2	1932/3	1933/4	1934/5	1935/6	1936/7	1937/8	1938/9	1939/40
Cyclical macro-marginal budget rate $\left[\dfrac{B^* - B}{Y^* - Y}\right]$	..	0.440	0.436	0.447	0.420	0.432	0.470	..	..	0.356	..
Ratio of autonomous expenditure to GDP†	0.194	0.194	0.198	0.200	0.182	0.189	0.189	0.200	0.205	0.220	0.330

Sources: As for table 7.2; data on unemployment benefits from working notes to Feinstein (1972).

Notes:
* Estimated on the same basis as the trend macro-marginal budget rate, account also being taken of the response of unemployment benefits to income variations.
† Autonomous expenditure comprises all items considered to be invariant to changes in economic activity and equals total central government expenditure (G^*) less outlay on unemployment benefits ($SIFB^*$).

At the beginning of the period an increase in GDP of £100 million would, at constant employment, have led to a rise in central government receipts of nearly £22 million; by 1932/3 this would have risen to £30 million, and by 1937/8 it would have fallen back to £27 million. If real GDP had grown at 2.25 per cent per annum – the assumed constant employment growth rate – receipts would have grown by approximately the same amount in 1929/30, but by 2.8 per cent in 1932/3 and slightly less in 1937/8, thus providing scope for increased expenditure and/or remission of taxation whilst maintaining an unchanged fiscal stance. In the absence of such countervailing action the fiscal stance would have tightened.

Table 7.3 gives estimates of the cyclical macro-marginal budget rate and the ratio of autonomous expenditure to constant employment GDP. Difficulty in obtaining a satisfactory statistical relationship for outlay on unemployment benefits against GDP has meant that estimates cannot be provided for all years (see appendix III), while stamp and estate duties have been excluded because of the difficulties of estimating a stable relationship between asset prices (the tax base for these duties) and GDP. Since they were highly cyclical their inclusion would raise the cyclical macro-marginal budget rate.

The evidence suggests the cyclical macro-marginal rate rose between 1929/30 and 1930/1 as the increase in eligibility for unemployment benefits, introduced in March 1930, made endogenous expenditure more responsive to income variations. The fall in 1931/2 reflected the return to the previous eligibility conditions and the reduction in benefit rates, while the increased rate in 1932/3 resulted from changes in the response of receipts – an increase in the cyclical macro-marginal tax rate more than compensating for a decline in the response of endogenous expenditure. Thereafter, the macro-marginal budget rate fell, rising temporarily in the mid-1930s with the extension of the unemployment benefits system, down to 1938/9.

On the basis of these estimates, it can be seen that the extent of automatic stabilization fell over the period; a deviation of GDP of £100 million from its benchmark level would have resulted in a change in the budget balance of £45 million in 1932/3 and £36 million in 1938/9, i.e. a 5 per cent deviation in GDP would cause a change in the budget balance of 2.3 per cent of GDP in the former year and 1.8 per cent in the latter. From comparison with estimates of the cyclical macro-marginal budget rates for the contemporary British economy (Ward and Neild 1978, 25, table 3.6), it would seem that the extent of automatic stabilization has changed only marginally over the past fifty years, although the ratio of autonomous expenditure to GDP has more than doubled over the intervening period and thus exerts a greater stabilizing function than in the 1930s.

The explanation of this surprising conclusion lies in conflicting developments on the receipts and expenditure sides of the budget. On the receipts side the aggregate tax elasticity (see table 7.2) was roughly comparable to that of the postwar period (Ward and Neild 1978, table 3.1), but since the ratio of receipts to GDP is approximately twice as high in the later period, the cyclical macro-marginal tax rate has been significantly higher. On the other hand, on the expenditure side, the cyclical macro-marginal rate appears to have fallen because of changes in the response of unemployment to income variations. Benjamin and Kochin's (1979) earlier claim that there was an historically high benefit–wage ratio between the wars, and that this induced large-scale voluntary unemployment, has now been largely discredited, 'the replacement ratios [being] much the same in both the inter- and the postwar periods' (Metcalf et al. 1982, 391 and table 1). Accordingly, since outlay on unemployment benefits only constituted between 1.0 and 1.9 per cent of constant employment GDP, the response of unemployment to a change of GDP must have been greater in the 1930s.

Ward and Neild (1978, 23, 25) calculate (for the late 1970s) that a 1 per cent deviation in Y from Y^* would result in a change in unemployment (within the first year) of only 0.22 per cent of the labour force, and further that a cyclical deviation of as much as 10 per cent from its trend value only gives rise to a change in outlay on unemployment benefits of 0.5 per cent of GDP. The situation in the 1930s differed significantly: for example, in 1930/1 the 4.4 per cent deviation in Y from Y^*, after a year of no deviation, resulted in a rise in the numbers unemployed of 7.5 per cent of the insured labour force and an increase in outlay on unemployment benefits of 1.2 per cent of GDP. Unemployment was thus more responsive to changes in GDP than in the postwar period: not only did unemployment adjust more speedily to a change in GDP but a relatively greater proportion registered as unemployed than in the postwar period, trends that reflect the different characteristics of the labour market between the two periods. In particular, a significantly higher pressure of demand in the postwar period, relative to that of the interwar period, has resulted in a marked fall in the output-employment elasticity (Matthews et al. 1982, table 10.1).

The conclusion suggested by these estimates is that during the 1930s adherence to the balanced budget rule was made more problematical by a budget sensitive to cyclical variations; the higher the cyclical macro-marginal budget rate the stronger the automatic stabilizing properties of the system and the greater the tightening that is necessary in the face of a cyclical downturn if a target budget balance is to be achieved.

5 THE FISCAL STANCE 1929–39

During the 1930s Britain alone among the major Western industrial economies eschewed 'resort to a policy of budget deficits to promote internal recovery' (Arndt 1944, 125). Instead, reliance was placed upon an active monetary policy, tariff protection, devaluation and specific intervention at a microeconomic level. As was shown in earlier chapters, the role accorded to budgetary policy as a stabilization instrument was limited: the principal objective was the maintenance of domestic and international confidence in the authorities' economic policies, and this dictated adherence to balanced budgets and orthodox financial principles. Consequently budgetary operations were potentially destabilizing, for the contemporary practice was to attempt to balance revenue and expenditure with little regard for autonomous fluctuations in economic activity.

As a subject for detailed study, the influence of fiscal operations on the course of economic activity during the 1930s has been somewhat neglected by scholars. With few exceptions, previous studies have tended to be rather cursory and superficial so that it is difficult to speak of a 'traditional interpretation' of budgetary policy during these years in any meaningful sense. Nevertheless, a consensus exists that policy was limited in its scope and objectives, and destabilizing in its operation. Richardson (1967, 211–12), one of the few writers to have attempted a serious assessment of the question, summarized his conclusion as follows:

> [The] government did not have a fiscal policy as such in the 1930s. The nearest it came to an attempt to control the public finances with a view to recovery was its stress on a balanced budget, not with the direct aim of stabilization but rather to restore business confidence at home and confidence in sterling and the government's ability to meet the crisis abroad . . . [Broadly] speaking, fiscal operations were destabilizing in their effects over the 1930s as a whole. The budget was balanced at the trough of depression, and this failed to impart a direct stimulus because expenditure was not increased. Later in the decade, when the economy was entering boom conditions there was a tendency for a budget deficit to develop because of the requirements of rearmament expenditure. This was the opposite of what was desirable on stabilization grounds. On the other hand, high levels of expenditure on rearmament and other items acted counter-cyclically in the recession of 1937–8, though this was not a conscious policy. . . . *British experience in the 1930s hardly provides a model of a counter-cyclical fiscal policy.* [emphasis added]

Using the conventionally defined budget balance (B_c in figure 7.1 and table 7.4) as an indicator of the setting of the budget, the following general features of 1930s budgetary policy are normally identified (see, for example, Aldcroft 1970a, 304–7, a standard text on the interwar period).

1 Budgetary policy was slightly reflationary in 1929 and 1930, the early stages of the depression, for despite increased taxation, expenditure growth was more rapid and the budget deficit widened.

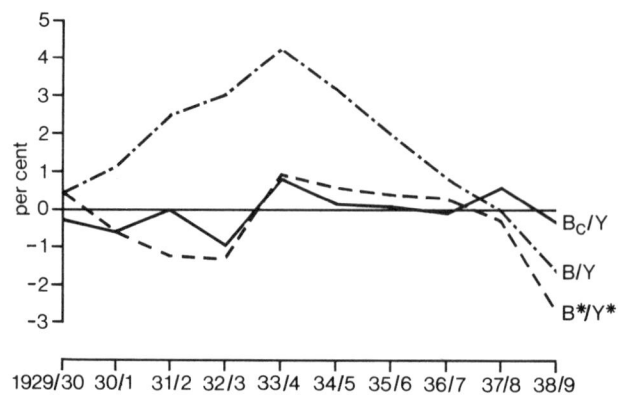

Figure 7.1 Budget balance as % of GDP 1929/30–1939/40
Sources: As table 7.4.

2 The severe tightening of revenue and expenditure necessary to balance the budget in 1931/2 (the trough of the depression) was highly deflationary, but these adverse effects were partially mitigated by the restoration of confidence, which followed from the restrictive measures, and the concomitant effects on business expectations.
3 The delay in remitting taxation and restoring the cuts in expenditure most probably retarded the onset and pace of recovery.
4 As a consequence of rearmament, rather than of a deliberate stabilization policy, budgetary policy became markedly expansionary from the later 1930s and ensured that the recession of 1937–8 was of short duration, and further, that the problem of abnormal unemployment of the interwar years was beginning to be resolved.

However, with the constant employment budget balance as our measure of changes in fiscal stance we can present a more exact and systematic exegesis of budgetary policy than the interpretation outlined above. Moreover the results obtained (summarized in table 7.4) would seem, at least for part of the period, to be at variance with the accepted view and thus suggest that some reinterpretation is appropriate.

For the period as a whole two general features are shown in figure 7.1 and table 7.4.

1 The differences between the budget balances at actual and constant employment, respectively B/Y and B^*/Y^*, are large, reflecting a variation of over 13 percentage points in unemployment rates amongst the insured labour force between the peak and trough years.
2 Changes in fiscal stance were extensive (a maximum change of approximately 6 percentage points between 1933/4 and 1938/9 in B^*/Y^*), a result not of attempts to stabilize activity by fiscal means, but from,

Table 7.4 Central government receipts, expenditure and budget balance: actual and constant employment 1929/30–1939/40

(% of GDP)	(T_c/Y)	(G_c/Y)	(B_c/Y)	(T/Y)	(G/Y)	(B/Y)	(T^*/Y^*)	(G^*/Y^*)	(B^*/Y^*)
1929/30	19.2	19.5	−0.3	21.1	20.7	+0.4	21.1	20.7	+0.4
1930/1	20.7	21.2	−0.6	22.1	22.7	−0.6	21.8	20.7	+1.1
1931/2	22.0	22.0	0.0	23.6	24.8	−1.2	23.8	21.3	+2.5
1932/3	21.9	22.7	−0.9	23.9	25.2	−1.3	24.5	21.5	+3.0
1933/4	21.1	20.3	+0.8	23.2	22.3	+0.9	24.0	19.8	+4.2
1934/5	19.8	19.7	+0.2	22.2	21.6	+0.6	23.1	19.9	+3.2
1935/6	19.9	19.9	+0.1	22.1	21.7	+0.4	22.7	20.7	+2.0
1936/7	20.2	20.3	−0.1	22.3	22.0	+0.3	22.7	21.9	+0.8
1937/8	19.9	19.3	+0.6	22.0	22.3	−0.3	22.3	22.3	0.0
1938/9	19.9	20.1	−0.3	22.0	24.7	−2.7	22.1	23.7	−1.6
1939/40	20.0	24.8	−4.9	21.9	35.1	−13.2	22.5	34.7	−12.2

(£m.)	(T_c)	(G_c)	(B_c)	(T)	(G)	(B)	(T^*)	(G^*)	(B^*)
1929/30	815.0	829.5	−14.5	893.9	876.5	+17.4	893.9	876.5	+17.4
1930/1	857.8	881.0	−23.2	915.1	939.3	−24.2	941.7	894.6	+47.1
1931/2	851.5	851.1	+0.4	914.5	960.2	−45.7	1,008.8	902.1	+106.7
1932/3	827.0	859.3	−32.3	903.9	954.1	−50.2	1,024.6	900.1	+124.5
1933/4	809.4	778.2	+31.2	890.0	856.7	+33.3	997.5	823.3	+174.2
1934/5	804.6	797.1	+7.5	899.3	873.5	+25.8	986.8	848.8	+138.0
1935/6	844.8	841.8	+3.0	935.7	919.7	+16.0	988.5	902.7	+85.8
1936/7	896.6	902.2	−5.6	990.0	975.3	+14.7	1,011.7	974.3	+37.4
1937/8	948.7	919.9	+28.8	1,051.5	1,067.2	−15.7	1,063.5	1,067.2	−3.7
1938/9	1,006.2	1,018.9	−12.7	1,114.1	1,251.3	−137.2	1,155.1	1,235.8	−80.7
1939/40	1,132.2	1,408.2	−276.0	1,241.0	1,990.2	−749.2	1,303.8	2,007.9	−704.1

Sources: The actual employment data are drawn from *Financial Accounts* and the working notes to Feinstein (1972); for the computation of the constant employment estimates, see appendix III.

firstly, striving to attain a balanced budget in the face of severe cyclical fluctuations in activity, and secondly, the imperative of rearmament which necessitated large-scale borrowing from 1937 onwards.

Depression 1929–33

Between 1929/30 and 1932/3 the budget balance (B/Y) deteriorated by 1.7 percentage points. In contrast, the constant employment balance moved into substantial surplus as the authorities attempted to balance the budget in the face of declining economic activity. This tightening (3.8 percentage points of GDP over 1929/30–1933/4) continued almost unabated until 1933/4, the remission of taxation in 1933 being insufficient to compensate for the severe tightening in 1931 of both receipts and expenditure.

The change in fiscal stance was achieved almost entirely by raising the ratio of receipts to GDP. In this respect it was comparable to the tightening of the period 1967–70 which, until recently, was the most severe of the postwar period – a change in the constant employment balance of nearly 7 percentage points of GNP, the expenditure ratio only falling marginally (Ward and Neild 1978, table 4.2). But since the size of the budget in relation to GDP was only half that of the postwar period, a given change in fiscal stance of (say) 2 percentage points of GDP required nearly a 10 per cent change in receipts in 1931/2 but less than 5 per cent in 1967.

The extent of the perverse fiscal action during the depression years can be said to depend on:

1 The percentage fall in GDP.
2 The response of the budget, as measured by the cyclical macro-marginal budget rate (b_y), to a change in GDP.
3 The extent to which discretionary action could be avoided by fiscal window-dressing.

GDP at constant factor cost fell by only 5 per cent over 1929–32, but the marked cyclical sensitivity of the budget to income variations ensured that even this small change resulted in a significant deterioration in the budget balance, although this was partially mitigated by increased taxation yearly from 1929 and cuts in expenditure in 1931. The increasingly deflationary stance adopted by the authorities in their attempts to maintain a balanced budget (B_c) was, however, significantly tempered by fiscal window-dressing – over 1929/30 to 1933/4 revenue (T_c) included £59.5 million of non-recurrent receipts while £39.1 million was borrowed. The authorities were thus able to avoid discretionary action totalling nearly £90 million, a figure approximately equivalent to an additional 6d. on the standard rate of income tax over the period. Following upon the already severe tightening that had occurred, the consequences of such a further increase in taxation would have been extremely serious.

The increased taxation and expenditure cuts (estimated full year effects of £81.5 million and £70 million respectively) imposed in September 1931 have generally been viewed as the most deflationary budget of the whole interwar period. The continuance of the crisis measures thereafter has also been seen as having retarded recovery (Aldcroft 1970a, 304–6): an impression substantiated by the change in the constant employment balance of 1.4 percentage points between 1930/1 and 1931/2 and a further 1.7 percentage points by 1933/4.

Many contemporaries, however, believed that by restoring confidence amongst business circles and the international financial community in the government's financial policy, the budget achieved a psychological stimulus which outweighed the direct restrictive effects (for example, Hicks 1938, 15; and Arndt 1944, 129). As was noted in chapter 5, confidence cannot be accurately specified or measured, and therefore the importance of this factor is difficult to establish; on somewhat stronger grounds, the authorities, and many writers since, believed that the balancing of the budget (B_c not B which continued to move into deficit until 1932/3) in 1931 and the consequent restoration of confidence permitted the cheap money policy,[10] which many see as the mainstay of recovery in the 1930s. Thus the 1931 budget was neutral or

> reflationary only because it led to the War Loan conversion and was accompanied by circumstances which caused or greatly assisted recovery. These circumstances were unusual and are unlikely to recur. In general, a policy of cutting expenditure and raising taxes will not alleviate but deepen a depression.   (*The Economist*, 11 June 1938, 593)

Furthermore, the War Loan conversion permitted the large fall in debt charge – a reduction of 30.4 per cent from £322 million in 1931/2 to £224 million in 1933/4 (see table 6.4, p. 102) – which formed the basis of the loosening of fiscal stance that occurred from 1934 onwards.

Whilst the dictates of a balanced budget restricted the scope for fiscal operations to be stabilizing in a depression, the central government's deflationary policies could have been partially offset by an expansion of public investment and local authority expenditure, both of which were outside the coverage of the conventionally defined budget. Gross fixed capital formation by public and semi-public authorities exerted a stabilizing influence during 1929–31, expanding (at 1930 prices) from £167 million to £198 million and thus nearly compensating for the decline in capital formation by the private sector from £266 million to £229 million. Thereafter, public investment was cut back sharply in 1932–3 as a consequence of the economy campaign, and thus in the two most critical years when fiscal stance was tightening public investment was destabilizing (figure 3.2A, p. 47). Total expenditure by local authorities followed a similar course, expanding during the first two years of the depression and then being seriously curtailed during 1931–4 (Peacock and Wiseman 1967, table A-20). Nor should the expansionary effects of these expenditures of 1929–31 be overstated, for much of the increased capital expenditure was financed out of additional current revenue and new borrowing was partially offset by simultaneous repayment of debt, while, in addition, expenditure was lowest in those areas with the highest unemployment (Hicks 1938, 126–7; Bretherton *et al.* 1941, 168).

Recovery 1933–7

Although there is disagreement over the precise impact of the government's deflationary policy in 1931–2, a consensus exists that the crisis measures were maintained too long, for once 'confidence had been restored, conditions were such that a reflationary fiscal policy could have materially assisted an early recovery' (Richardson 1967, 220). Within the constraint imposed by the prevailing orthodoxy, the timing of budgetary relaxation was delayed by two factors: first, the yield of taxes on income (which constituted 30 to 40 per cent of total receipts) was slow to respond to recovery, and secondly, whilst in the early stages of the recovery the total numbers unemployed fell rapidly, there was a proportionately smaller effect on outlay on unemployment benefits charged to the budget as conventionally defined. The first factor is explicable in terms of the lag between earnings and assessment for income and surtax; the second derives from the rather complex administrative arrangements governing outlay on unemployment benefits.

Unemployment amongst insured persons reached a peak of 2.979 million in January 1933, falling rapidly to 2.288 million by the end of the year, a reduction of 23.2 per cent. This fall was accompanied by a marked reduction in total outlay on unemployment benefits, but because of the nature of the central government's contribution to the unemployment benefits system, its contributions fell proportionately less than the reduction in outlay of the system as a whole.

From October 1931 onwards central government contributions took three forms.

1 Payments to the Unemployment Insurance Fund on the basis of equal thirds contributions from the state, employers and employees.
2 Responsibility for the whole cost of transitional payments (unemployment assistance from 1935).
3 The debt of the Unemployment Insurance Fund having reached its statutory maximum of £115 million, the Exchequer was obliged to meet by a deficiency grant any shortfall in revenue relative to expenditure.

Between March and December 1933 that part of the unemployed for which central government was fully responsible fell far less (by 11.9 per cent) than those receiving benefits from the Unemployment Insurance Fund (a reduction of 28.2 per cent) for which only part of the charge was borne by the budget. The burden of unemployment charges on the budget was thus slow to respond to recovery: while the average numbers unemployed fell by 24.3 per cent between 1932/3 and 1934/5, the unemployment charge on the budget only fell by 15.5 per cent.

As a surplus began to accrue to the Unemployment Fund this had to be allocated to redemption of the Fund's debt. Given the budget identity in use, such transactions did not appear in the budget accounts, just as in 1929–31 borrowing had also been excluded. A surplus began to accrue from June 1933 onwards so that the burden of the deficiency grant no longer fell on the budget, the net effect on the budget being a result of two factors.

1 The numbers of insured unemployed (corresponding to the short-term unemployed) fell faster than those receiving transitional benefits (essentially the long-term unemployed), a usual occurrence in a cyclical upturn.
2 The effects of the change in eligibility for insurance benefits – introduced in October 1931 as an economy measure – were beginning to lead to the transference of the unemployed from insurance benefits to transitional benefits.

Revenue adjusted for non-recurrent receipts (T) continued to be depressed until 1934/5, falling by 2.7 per cent over 1931/2 to 1933/4, but expenditure (G_c) fell far more rapidly (by 8.6 per cent) over these years, so that a substantial surplus (B_c) was achieved in 1933/4 which permitted a loosening in fiscal stance from 1934 onwards. As was shown in chapter 6, this change was occasioned solely by the reduced debt charge on the budget, resulting from lower interest rates and the near abandonment of sinking fund payments. Remission of taxation and restoration of the expenditure cuts followed gradually in the budgets of 1934 and 1935, but the scope for relaxation remained very tight, for although receipts were beginning to reflect the recovery of economic activity, they were outpaced by the growth of expenditure as rearmament began to dissipate the gains that should have followed from recovery.

The extent of this relaxation is measured by a 2 percentage points change in the constant employment balance between 1933/4 and 1935/6, far less than the tightening of the previous period. This change in fiscal stance resulted almost equally from variations in the ratio of receipts and expenditure to GDP, the former reflecting remission of taxation, the latter the restoration of the expenditure cuts and the growth of rearmament expenditure. Overall the direct contribution of fiscal policy to recovery was extremely limited. By 1935 fiscal stance had changed comparatively little since the depression years, the relaxation had been delayed until long after the onset of recovery, and public investment had been destabilizing in the early stages of recovery (though in its later stages, public investment did grow strongly – see figure 3.2A, p. 47). Against these factors, however, must be placed the undoubted contribution to recovery of the restoration of confidence and the cheap money policy, both deriving from the apparent adherence to budgetary orthodoxy.

Recession and rearmament 1937–9

The final phase of budgetary policy was inextricably connected with the needs of rearmament. Total defence expenditure increased from £136.9 million in 1935/6 to £265.2 million in 1937/8 and had reached £1,142 million by 1939/40, when it constituted 19.8 per cent of constant employment GDP (see table 7.5). The growing importance of rearmament expenditure was reflected in the change in fiscal stance over these years.

Table 7.5 Summary figures of defence expenditure 1929/30–1939/40

	Total defence expenditure*		
	(£m.)	as % of central government expenditure (G*)	as % of constant employment GDP
1929/30	113.0	12.9	2.7
1930/1	110.5	12.4	2.6
1931/2	107.3	11.9	2.5
1932/3	103.0	11.4	2.5
1933/4	107.9	13.1	2.6
1934/5	113.9	13.4	2.7
1935/6	136.9	15.2	3.1
1936/7	186.2	19.1	4.2
1937/8	265.2	24.9	5.6
1938/9	400.2	32.4	7.7
1939/40			
(April)	628.8	..	..
(September)	1,249.0	..	..
(outturn)	1,142.0	56.9	19.8

Sources: Defence expenditure from IIMSO (1940, table 151; 1948, tables 253–4) and PRO (1940); GDP from table 7.1.

Notes:
* Expenditure covered by revenue, borrowing under the Defence Loans Acts, 1937 and 1939, and the Vote of Credit granted on 3 September 1939. In addition to the expenditure of the three defence forces, expenditure on civil defence and food storage also included.

The period of economic recovery 1932–7 had seen a limited relaxation in fiscal stance, a change in the constant employment balance of just over 4 percentage points of GDP, while the years 1937/8 to 1939/40 saw a change of over 12 percentage points. The ratio of receipts to GDP remained constant over this period, although tax rates were increased yearly from 1936, and the change in fiscal stance reflected the rise in the expenditure ratio as military outlays were greatly expanded.

The timing of this change in fiscal stance was most fortunate. Despite the absence of a formal commitment to an active counter-cyclical fiscal policy by the authorities, fiscal operations did act to mitigate the recession of 1937–8. While the rearmament programme was eventually to prove itself a most effective demand stimulus, being 'the greatest public works programme ever devised in time of formal peace' (*The Economist*, 22 April 1939, 184), it had long been appreciated that the scope for manipulating rearmament was limited: 'consideration[s] of business cycle policy' could not take precedence over 'the duress of [the] international situation' (Balogh 1936, 86).

Bretherton *et al.* (1941, 92) estimated that unemployment amongst insured persons might have risen as high as 3 million, compared with its actual figure of 1.8 million, if the authorities had decided to balance the budget in 1938/9 rather than borrow over £120 million for rearmament. Thus, they contended, 'The depression would ... have become more severe than that of 1932 and presumably would have increased in length too.' More recent research, by M. Thomas (1983, 571), who has used a social accounting matrix as a tool to analyse the income effects and employment creation of rearmament, suggests that this conclusion 'somewhat overstates the effects of rearmament', though 'the overriding analysis holds'.

It is of importance that the growth of rearmament expenditure and the decline in private sector demand were not exactly synchronized. The recession was able to develop for some months before fiscal operations became of sufficient moment first to stabilize activity and then to stimulate recovery (see *The Economist*, Trade Supplements, 24 September 1938; 25 February 1939). Employment-creation by the rearmament programme rose over threefold from 1935–8, generating an additional million jobs.[11] The principal sectors directly affected by rearmament (the engineering trades, shipbuilding, iron and steel) were, of course, those which had suffered employment losses from the fall-off in exports (M. Thomas 1983, 567, 570), the dominant feature of the 1937–8 recession.

By the spring of 1939 both the authorities and economic commentators were agreed that recovery was progressing strongly and that the abnormal unemployment – the 'intractable million' – which had plagued the interwar economy was being reduced as a result of rearmament. Nor was this just a stimulus to aggregate demand; there was also some redirection of demand to the depressed areas, where defence contracts had been specifically placed, though the extent of this can be overstated (Middleton 1985).

The change in fiscal stance between 1938/9 and 1939/40 ensured the achievement of full employment towards the end of 1940. There is evidence, however, that full employment would have been attained some months earlier had it not been for the outbreak of war which temporarily halted the progress of recovery. Unemployment had fallen rapidly from 2.134 million to 1.295 million between January and August 1939, but had risen thereafter as a consequence of the disruption produced by the onset of war, and it was not until March 1940 that unemployment had recovered to its August 1939 level.

6 CONCLUSIONS

The overall influence of fiscal operations during this period is difficult to evaluate since modern (non-monetarist) objectives and targets of budgetary policy are at variance with those of the 1930s. Within the limited role accorded at the time to budgetary policy as a stabilization instrument, policy can be judged to have been not unsuccessful, for, with the exception of the débâcle of 1931, fiscal operations provided a stable environment for business and permitted an expansionary monetary policy, conditions conducive to recovery. Thus, we might agree with Sabine's (1970, 285) conclusion that, while budgetary policy was 'pitched in a minor key', it nevertheless 'played a vital, if unspectacular part in the limited recovery of 1933 to 1936 by a delicate combination of inflatory and deflatory measures'.

It is when fiscal influence is appraised with reference to Keynesian objectives of budgetary policy, objectives formulated and developed during the 1930s in response to the limitations and unsatisfactory macroeconomic impact of existing policy, that its deficiencies and destabilizing characteristics become evident. This, of course, was the inevitable consequence of adherence to the balanced budget rule, which compelled an overriding of the automatic stabilizers whenever an endogenous or exogenous demand shock threatened budgetary stability.

In this respect there is also an obvious parallel between 1929–33 and 1979–83. The first Thatcher administration's pursuit of a constrained PSBR target (the modern equivalent of the balanced budget rule) not only marked a complete repudiation of conventional Keynesian demand management objectives and policy instruments, it also compelled them to override the automatic stabilizers once the restrictive stance of monetary and fiscal policy was actually made manifest in an increasingly depressed real economy. A further tightening of policy was then necessary, this in turn exacerbating the depression and – through the operation of the automatic stabilizers – forcing additional restrictive measures if the PSBR and monetary targets were to be attained (Buiter and Miller 1981). That a government in a post-Keynesian world can pursue such a course so resolutely, face and seemingly overcome an opposition more informed and vocal than that of the earlier 'great' depression, makes more comprehensible the events of 1929–33. Such parallels are considered further in chapter 9.

To return to our discussion of the 1930s, the foregoing study suggests that the traditional interpretation of budgetary policy during this period requires modification on two counts.

1 The budget balance at actual employment (B_c or B) is an extremely misleading indicator of changes in the setting of the budget. In the early years of the depression it appears to signify a loosening of fiscal stance whereas, in fact, as indicated by changes in the constant employment balance, budgetary policy was becoming progressively more restrictive.
2 The traditional interpretation, that the direct deflationary effects of the September 1931 budget were outweighed by the restoration of confidence, whilst intuitively appealing, should be subject to serious scrutiny. The extent of the tightening in the depression and early recovery periods was severe, and consequently any recovery of private sector demand induced by the restoration of confidence would have had to have been considerable to compensate for the contraction of public sector demand.

Until the advent of the 'new classical macroeconomics' in the 1970s, and its undermining of the foundations of Keynesian stabilization policy, few would have disagreed that in the conditions of the 1930s, with its heavy unemployment and falling price level, 'recovery proceeded less strongly and rapidly than it would have done with more enlightened budgetary policies' (Winch 1972, 218). The recent reaction against deficit-finance in certain quarters, and the relevance of the modern debate to the 1930s fiscal policy debate, are considered in the next chapter in connection with our discussion of the 'Treasury view'. In earlier chapters we saw that an expansionary fiscal policy was not pursued because of adherence to budgetary orthodoxy and an implicit faith in the potency of market forces. Other factors were also of importance, for had more 'enlightened' policies been adopted the nature of the unemployment problem of these years was such that fiscal policy would have had to have been supplemented by selective demand management measures. In particular, an active regional policy would have been required while, in the circumstances of the abnormally depressed level of world trade, a higher level of activity would have resulted in balance of payments problems.

CHAPTER EIGHT

THE 'TREASURY VIEW' AND PUBLIC WORKS

The interwar 'Treasury view' on public works and deficit-finance as appropriate policy responses to deficient demand and mass unemployment has long been a subject of interest to economists and economic historians. The resulting verdict of history has been far from favourable to the 'Treasury view', for the judgement quickly passed into orthodoxy that the Treasury's position was theoretically untenable, easily discredited and unworthy of further serious study.

Such judgements, of course, were not unaffected by the Keynesian revolution. While cycles of historical interest suggest that they would be subject eventually to reappraisal, the present would seem to be particularly appropriate for such an exercise. Recently there has been a discernible revival of interest in the 'Treasury view' as the monetarist counter-revolution in theory, and its partial translation into the current monetarist policy experiment, has generated a certain inquisitiveness about possible theoretical–policy antecedents. (The new classical macroeconomics may also provoke similar historical enquiry.) Nor have the Keynesians remained free from such motives, although in this case their ambitions have been rather different, indeed diametrically opposed: to reaffirm the orthodox critique of the 'Treasury view' as part of their attempted exoneration of conventional demand management and the counter-attack on the new monetarism (Kaldor and Trevithick 1981, 1–2).

Hitherto, both monetarists and Keynesians have assumed much about the 'Treasury view', but never attempted its detailed specification. Nor for that matter have economic historians, although there is a wealth of literature on the subject.[1] A review of the 1930s public works debate, and a more historically accurate specification of the Treasury's position, is thus long overdue. Such a review, the focus of this chapter, also permits the 1930s fiscal policy debate to be viewed from a much broader perspective than that of previous chapters, this in turn enabling us to draw conclusions about the form and progress of economic management in Britain by 1939.

1 THE CASE FOR PUBLIC WORKS

The proposal that, in a depression, public works might provide a useful employment stimulus has a long lineage. In Britain, their first active use on any substantial scale came in the early 1920s; conceived of as a purely temporary relief measure, there later developed dissatisfaction with their effectiveness, and increasingly they were opposed on theoretical grounds. By the later 1920s, this opposition had supposedly hardened into a dogma, the so-called 'Treasury view', whereby loan-financed expenditures were regarded as diversionary or inflationary and thus provided no net addition to employment.

While the development of the pre-1929 'Treasury view' is a subject of considerable interest in its own right, we can begin with the policy debate generated by the 1929 general election: the issues there raised embraced those that had been developing in previous years, while the form of this debate was to be crucial in the way that it influenced subsequent events.

Unemployment dominated the 1929 general election, and dominating the unemployment debate was Lloyd George's pledge that:

> If the nation entrusts the Liberal Party at the next General Election with the responsibilities of Government, we are ready with schemes of work which we can put immediately into operation, work of a kind which is not merely useful in itself but essential to the well-being of the nation. The work put in hand will reduce the terrible figures of the workless in the course of a single year to normal proportions, and will, when completed, enrich the nation and equip it for competing successfully with all its rivals in the business of the world. These plans will not add one penny to national or local taxation. (Liberal Party 1929, 4)

The enormity of this pledge, and the extravagant form in which it was expressed, pose problems for the historian: for example, since this pledge formed the core of the Liberals' election manifesto, how strict should one be in interpreting the claims made for the proposed programme; how does one make the divide between the excesses of a general election campaign and the real issues, of theory and policy, that separate the respective parties?

Mention ought also to be made of the origins of the Liberal programme. This was the product of a remarkable collaboration between politicians and economists, its origins going back to Lloyd George's advocacy, in 1924, of public works in the *Nation and Athenaeum*, the organ of the more progressive Liberals who attempted to steer a course between *laissez-faire* individualism and collectivism. In the debate that followed, a new approach to economic management began to be conceived which, on the initiative of the Liberal Summer School, eventually found full expression in *Britain's Industrial Future* (the 'Yellow Book') published in February 1928. This has been described 'as the most farsighted policy document produced by any political party between the wars' and as having 'pointed to a practical compromise between the irresponsibility of unfettered capitalism and the rigidities of theoretical socialism' (Campbell 1977, 201). The Liberals' 1929 election manifesto, known as the 'Orange Book', was essentially the 'National Development' chapter of the 'Yellow Book', rewritten in a more popular and challenging form.

Thus the Liberal programme was rather more than just a large-scale, but temporary, public works programme: it derived from a larger and more comprehensive programme of economic and political action which would have permanently enlarged the role of the state. The various responses to the Liberals' proposals must, therefore, be seen in the light of the implications of accepting such a large-scale public works programme.

Turning now to the details of the programme; for the Liberals, a necessary starting point was that

> individual enterprise alone cannot restore the situation within a time for which we can wait. The State must therefore lend its aid and, by a deliberate policy of national development, help to set going at full speed the great machine of industry. (Liberal Party 1929, 9)

This approach to the unemployment problem of the 1920s, essentially one of undertaking a short pump-priming exercise based on 'national development', stood in stark contrast to that of both the Conservative and Labour Parties who, by the later 1920s, had become committed to a long-term employment policy based on the recovery of industry through its normal channels (Skidelsky 1967, 51).

The Liberals' public works programme is summarized in table 8.1. For analytical purposes it can be discussed under three headings:

1 The unemployment schemes themselves.
2 The soundness of their unemployment theory.
3 The financial feasibility of the proposed programme.

The first may be considered very briefly. All the schemes were justified by the argument that there was ample scope for a national development programme, so constituted and totalling £250 million (a programme

Table 8.1 Liberal Party's 1929 public works programme

	Direct employment (primary)		Cost (£m.)
	Within the first year of the scheme commencing operation	Within the second year	
	(man-years)	(man-years)	
Roads and bridges	350,000	375,000	145.0
Housing	60,000	60,000	34.5
Telephone development	60,000	60,000	30.0
Electrical development	62,000	62,000	31.0
Land drainage	30,000	30,000	. .
London passenger transport	24,000	24,000	11.0
TOTAL	586,000	611,000	251.5

Source: Liberal Party (1929, 52).

representing approximately 6 per cent of 1929 GDP), because the government, particularly in the case of roads and housing, was deliberately and unnecessarily restraining public investment; and further that these programmes, for which detailed plans had already been drawn up, 'would begin to absorb Labour within three months of the adoption of this policy, and would before the end of twelve months reduce the numbers of unemployed workers to normal proportions' (Liberal Party 1929, 9). As will become evident later, this claim was particularly contentious.

With reference to (2) above, and in anticipation of Treasury criticisms, it was argued:

> There is no fixed fund of employment. . . . In special circumstances like the present, private investment may not be forthcoming on a sufficient scale; and yet there may be work waiting to be done which is either outside the sphere of private enterprise, or which private enterprise unassisted cannot be expected to undertake. . . . If State enterprise is invoked in directions in which it will not conflict with or displace private enterprise, it has no less effect in increasing employment than that of any other enterprise. Indeed, having as a prime consideration the provision of employment, it can be so chosen that a maximum of employment is provided for a given expenditure.
>
> (Liberal Party 1929, 54)

This point was then further developed with regard to the supply of loanable funds, evidence being presented that the ratio of time to demand deposits had increased as a result of depression. Upon this foundation, the pamphlet then pursued to its logical extreme what it believed to be the Treasury's position:

> If capital is not available for the absorption of the unemployed on a policy of national development, then it is not available for their absorption at all; unless, of course, the credit of the British Government, restored at such a cost, is inferior to that of the ordinary private enterprise! (Liberal Party 1929, 56–7)

The pamphlet concluded that not only was the supply of savings sufficient to finance the programme without prejudicing (in effect crowding-out) private investment, but that the schemes would be partially self-liquidating: the anticipated permanent reduction of unemployment by 0.75 million resulting in a saving to the Unemployment Fund of £30 million per annum and an increase in tax receipts of £8–10 million per annum.

These, very briefly, were the principal elements of the Liberals' case; mention should next be made of Keynes and Henderson's supporting pamphlet – *Can Lloyd George Do It?* Whilst this was published prior to the government's reply to the Liberal pamphlet – although not early enough for the government to take account of it – it is of importance, for it attempted a more refined exposition of the general case for public works and sought to anticipate many of the government's criticisms.

Two aspects, in particular, require note. First, some writers – for example, Harris (1948, 52) and Skidelsky (1967, 54) – have identified a crude multiplier mechanism within the pamphlet, one that led the authors to conclude that 'the effects on employment of a given capital expenditure would be far larger than the Liberal pamphlet assumes' (Keynes and Henderson 1929, 107). Secondly, in their treatment of the not unconnected questions of the cost of the programme and the availability of funds to finance it, they estimated that, on the basis of a programme totalling £250 million, the annual cost to the budget would be as low as £2.5 million when full account was taken of the self-liquidating nature of the projects. On the question of the availability of the requisite funds, Keynes and Henderson (1929, 115) emphatically rejected the notion that 'money raised by the state for financing productive schemes must diminish *pro tanto* the supply of capital available for ordinary industry', since if this were the case, any new expenditure would divert resources from other uses.

Thus Keynes and Henderson's rejection of crowding-out followed along the same lines as that of the Liberal pamphlet, viz. that this was not a possibility at a position of less than full employment. There was, however, one new feature, for they questioned the assumption held by both the Liberal pamphlet and the Treasury that public works could not be supported by an accommodating monetary policy. The importance of this point will become clearer later, when we are considering the Treasury's position.

2 THE 'TREASURY VIEW' 1929-30

The 'Treasury view' was not just a theoretical view. In this section we show that it embraced wide-ranging technical, administrative and political objections to public works. To the Treasury, these objections constituted the disruptive intermediary which prevented the theoretical potentialities of public works from being translated into practical and effective results. We can consider the neutralizing mechanism – first introduced in chapter 5 – in more detail later, but in essence it was that large public works programmes caused a loss of confidence, which led to an adverse change in liquidity preference, and there resulted a form of psychological crowding-out. In this interpretation a large loan-financed public works programme still had no substantial net effect on employment, but the sequence of events and causes of crowding-out were rather different from those accepted hitherto.

In chapter 5 the argument was advanced that the theoretical basis underlying adherence to balanced budgets has been misinterpreted; this would also seem to have been the case for the 'Treasury view'. At no time did the Treasury doubt, *ceteris paribus*, that in the short term state expenditure could raise aggregate demand and employment. Rather, their objections were twofold. First, they contended that a number of constraints would operate to neutralize the favourable effects of state expenditure if it was on the scale envisaged by the Liberals (objections not applicable to smaller-scale projects). Secondly, such a course was undesirable because it failed to offer a permanent solution to heavy unemployment. It was here, with the second set of factors, that in 1929 and thereafter, there were deep-seated theoretical differences between the Treasury and the 'new' economics.

The rejection of the 1929 Liberal public works programme has traditionally been ascribed rather more to the dominance and stultifying influence of the 'Treasury view', and rather less to the programme's technical deficiencies, and the widespread mistrust of it as a mere electioneering stunt (Williamson 1982, 402). The 'Treasury view', as expressed in the White Paper *Memoranda on Certain Proposals Relating to Unemployment* (HMSO 1929, hereafter *Memoranda*), has further been interpreted as deriving from classical economics with its implicit assumption of full employment and a fixed fund of savings.[2] Yet, this interpretation has been too readily accepted: as will now be suggested, the theoretical basis of the 'Treasury view' has been misconstrued, and the whole basis of the 1929 policy debate interpreted too narrowly.

It is generally held that the 'heart of [this] White Paper lay in the Memorandum prepared by the Treasury', and that this 'comprise[d] a rag-bag of objections to public works which [gave] the impression of proving too much' (Winch 1972, 119). In fact, the White Paper, although a coherent unity, divides distinctly into three parts: a consideration of the labour supply available for public works; a comment on the practicality of the proposed schemes; and the Treasury memorandum on the finance of the proposed programme. This document represents a general Whitehall view, rather than a purely Treasury view; it reflected the 'past experience of public works . . . and was a description of what in fact ha[d] been found often to happen' (Hicks 1938, 222). Nor would the available evidence support the view that these practical objections were without substance, a mere screen for more fundamental, and largely indefensible, theoretical objections.

We can begin by looking at the supply of unemployed labour. In chapter 2 the argument was advanced that, apart from the well defined period of general demand deficiency (1930 to mid-1933), the characteristics of interwar unemployment were such as to cast doubt on the suitability of a centrally directed public works programme as a means of effecting a *permanent* stimulus to employment. Such was also the opinion of the Ministry of Labour in their contribution to the White Paper.

Their memorandum opened with the criticism that the Liberals' plans assumed a constant figure of 1 million unemployed whereas during the course of a year the Live Register would contain 3–4 million persons and that:

> At no time would all on the Live Register be willing or able to accept whatever alternative employment is offered. This fact is fundamental to the whole question of the extent to which the State need or can profitably provide a substitute employment market. (*Memoranda*, 4)

This point was illustrated by the data reproduced in table 8.2.

Although the potential available male labour supply was 0.44 million it was contended that further reductions were necessary because of the nature of the works schemes (primarily roads) and the geographical and occupational immobility of labour. When these adjustments were made, only 0.25–0.30 million persons were available for direct employment (*Memoranda*, 7), a figure that fell far short of the 0.586 million that it was anticipated would be directly employed on the Liberal programme. Thus, even if the Ministry of Labour had been unduly pessimistic in their estimates,[3] the criticism is valid that the Liberal proposals overstated the extent of a certain category of unemployment, misunderstood the dynamics of the labour market, and failed to appreciate the difficulty of matching labour (both occupationally and geographically) required for the schemes to the available labour supply.

Table 8.2 Composition of insured unemployed April 1929

		Unemployed (m.)
Insured unemployed in Great Britain, 22 April		1.144
deduct:		
Women and girls	0.224	
Boys under 18	0.025	
Men temporarily stopped	0.157	
70% of casual workers	0.054	
75% of men over 50	0.123	
Disabled or physically defective men under 50	0.020	
Men unsuitable by nature of present occupation	0.100	
	0.703	
Total available for employment on works programmes		0.441

Source: HMSO (1929, 6).

The Ministry of Labour did not object to public works as such, merely to the form and magnitude of the Liberal programme. Two fundamental points emerge from their analysis.

1 At the time of writing the UK economy had not yet been affected by the world depression, indeed it was approaching a cyclical peak in employment. Accordingly, their criticism would seem valid that whatever the Liberals might have stated, the programme implicitly assumed a high level of cyclical unemployment (it made no analysis of the unemployment problem as such), whereas the real problem was structural.
2 It was believed that the completion of the schemes would create a serious demobilization problem, i.e. that the public works would not have secondary and tertiary effects on employment which by raising demand would induce the reabsorption of the primary direct employment thus released. Thus it would appear that the Ministry of Labour took no account of the multiplier (a concept implicit in much of the literature but not yet empirically or formally derived). In fact, the multiplier effect was discounted on the grounds that the types of projects selected could not aid the export industries, nor would they stimulate other 'normal' channels of industry (i.e. structural change) because of the adverse effect on confidence, and thus on private sector investment, of such a large-scale public works programme (a point taken up in the Treasury memorandum).

There then followed memoranda on the various schemes, mainly concentrating on the road programme which constituted nearly 60 per cent of the total proposed expenditure. The criticisms levelled against the road programme echo those made against all the other schemes:

> The pamphlet is novel only in the scale of its proposals and the rate at which it is claimed that they are to be carried out. A volume of work which, even if it were all desirable, would take at least a decade to execute economically and efficiently is compressed into the short period of two years, within which it would not be practicable to spend a sum of £145 millions.
> ... the obstacles to any such concentration of work as it proposes are, short of dictatorship, insuperable whatever powers of overriding private interests and the autonomy of local authorities were obtained.
> (*Memoranda*, 17)

In the Ministry of Transport memorandum we may discern three types of criticism of the Liberal proposals (which were mirrored to a similar degree in the memoranda of the other departments). First, the Liberal figure of 5,000 man-years of primary (direct and indirect) employment per £1 million expenditure was questioned, and a more realistic figure of 4,000 man-years substituted, although even this was accompanied by the caveat that this might also be an exaggeration since not all indirect employment was additional (*Memoranda*, 19–20). Secondly, and of more importance, the central criticisms focused on the administrative and technical problems associated with the implementation of such a large public works programme over the time scale envisaged by the Liberals. As was shown in chapter 3, appeal to such considerations was not a diversionary tactic by an obscurantist bureaucracy: these were issues of substance, themselves sufficient to prevent the adoption of the Liberal proposals or the attainment of the expected favourable employment effects.

Amongst the factors referred to, emphasis was placed upon the delays involved in planning schemes so that the Liberal programme was 'not practicable with regard to efficiency and economy', there were considerable lags before schemes came into full operation and reached their maximum employment effects, and the programmes would not be entirely a net addition to expenditure since some of the work would have been undertaken anyway (*Memoranda*, 23).

In justification of the dismissive tone of the Ministry of Transport's memorandum, it is important to understand that the Liberal Party had few detailed plans for the projects themselves and thus the time period over which the projects were to affect unemployment were quite unrealistic. Keynes and Henderson (1929, 87) may have argued that 'Behind Mr. Lloyd George's pledge there lie four years of minutely detailed preparation, and ... a severe and lengthy process of thought and study', but the Ministry of Transport thought differently. For example, the Dartford-Purfleet tunnel project had been cited by the Liberals as one that could be started within three months (Liberal Party 1929, 20); yet according to the Ministry:

> For this scheme there is only a preliminary report by consulting engineers with four sheets of drawings attached. The preparation of full engineering details necessary to enable tenders to be obtained would require about a year's work and study; and Parliamentary powers would have to be obtained. It is, therefore, difficult to see how work could at best be begun in less than 18 months.
> (*Memoranda*, 22–3; PRO 1929a)

To a greater or lesser degree this was a criticism that was equally applicable to all the other schemes proposed by the Liberals.

The rejection of the Liberal case on these grounds was undoubtedly politically expedient at the time; whether permissible, when viewed within a longer historical perspective, is, however, a different question. As is now more clearly appreciated, opposition parties, by being denied access to the facilities with which to draw up 'practical' programmes, labour at a disadvantage in such matters. Further, it is arguable that radical policy alternatives have as a result gone by default, neither receiving the attention demanded by free democratic deliberation nor by the recurrent difficulties of the British economy. Our interpretation of the 1929 policy debate is thus dependent in part upon the weight we ascribe to those factors relative to the undoubted political opportunism which underlay the Liberal programme.

To turn now to the Treasury memorandum, here also there was no opposition to public works as such, merely to the Liberal programme as constituted. Moreover, there was agreement that public works should be financed 'without resort to inflation' (*Memoranda*, 45; Liberal Party 1929, 62), by which they meant that the additional expenditure would be covered by bond sales to the non-banking sector and not by money creation. The difference between them lay in the fact that the Treasury believed that this borrowing would impinge on the supply of capital available to private industry, whereas the Liberals subscribed to the view that the borrowing would be covered by idle balances existing in a depression, a reduction in net overseas lending, and the savings to the budget consequent upon the higher level of employment generated by the fiscal stimulus.

On this difference in analysis, the Treasury's view is usually interpreted in Ricardian terms: that an increase in government expenditure had no effect on total employment because it would crowd out a comparable amount of private sector investment (for example, Winch 1972, 118). In fact, analyses of the 'Treasury view' solely in these terms have created a very misleading impression, for their approach to the question was rather more complex and derived from a concatenation of theoretical and practical considerations.

In pursuing these revisions to our understanding of the 'Treasury view', we need at this point to introduce Hopkins's (1930) evidence before the Macmillan Committee as a supplement to the 1929 Treasury memorandum. This is a crucial additional source: one well known, yet strangely neglected, or dismissed as of no great moment to our appreciation of the Treasury's position.

It has generally been argued that the Treasury's theoretical analysis ignored both the multiplier effects of, and social rate of return on, public investment (Youngson 1969, 296; Winch 1972, 120–1). Whilst the multiplier was not formally specified until 1931 (Kahn 1931), it was undoubtedly implicit in much of earlier economic literature; a similar judgement can also be made about the social rate of return.[4] Hopkins, in his evidence before the Macmillan Committee, showed an awareness of both concepts, but nevertheless discounted them as inapplicable, given the current facts of unemployment, and inoperative, when considering a programme of the magnitude and type proposed by the Liberals.

Hopkins's analysis took as its starting point the difficulties of the staple export industries, difficulties which had been exacerbated by the characteristics of the depression after 1929. From this standpoint, two objections were advanced against large-scale public works. First, even assuming that the schemes were feasible, they 'would concentrate employment in a marked degree upon individual trades which [were] neither unsheltered nor unprosperous ... and while increasing employment and profit making there would be little or nothing for the depressed basic trades'. Secondly, this concentration of employment would result in supply bottlenecks, generating cost pressures, which would then be transmitted throughout the economy. The final effect would be a worsening of the already diminished competitiveness of the export sector, and perhaps also increased import penetration: serious consequences given the then prevailing gold standard, and the precarious external balance (PRO 1930f, 6–7).

In turn, these objections followed from two central tenets of interwar Treasury economic thinking. First, the Treasury were antipathetic towards the notion, implicit in Keynes's and others' writings, of the homogeneity of demand impulses, a reflection of their essentially microeconomic or structural diagnosis of the unemployment problem and of the way in which they viewed income generation. The concept of 'industry', in the aggregate, was rejected as a mere abstraction, one that led to potentially destabilizing policy actions (PRO 1930b; d). Secondly, and not unconnected, was the belief in what might be termed the 'normal channels of trade', the policy implications of this being that public investment was a complement to that of the private sector, not a substitute for it. Here the textual evidence is far from conclusive, but it would appear that the Treasury held the position that public works on any substantial scale distorted the course of economic activity from its normal channels (determined by relative prices), made the ultimate transition to normal employment patterns more difficult, and forced periodic reflationary stimuli in order to permanently sustain the higher level of employment (PRO 1935a, para. 4). Such a position bore a strong resemblance to Hayek's writings at that time, and thus had a certain intellectual pedigree.[5]

Finally, we return to the Treasury's dismissal of the economists' contention that a public works programme gained additional justification from its positive social rate of return. The Treasury's reasoning should by now be clear: while they accepted the logic of this argument at the level of the individual project, they questioned its validity at the macro level, where a general reaction against the programmes might be expected, this leading to the establishment of forces which acted to neutralize at the national level any local benefits accruing from the schemes.

3 AN *IS-LM* MODEL OF THE 'TREASURY VIEW'

The foregoing broad discussion of the 'Treasury view' made clear that their conception of crowding-out had certain unique features, features which, it will be argued, bear a closer resemblance to the Keynesian rather than the monetarist view of crowding-out. These issues are now further explored using comparative static equilibrium analysis in an *IS-LM* model as a means of identifying the significant features of the standard Keynesian, monetarist and 'Treasury view' models.[6] Such an approach, of course, is not without its difficulties, in that the *IS-LM* apparatus has severe limitations as an analytical tool, it cannot capture all the significant features of the three models, and the standard forms of the Keynesian and particularly monetarist models are themselves the subject of debate.[7] Nevertheless, it is a valid analytical tool in view of both the limited purpose of the exercise here attempted and the need to counter what the author discerns to be an oral tradition about the 'Treasury view' which implicitly makes use of such an analysis.

We begin with the Keynesian model, two variants of which are represented in figure 8.1A-B. The former can be taken as an approximation to Keynes and Henderson (1929), the liquidity trap portrayed (that of a money demand function having infinite interest elasticity) being an important component of Keynes's later, *General Theory*, arguments for favouring fiscal initiatives. In this extreme model the fiscal stimulus generates increased income but is not subject to monetary feedbacks through higher interest rates. The second variant represents the more normal 'textbook' case where the economy is close to full employment

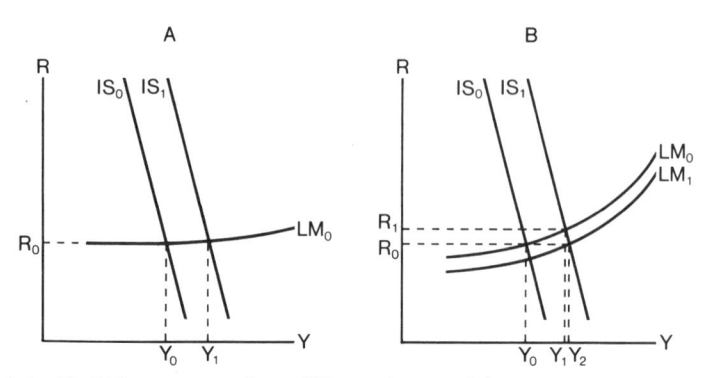

Figure 8.1 IS–LM representation of Keynesian models

and where the *LM* schedule is more steeply gradated. (There is evidence that the demand for money was never infinitely interest elastic between the wars – see, for example, Mills and Wood (1977), figure 1; the operation of a liquidity trap, therefore, being most unlikely.) In both variants fiscal policy is all-powerful but monetary policy not impotent. In figure 8.1A a shift from IS_0 to IS_1 (the public works programme) increases equilibrium income from Y_0 to Y_1 but leaves the interest rate unchanged at R_0; in figure 8.1B the shift in the *IS* schedule (to IS_1) increases equilibrium income as before (from Y_0 to Y_1) but raises interest rates (from R_0 to R_1), thus causing some crowding-out, albeit that the assumption is made in the Keynesian model that the fiscal policy multiplier exceeds unity. An accommodating monetary policy (the shift from LM_0 to LM_1) then restores the previous interest rate level (R_0) and permits a higher level of income (Y_2).

We turn next to monetarist models, possible configurations of which are represented in figure 8.2A–C. Model A can be viewed as an extreme case, one founded upon a crude quantity theory, where the *LM* schedule is vertical by virtue of the assumption that the demand for money is wholly insensitive to interest rates. In this model fiscal policy is impotent. It cannot alter the level of real income (only the composition of aggregate demand); its influence is upon the price level and interest rates. In addition, since nominal income can only be changed if the quantity of money changes, an exogenous change in consumption and investment behaviour (which shifts the IS schedule) will still not alter income. In the light of the judgement that the Treasury in the 1920s adhered to a classical economic framework (Hancock 1960, 310–11), this model could be taken as an accurate specification of the 1929 'Treasury view'.

Similarly model B, another extreme case, where the original equilibrium position is one of full employment ($Y_0 = Y_F$), might be taken as describing the 'Treasury view', that is if Keynes's (1929) criticism that the

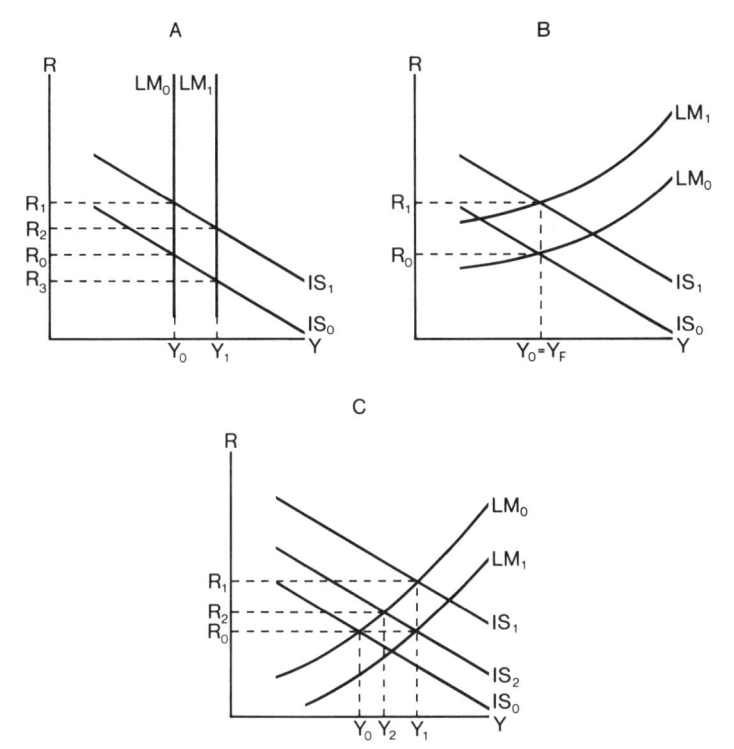

Figure 8.2 IS–LM representation of monetarist models

Treasury's position implicitly assumed full employment is judged to be valid. In this model, the shift in the *IS* schedule (to IS_1) generates excess demand in labour and product markets, thereby increasing prices, and resulting in a leftwards shift of the *LM* function (to LM_1) to restore monetary equilibrium with the lower stock of real balances, the consequent higher interest rates paring back consumption and investment and thus eliminating excess demand.

Model C, however, claims no historical antecedents, and instead represents a possible modern 'textbook' monetarist position. A similar configuration to figure 8.1B, except that the slopes of the *IS–LM* schedules reflect monetarist rather than Keynesian assumptions about both the interest elasticity of investment demand and the demand for money, in this model an expansionary fiscal policy results in crowding-out of two forms: the first, as established in figure 8.1B, where the demand for additional transaction balances consequent upon the shift to IS_1 raises the interest rate (to R_1); the second, a wealth effect, whereby the sale of bonds to finance the budget deficit raises interest rates, thus reducing the value of the outstanding stock of bonds held by the private sector, with, as a result, reduced consumption and investment (a shift from IS_1 to IS_2). A lower interest rate regime, and higher level of economic activity, are then attained by an accommodating monetary policy which shifts LM_0 to LM_1, restoring the interest rate to R_0 and yielding an income level Y_1.

A further set of arguments needs to be introduced before we can return to our discussion of the 'Treasury view'. The reaction against fiscal policy of the monetarist counter-revolution of Friedman and others was only the first intellectual challenge to the post-Keynesian neo-classical synthesis. More recently, a second challenge has arisen: that of the case for fiscal impotency as put by the new classical macroeconomics, associated with the works of Lucas, Sargent and Barro (for a survey, see Barro 1981).

Retrospectively, this first, monetarist challenge appears straightforward. To quote Friedman, 'I regard the description of our position as "money is all that matters for changes in *nominal* income and for *short-run* changes in real income" as an exaggeration but one that gives the right flavour of our conclusions' (cited in Tobin 1974, 79). The new classical macroeconomics 'is theoretically and politically a more sweeping departure, and in many respects it is an alternative to monetarism as well as to Keynesian macroeconomics'.

> Monetarism Mark I said that, as between fiscal and monetary policies, only money really matters; the new classical macroeconomics says that no macroeconomic policy systematically alters the real course of the economy. Monetarism Mark I favoured stable monetary growth above other monetary rules; the new doctrine implies that any predictable policy will have the same real consequences as any other. Monetarism Mark I endorsed floating exchange rates; the new position is that the exchange rate regime does not affect real outcomes. Monetarism Mark I acknowledged that shocks, other than those administered by government policy, could displace the economy for significant periods from full employment or from the 'natural rate of unemployment'. It agreed with the Keynesians that discretionary policies could work in principle but disagreed about their practical necessity and desirability. The new school denies disequilibrium and denies that policies can help or speed the natural processes of stabilization. (Tobin 1980, 21–2)

This second challenge to Keynesian macroeconomics, one which is a direct descendant of the interwar Austrian school of business cycle theory associated with Hayek (1933) and Haberler (1939), seeks to explain macroeconomic behaviour within a classical theoretical framework characterized by optimizing behaviour (rational expectations) and continuous market clearing. The issues raised by this revisionist school are both extensive and complex, the subject of much debate. Our discussion will be limited to those issues directly pertinent to the historical object of our analysis, not to the full debate.

Mention should first be made of the 'Ricardian equivalence theorem' (see Barro 1974), an offspring of rational expectations which has led to the revival of the old (Ricardian) argument that fiscal policy is impotent because of the equivalence of debt and taxes. More specifically, the theorem asserts that forward-looking life-cycle consumers anticipate higher taxes in the future to service current bond-financed government deficits, thereby increasing their savings by an amount equivalent to the new bonds. This robs deficit-financing of all macroeconomic effect. The *ex ante* crowding-out also makes irrelevant the more general crowding-out through interest rates, portfolio and real balance effects.

After extensive scrutiny, the argument that government bonds are not net wealth remains highly suspect, on both conceptual and econometric grounds (Tobin 1980, 31, 54–67; Feldstein 1982). Nevertheless, it is of interest to our historical discussion. Earlier it was shown that during the 1933 budget debate the Treasury publicly maintained the view that if the budget was deliberately unbalanced any possible expansionary effects might be vitiated by the expectation of a future higher tax burden. Without claiming too much, for the Treasury did not elaborate upon this argument, there is the possibility that the neutralizing mechanism was an increase in savings as consumers and businesses revised their expectations and adjusted their spending to the consequences for future taxation of government policy.

This, in turn, leads us to the broader new classical macroeconomics literature on the consequences of expectations about policy (see Lucas 1976). It is now accepted that the private sector response to a change in taxes or transfers will depend upon expectations of the duration of the income change, whether transitory or permanent. More fundamentally, when economic behaviour depends upon expectations of economic behaviour, the effects of policy in one period and economic structure cannot automatically be applied to another age or structure. Thus, even if Keynesian stabilization policies were successful in maintaining full employment until the late 1960s, no useful guide is offered to the possibilities for successfully applying such policies in interwar Britain – the earlier age being marked not just by a different economic structure but also by pre-Keynesian expectations of the behaviour of the private and public sectors.

In the early 1930s, when fiscal policy was founded upon the balanced budget rule, the appearance of a deficit during the depression led to expectations of higher taxation, this exacerbating depression through its effect upon private sector expenditures. Conversely, in the postwar period, during the phase when fiscal policy was the central instrument for securing full employment, tax increases were not expected in recessions, private sector expenditures thus supporting the policy stance. In a study of the postwar US economy, Baily (1978) has shown how the behaviour of the corporate sector was quite different in the mid-1960s, when it was expected that an active stabilization policy would secure full employment and high growth, from earlier periods, when other objectives prevailed; and that rational expectations of monetary and fiscal policies not only do not nullify the intended influence of these policies but actually reinforce their effect upon economic stability. On this reasoning, it is clear that, for example, the case of the US economy in the 1930s, where the 'New Deal' and deficit-finance failed to stimulate full recovery, had an important demonstration effect for business and policy-makers alike. Without a positive demonstration of fiscal policy's potency – in the context of a largely unregulated market economy, rather than in, say, Nazi Germany – it is difficult to conceive of the creation of expectations which would so mould private sector expenditure behaviour as to allow fiscal policy's effectiveness.

One further set of propositions of the new classical macroeconomics requires mention: that of the implications for policy of the belief in continuous market clearing by price. This is founded upon a resumption of the classical belief in the flexibility of prices and the ability to clear markets, especially the behaviour of wages and prices in preventing excess labour supply. According to this view the labour market is always cleared, the economy never deviating from full employment equilibrium. This requires that the trade cycle be explained, not in Keynesian terms, but as a consequence of inadequate information and exogenous random shocks. Since markets are always being cleared, no excess supply (or demand) can exist to be erased by aggregate demand policies. Thus, 'Policy can never make more than a transient difference to real outcomes, and anyway the transient difference is always a non-optimal distortion' (Tobin 1980, 41).

On such a view, therefore, a stabilization policy would have been neither possible nor desirable in interwar Britain. The Treasury, whose conduct of policy in the early 1920s suggested an implicit belief in wage/price flexibility and some sort of 'hidden hand', were still relatively optimistic as late as 1929 that wage/price rigidities could be overcome (*Memoranda*, 52–3), but by the later 1930s they had resigned themselves to the implications of real wage resistance for economic management. While a full new classical macroeconomic analysis has yet to be attempted for interwar Britain, we can anticipate future developments in this field.[8] For the present, Broadberry's (1983, 469) researches into the interwar labour market suggest that any 'relative price changes, signalling a transfer of resources [between sectors] . . . were . . . swamped by quantity signals in the form of reduced aggregate demand'.

Our specification of the 1929 'Treasury view' can now be conducted in two stages: first, and as before, through the *IS–LM* framework; secondly, by the explicit incorporation of a balance of payments sector.

THE 'TREASURY VIEW' AND PUBLIC WORKS   161

The first stage in the analysis is represented in figure 8.3A. Both the *IS* and *LM* schedules are drawn as interest responsive (elastic), this a legitimate assumption in light of the Treasury section of the *Memoranda* and the tenor of Hopkins's (1930) exposition before the Macmillan Committee. Thus the *IS* schedule reflects essentially monetarist assumptions about the interest responsiveness of investment demand, the *LM* schedule Keynesian assumptions about the interest elasticity of the demand for money, while the aggregate supply function reflects Keynesian assumptions about the short-term supply schedule in face of an expansion of aggregate demand.

The dynamics of figure 8.3A are as follows. The first stage, the shift from IS_0 to IS_1, describes the public works programme which, *ceteris paribus*, raises equilibrium income to Y_1 but also increases interest rates to R_1 and prices to P_1, the latter the consequence of increased demand in face of an upward sloping aggregate supply schedule (shown in the second part of figure 8.3A). This would be the final equilibrium position if the *ceteris paribus* condition was fulfilled (as in figure 8.1); that it was not lay at the heart of the 'Treasury view'. This condition would have been fulfilled, if the shift in aggregate demand had operated through the

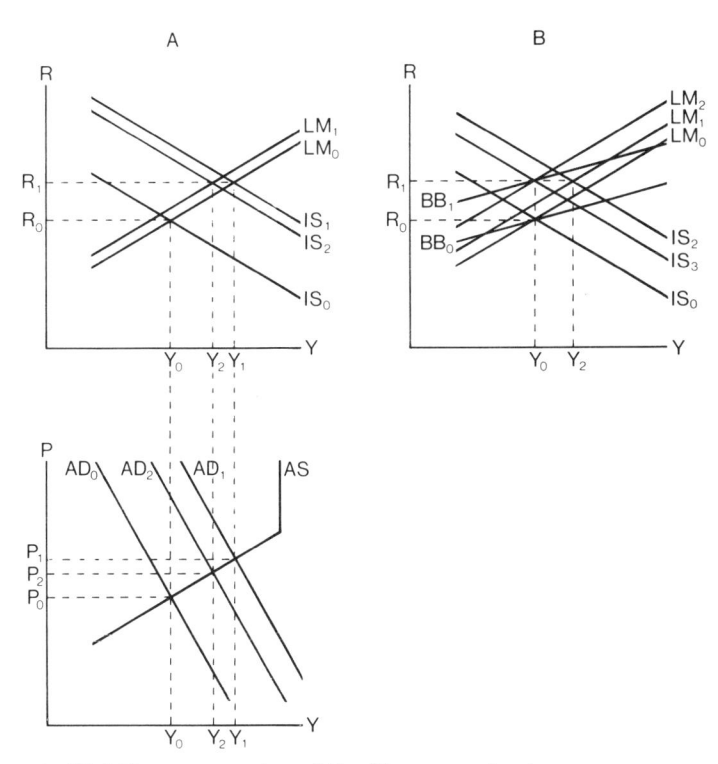

Figure 8.3 *IS–LM* representation of the 'Treasury view'

'normal' channels of trade (as noted earlier), or even through a rearmament programme. For example, as regards the latter, Hopkins was to note in 1937:

> In financial quarters throughout the world (where perhaps more than anywhere else the credit of a nation is made or marred) borrowing for a current purpose which merely provides for men in idleness is regarded as one of the worst forms of borrowing, but borrowing for armaments ... is regarded as unfortunate, no doubt, but still respectable.
> (PRO 1937b)

Thus the 'Treasury view' concerned the operation of additional forces, or in our analysis, the imposition of further sequences within the *IS–LM* model, which neutralized the initial expansive shift of the *IS* schedule; what were earlier termed disruptive intermediaries. These centred upon two Treasury judgements: that 'Keynes, with all his brilliance, appears frequently to misunderstand the psychology of the markets' (PRO 1938g); and that 'the atmosphere in which [public works] schemes may be undertaken will itself condition the immediate consequences which they produce' (Hopkins 1930, 20). These disruptive intermediaries assumed two forms.

First, account needs to be taken of a leftwards shift of the *IS* schedule, from IS_1 to IS_2, this a deflationary reaction to the announcement and introduction of the public works programme, a reaction composed of two distinct elements. The first relates to the adverse confidence effect upon the business community noted above, whereby entrepreneurs view the programme as creating a highly artificial situation, this resulting in a revision of their perception of future profitability and thus a leftwards shift in their investment demand schedule. The second, to the fact that the programme was concentrated upon a narrow range of industries (facing upward sloping marginal cost schedules) and that this would, in aggregate, generate shortages and price rises which would tend to cause some curtailment of private, and perhaps even public, sector investment.

Secondly, the deflationary consequences of the initial fiscal stimulus were compounded by a leftwards shift of the *LM* schedule to LM_1. With this shift the operative process is more difficult to discern, less susceptible to exact theoretical specification, not only because the 'Treasury view' was 'not ... capable of being put in the rigid form of a theoretical doctrine' (Hopkins 1930, 20), but also because it was founded upon a judgement:

> I should have thought that a scheme of this kind so far from setting up a cycle of prosperity would produce a great cry against bureaucracy ... and so far from it producing a general willingness to invest in these vast Government loans I should have thought that the loans would have to be put out at a very high price. (Hopkins 1930, 18)

This judgement is deemed impossible to substantiate, because the Liberal programme was never introduced; consequently Keynes and later writers have dismissed it, too easily in fact, for whilst the 'Treasury view' appealed to a counterfactual argumentum, in early 1931,

> The sensitive state of public feeling was shown by the fact that a rumour that the Government was about to float a large development loan caused an appreciable fall in the funds, and Snowden had hastily to announce that he had no idea of going in for a spectacular loan for this purpose. (Grigg 1948, 244)

To say that a similar, albeit more serious, reaction would have been unlikely in 1929 is both to view history unimaginatively and to deny the strong political and economic objections to the Liberal programme expressed by influential groups other than the Treasury.

From this Treasury judgement upon the state of confidence, it follows that the *LM* schedule shifts leftwards in response to a change in liquidity preference (a lessened preference for bonds) induced by the initial fiscal stimulus, the operative intermediary here being a fear of inflation. As with the shift in the *IS* schedule, this reaction was also composed of two distinct elements. The first relates to the adverse confidence effect of the financial community noted above, whereby bond-holders viewed disfavourably the government's departure from fiscal orthodoxy, doubted the logic of the Keynesian case, and judged that unbalanced budgets could not be indefinitely financed from bond sales to the non-banking sector without an eventual crisis and resulting inflation. The second, to an increased preference for equities relative to gilt-edged, this a response to the inflation expected to be generated (by real causes) as a result of the pursuance of the Liberal programme. A third element, that of a possible diversion of funds overseas, is left for consideration in the next part of our analysis.

The present stage of the analysis can be summarized thus: commencing at an equilibrium position Y_0 (in figure 8.3A) the application of a fiscal stimulus fails to effect a commensurate increase in income because it sets in chain a sequence of deflationary forces which act to offset, or even completely neutralize, the initial increment to demand. The multiplier thus lies within the range zero to less than unity (for nowhere in the Treasury papers is it suggested that it is negative); and in figure 8.3A it is represented as positive, for Y_2 the final equilibrium position exceeds Y_0. Its exact value, however, is uncertain and the position of Y_2 is perforce largely arbitrary; a more definite value only becomes possible as we now transform the model to incorporate explicitly a balance of payments sector.

In figure 8.3B the original specification of the 'Treasury view' is extended so as to incorporate an external sector, this because only through a transformed model can all the elements of the 'Treasury view' be captured and previous misspecifications be rectified. In figure 8.3A the working through of the fiscal stimulus not only raised incomes but also interest rates, thereby attracting an inflow of funds to London which, *ceteris paribus*, would move the balance of payments into surplus. As with the shift of the *IS* and *LM* schedules in face of a fiscal stimulus detailed earlier, the *ceteris paribus* condition about the balance of payments is similarly invalid; rather, three forces would make for a move into deficit.

1 The higher domestic price level (P_2 at income Y_2), given the fixed exchange rate, would act against exports but encourage imports, thereby worsening the deficit on merchandise trade account.
2 The British government's failure to adhere to the strict standards of budgetary orthodoxy expected of it by the international financial community might, the Treasury argued, lessen the attractiveness of London as a repository for overseas funds and even lead to a capital outflow, this despite the higher interest rates now prevailing.
3 Exports would be further affected at second remove, this by an indirect mechanism whereby higher interest rates would restrict the demand for loans by developing countries, these loans being considered an important eventual source of demand for British exports.

Having outlined the balance of payments implications of the public works programme we can now return to figure 8.3B which summarizes the theoretical, and practically based, principles which underlay the 'Treasury view'. Commencing with the initial equilibrium position Y_0R_0 (and with BB_0, the schedule which describes the balance of payments, representing both internal and external balance at this equilibrium position), the effect of the public works programme is to shift the *LM* schedule to the left (from LM_0 to LM_1) and the *IS* schedule to the right (from IS_0 to IS_2), and to result in the partial equilibrium position Y_2R_1. The external implications are now introduced: the public works programme results in a further leftwards shift of both the *LM* and *IS* schedules (to LM_2 and IS_3 respectively) which, in turn, shifts the balance of payments schedule leftwards to BB_1 because induced price changes alter the exchange rate. The final equilibrium position is thus shown as Y_0R_1, the same level of income as pertaining before the introduction of the public works programme, but now associated with higher interest rates and a changed composition of aggregate income, changed as between private and public sector activity and as between exports and domestically consumed output. Given the already weak export position, and the associated regional problem, the adverse consequences of a fiscal stimulus were thus potentially serious.

The final equilibrium position, here shown as Y_0R_1, cannot be established *a priori*: in our representation of the 'Treasury view' crowding-out (in all its various forms) is taken as complete in its effects, for this is what is suggested by a careful textual analysis of the available evidence. Nevertheless, *super* crowding-out (a negative multiplier, resulting in a final equilibrium position of less than Y_0) cannot be discounted given the centrality of confidence in the process outlined above. By virtue of the difficulties of counterfactual verification, this possibility cannot usefully be further investigated; further comment, however, is required, and made possible in light of our specification of the 'Treasury view', upon the role played by an accommodating monetary policy in the process of adjustment to the public works programme.

From figure 8.3B it follows that a monetary expansion (to offset any induced increase in liquidity preference) could, *ceteris paribus*, shift the *LM* schedule back to the original position, thereby both raising incomes and permitting lower interest rates. If our specification of the 'Treasury view' is valid, then there is also substance to the Treasury's insistence that only monetary policy could increase aggregate demand, an insistence given added weight by compelling political forces also making for a preference for monetary instruments. In light of this, it is possible that Keynes and Henderson (1929), in urging an accommodating monetary policy as a supplement to the public works programme, anticipated or implicitly acknowledged that adverse confidence effects might operate and could only be overcome by monetary action.

4 THE 'TREASURY VIEW' 1931–9

Before discussing the development of Treasury thinking after 1931 we should briefly note the 1929–31 (minority) Labour Government's experience of actually conducting a large-scale public works programme. This experience confirmed the 'Treasury view', and influenced the public works debate for the rest of the 1930s.

Labour's public works programme differed substantially from that proposed by the Liberals; it was financed from current revenue, undertaken by local authorities (with little central planning), and composed of remunerative projects. Its magnitude was thus limited from the outset. These constraints aside, the policy was still deemed to have been unsuccessful (PRO 1932a; 1933b; k): its employment effects were judged to have been small in relation to expenditure, it had taken a long time to come into operation, and the stock of available remunerative projects was quickly exhausted. By June 1930, a full year after taking office, schemes approved only totalled £110.1 million, while even a year later, at their peak, schemes actually in operation totalled but £107.7 million (on an annual basis). These gave primary direct employment to 61,165 persons; assuming an equal amount of primary direct to indirect employment and an employment multiplier of 1.5 (this most probably an over-estimate – see p. 177), employment equivalent to only 10.9 per cent of the total numbers unemployed had been generated after two years sustained effort (Middleton 1983, 361 and figure 1).

These results were criticized by Lloyd George, Mosley and others as totally inadequate, a reflection of the government's conservatism, obstructionism and lack of real commitment to the policy. Within Whitehall, however, where it was believed with some justification that the policy had been pursued to the fullest extent possible, the conclusion drawn was that the programme's poor results vindicated Whitehall's earlier objections to large-scale public works.

As with the refusal to promote recovery by deficit-finance, Britain almost alone amongst the major Western countries decided against an active public works programme as part of its domestic recovery policy after 1931.[9] The previous public works experiment terminated with the emergency budget measures of September 1931, and thereafter was not repeated, this despite both widespread opposition to the apparent embargo on public works and the regained freedom afforded by the quietus of previous policy constraints (such as the gold standard).

The tenacity with which ministers and officials continued to oppose public works throughout the 1930s has long been attributed to the pervasiveness and diuturnity of the 'Treasury view', and as evidence of the fact that 'the ideas of Keynes had almost no effect on Government policy in this country before 1939' (Youngson 1969, 293). Recently, however, this view of Whitehall's continued theoretical orthodoxy has been challenged, and substantially modified, first by Howson (1975), and later by Howson and Winch (1977). Such a revision can be taken too far; while the evidence does not support Hutchison's (1978, 155) sweeping statement 'that both the Treasury and the Bank were largely converted to "Keynesian policies" . . . *at least a year before the publication of The General Theory*', there is sufficient evidence for the more limited conclusion, that, in the realm of monetary policy, Treasury economic thinking was increasingly influenced by Keynes's and other economists' policy advice.

As regards fiscal policy, and public works in particular, Howson and Winch (1977, 134–48) have established that by the later 1930s the Treasury were prepared to countenance public works as a stabilization instrument in any possible future recession. By contrast, Peden's (1980, 6) researches led him to conclude that prior to the Second World War 'the Treasury remained sceptical about the use of public works as a cure for unemployment'. As will now be shown, there is no necessary contradiction between these two views: the case rests on the motives for, and permanence of, the change in Treasury policy.

The National Government's unemployment policy came under serious and concerted attack in 1933 and 1935, as represented by the reflationary programmes proposed by Keynes in *The Means to Prosperity* and Lloyd George in his 'New Deal'. On both occasions, the government's response

THE 'TREASURY VIEW' AND PUBLIC WORKS 167

was to allow a limited expansion of public works expenditures, whilst rejecting the general case for large-scale loan-financed expenditures. This relaxation of Treasury opposition was thus more apparent than real: it was largely a response to certain political pressures – the need to mollify the more progressive government backbenchers, pacify the Opposition, and be seen to be taking account of the change in public opinion since the 1931 crisis measures – and an acknowledgement of the opportunities afforded by gradually improving economic conditions. There was no discernible lessening of the theoretical objections to public works. On the contrary, the Treasury's internal discussions of Keynes's *The Means to Prosperity* reveal the genesis of a new theoretical objection, one concerning the monetary prerequisites for effecting a stimulus to demand by fiscal means.

There is strong evidence to suggest that the Treasury had anticipated the debate that was to occur between Keynes and Robertson on the question of the validity of the comparative equilibrium approach of the *General Theory*. Throughout the *General Theory*, the explanation of an increase in aggregate demand generated by loan-financed expenditure was couched solely in terms of current savings; the other two potential sources of finance – idle balances and an increased money stock – were excluded from consideration. As Trevithick (1978) says, this 'jeopardised . . . the internal consistency of the *General Theory*' for it introduced 'an unfortunate circularity of reasoning in the analysis': if current savings are the sole source of finance then 'an increase in investment requires an increase in savings before it can become effective, but the increase in savings will only be forthcoming as a *result* of an increase in income.' Thus 'an additional, though temporary, source of finance' was required 'to permit the process of expansion to get under way'. The Treasury had long maintained such an argument, that an increase in the money stock was required. For example, when meeting Chamberlain in March 1933 to discuss his *Means to Prosperity* proposals, Keynes was asked the following question (drafted by Phillips):

> If you contemplate a really large expenditure to be raised at once (say £m50 or £m100 in the next few months), are idle balances sufficient and will they be enticed into use by Government bonds . . . except at a price which will set back interest rates a great deal? (It is no good saying that the [public] works will produce the savings for investment, for ex hypothesis the borrowing precedes the works.) (PRO 1933e, para. 11)

This point was finally admitted by Keynes after a long and interesting debate with Robertson, in which Keynes changed the emphasis of his argument away from the 'simple "investment determines savings" formula towards a more complex position which acknowledges the interaction between money, savings and investment in a process of disequilibrium adjustment'. Thus Keynes eventually held that crowding-out, or as he put it 'congestion in the capital market', would result unless the policy calculated to permanently raise activity actually came in two stages:

> Increased investment will always be accompanied by increased savings, but it can never be preceded by it. Dishoarding and credit expansion provides not an *alternative* to increased saving, but a necessary preparation for it. It is the parent, not the twin, of increased saving.
> (Keynes 1973, 284–5, cited in Trevithick 1978)

This theoretical position continued to guide Treasury thinking until at least the end of the 1930s (see, for example, PRO 1935e; 1939d). In addition, underlying the Treasury's extreme reluctance, first, to allow the resumption of work on the projects temporarily abandoned in late 1931, and then to support a radical change in policy involving the use of public works as a recovery device, was the fear that such a course of action would conflict with the government's monetary policy and consequently jeopardize recovery. Thus the question of confidence continued as a major obstacle for those seeking to advance the theoretical case for public works, an obstacle which was largely insurmountable, given its imperfectly specified determinants, and the visible benefits accruing from cheap money.

Later however, in 1937, a change in Treasury opinion has been identified, a change which Howson and Winch attribute to the growing influence of Keynesian policy prescriptions. This concerned the Treasury's approval (in theory) of a counter-cyclical public works programme to combat the recession that was anticipated as following, first, the run down of house-building, and later, the end of the rearmament programme.

On the basis of *a priori* logic a change in official attitudes towards public works at this time would appear perfectly plausible, given that economists had become more united in their support for, and more convincing in their theoretical justifications of, public works, while the favourable effects of rearmament expenditures on employment could be taken as a demonstration of the legitimacy of the general case for deficit-financing. The empirical basis of these influences has been well documented (Winch 1972, ch. 9), but their *actual* influence on the course of events has by no means been proven, for the question at issue is not so much that the Treasury came to support what appears to be a Keynesian policy measure (a policy in fact never pursued because of the war), but whether in actuality this was a change of any particular long-term significance, and whether the operative forces at this time were rather less theoretical developments and rather more the interaction of changing political and economic circumstances occasioned by rearmament.

In pursuing these arguments, our starting point is with the form of the public works programme approved by the Treasury and Cabinet. After investigation by an interdepartmental committee, it was concluded 'that the contribution which the Government [might] make towards stabilising employment by a skilful timing of the capital expenditure for which it is responsible is not unimportant; though on the other hand it is not on so considerable a scale as to solve the problem', and that with 'normal' public investment at £250 million per annum discretionary adjustments of −£20 million and +£30 million might be made in years of 'abundant employment' and 'depression' respectively (PRO 1938a). The programme finally approved in January 1938, some four months after the onset of recession, was thus small in relation to any likely cyclical disturbance: there were to be no substantial additions to the volume of planned public investment, merely an alteration in its medium-term time profile; it was to be financed by local authorities as previously, not by a large central government loan; and the commitment remained to balance budgets once the rearmament programme was completed.

The only policy innovation of any substance was the May 1938 circular to local authorities which requested that they compile five-year forward investment plans. This has been seen as a 'great advance', a first step in the lessening of administrative constraints (Bretherton et al. 1941, 198–9). Yet, at the time, commentators were rather less sanguine, believing that it was indicative not so much of a commitment to counter-cyclical public works as to an attempt to expedite the rearmament programme by controlling local authority investment on the basis of the information acquired as a result of the circular (The Economist, 14 May 1938, 347).

By mid-1937 sustained pressure for contra-recession measures was being generated both by the economists and by a more broadly based, and ultimately more significant, body of political opinion. A future recession was widely forecast, and the view that it could at least be partially mitigated by government action had gained wide currency. This wider opinion, of course, was in part formed by the contemporaneous (theoretical) debates amongst economists. It was also, however, deeply influenced by empirical considerations, namely the recognition that the measures of 1929–31 had been fatally flawed by overhasty planning (forced by the necessity for immediate action) and easily overwhelmed by the strength of autonomous deflationary forces, whereas if such measures were planned in advance their future effectiveness would be improved accordingly.

These various pressures were most clearly and effectively expressed in House of Commons debates from the autumn of 1937 onwards, debates which became more acrimonious as recession became apparent rather earlier than originally feared, as government failed to respond with a satisfactory policy statement on public works, and instead gave the appearance of 'relying upon the acceleration of the defence programme to fill the growing gaps in private enterprise' while giving no real consideration to the period after the ending of the programme (*The Economist*, 26 March 1938, 677). Nevertheless, as we have seen, government was not inactive. It was, however, cautious: the Treasury were anxious that any statement about public works should lay stress upon

> the need to avoid adding to the already excessive demands upon labour in the building & allied trades & not upon the need to have something in store for the 'slump'. Experience shows how easily business sentiment is influenced & if anything is said that leads to the feeling that the Gov[ernment] agree with those economists who see an imminent slump, many people may shift their plans accordingly and bring about the very thing we all want to avoid. (PRO 1937d)

Once the onset of recession had been recognized, the government's tactics were modified: pronouncements were now made that this was but a temporary setback (*Hansard* 1938), and, implicitly, reliance was placed upon rearmament expenditures to stabilize activity 1938–9. Had war not then intervened, contra-recession measures would almost certainly have been applied when necessary after 1941. The decision to finance rearmament partly by borrowing had created a precedent with serious political repercussions: 'If you can do that for armaments you are going to have great difficulty in persuading the working men of the country that it is a wrong policy to borrow for real assets in public works' (*Hansard* 1937, col. 202). The prospect of a general election in late 1939 or 1940 gave added leverage to those pressing for the forward planning of contra-recession measures.

Treasury documents for 1938–9 show, however, that any such public works effort would have been of limited magnitude, that the individual projects would have had to be 'productive', and that the Treasury were far from accepting the argument that the example of rearmament expenditures served to vindicate the general case for large-scale public works. Whilst the favourable employment effects of rearmament were not in dispute *per se*, it was contended that the higher level of employment could not be permanently maintained without further reflationary stimuli. In addition, fears were also being expressed in various quarters that the rearmament programme, by artificially stimulating the staple industries once more, was retarding structural change and exacerbating the long-term difficulties of the depressed areas (see, for example, PRO 1939e; g; Dennison 1939, 159).

By the eve of the Second World War, at least on the issue of public works, there were still substantial differences between the Treasury and Keynesian views: the meeting of minds did not come until after the onset of war. But even then, there remained residual doubts about public works, doubts which stemmed from the interwar experience of this policy instrument (PRO 1942a; b). Moreover, the recent research of

Booth (1983) and Peden (1983a) strongly suggests that the Treasury's conversion to Keynesian peacetime demand management was protracted, not achieved early on in the war as was previously thought.

The Howson and Winch thesis has thus been found wanting, the traditional interpretation of the limited influence of the 'new' economics upon policy before the Second World War reaffirmed. This conclusion is given added force by the absence both of pressures from organized business for an active management of demand – the Treasury thus being under no compulsion to deviate from orthodoxy – and of official national income statistics until 1940–1 to assist such management. As regards the latter, further research is needed into why Britain did not participate at an official level in what Patinkin (1976) has termed the 'statistical revolution' in national accounting procedures, a revolution of comparable importance to the theoretical Keynesian revolution. At this stage, two reasons suggest themselves, neither of which lend credence to the Howson and Winch thesis. First, that until 1937 or thereabouts the government believed that its fiscal operations had little or no effect on the level of demand (because budgets were balanced) and thus there was no need for data on national income and its components. Secondly, that national income accounting procedures are based upon an aggregative approach to economic management, an approach not accepted until changed conditions forced it upon the Treasury during the Second World War.

5 CONCLUSIONS

With our specification of the 'Treasury view' now complete, we can return to the questions posed earlier in this chapter, namely those concerning the search for possible theoretical–policy antecedents to the current monetarist position, and to our statement that the Treasury's thinking actually bore a closer resemblance to the Keynesian rather than the monetarist view of crowding-out.

We have seen that the Treasury, far from holding to a simple classical economic position, did not implicitly assume full employment, and therefore cannot be criticized on these grounds. Their position was different both from that of Keynes, and from that of the new monetarists who have looked not to psychological crowding-out as the mechanism that neutralizes fiscal operations but to crowding-out due to the interest inelasticity of the demand for money function, to rational expectations, to wealth effects and to the natural rate of unemployment hypothesis.

Whilst the 'Treasury view' offers little of substance to the modern monetarist position, and certainly does not constitute a legitimate theoretical–policy antecedent, there are connections of importance with the Keynesian position, or more correctly with Keynes of the *General Theory*, for here it is necessary to invoke Leijonhufvud's (1968) distinction between Keynes and the Keynesians.

These connections relate to the issue of confidence, and its supposed neutralizing effects upon a public works programme, where it is arguable that, in contrast to the impression given by the historical record, there was in fact a large measure of common ground between the Treasury and Keynes. This common ground, of course, never found expression, this for two reasons. First, Keynes's independent position as an economic critic with no political responsibilities inevitably led him to place less emphasis upon the confidence issue than did the Treasury, who had to consider wider issues and whose natural caution made them anxious to avoid any possibility of financial collapse. Secondly, Keynes's temperament, polemical style and attempts to reach and influence a wide audience too often led him in his policy advice to discount the confidence issue, not because he viewed it as unimportant, but because he felt compelled to generate an optimistic aura to his policies. This optimism was contrived – perhaps necessarily so in the circumstances – because, when a financial crisis threatened in 1931, Keynes gave advice on the confidence issue which accorded with that of the Treasury (PRO 1931d), and because in the *General Theory* he showed both a perceptive understanding of the determinants of confidence and how, if there be an 'upsetting [of] the delicate balance of spontaneous optimism' induced – for whatever reason and however irrationally – by a public works programme, liquidity preference and the marginal efficiency of capital schedule could both be adversely affected, thus neutralizing the expansionary effects of the programme (Keynes 1936, 120, 162).

Keynes saw the extirpation of this irrationality as one of his principal tasks; the Treasury did not. This raises the interesting question, for which there is no answer, of the direction of association between the 'Treasury view' and the confidence issue: the Treasury appealed to this issue as a critical foundation of its position, yet by virtue of that appeal they strengthened the very conditions – by reinforcing in the minds of entrepreneurs and financiers the dangers of 'unsound finance' – which both supported their position and made more difficult the possibilities for a successfully expansive fiscal policy. An impasse was thus reached, one only terminated with the changed conditions wrought by the Second World War.

CHAPTER NINE

CONCLUSIONS

Before the First World War, when the public sector's direct claim upon resources was small, governments could ignore with impunity the macroeconomic impact of their fiscal operations. The enlargement of the public sector after 1914 quickly forced the authorities to consider the macroeconomic consequences of their fiscal actions. The decision to actively manage demand, however, was neither an immediate nor inevitable consequence of this. While the war-induced changes in the technical interaction of the budget and the real economy were an essential precondition for such a decision, it was political developments that determined the pace and form of progress towards the managed economy.

It has been shown that by 1939 fiscal and other instruments were being used to actively manage aggregate demand, but that this was not evidence of official acceptance of Keynesian principles of demand management. While 'increased public expenditure, albeit not the kind advocated by the economists, did indeed combat the slump' of 1937–8 (Howson 1975, 139), government was still far from accepting as one of its 'primary aims and responsibilities the maintenance of a high and stable level of employment' (HMSO 1944, 3). Thus we need to acknowledge that rearmament engendered rather special circumstances in the later 1930s, ones in which a retrospective assessment may lead us to infer erroneously that the effects of a policy were actually intended at the time of its inception. Deficit-finance after 1937 may well have created a precedent for later peacetime economic management, but that was not the authorities' intention.

The form of economic management prevailing by 1939 can be specified using the following standard formulation of the principal objectives of postwar macroeconomic policy:

1 Full employment.
2 Balance of payments equilibrium.
3 Reasonable stability of prices.
4 A satisfactory rate of economic growth.

Although axiomatic that any commitment to 'full' employment still lay in the future, there had none the less occurred important changes in official and ministerial thinking about unemployment since the early 1920s. For example, the belief in the market's efficacy, constantly alluded to in the 1920s, had by the mid-1930s definitely been superseded by a more pessimistic philosophy which ascribed a much enlarged role to government and recognized the case for stabilization.

Such progress is vividly illustrated by a comparison between the recessions of 1920–1 and 1937–8, the former being exacerbated by government fiscal and monetary policies, the latter eventually overcome by fiscal policy, albeit under the guise of rearmament. In the intervening period the authorities had become much more self-confident about their ability to influence the economy. This was essential if they were ever successfully to assume a full demand management responsibility. Similarly, they had to overcome their previous inhibition, akin to a self-denying ordinance, about bearing the responsibility for generating public expectations of the government's prowess at economic management. In time, political competition would no doubt naturally have produced this result, the political parties eventually coming to appreciate the substantial rewards available in return for successful economic management. Finally, the political preference for monetary rather than fiscal instruments had also to be overcome. This was to prove a more intractable problem.

The management of the external account, in one form or another, can be regarded as one of the oldest economic functions of government. It was certainly to be an important responsibility in the 1930s, for, as was shown in chapter 2, the external balance was precarious throughout the period. It is arguable that after 1931, with the gold standard abandoned and no longer exercising its reactionary influence, the authorities' management of the external account was more ambitious, flexible and successful than their domestic economic management.[1] Thus the Exchange Equalization Account, established in 1932 to regulate sterling's managed float, represented a considerable policy innovation, as did the periodic attempts to undervalue sterling in order to promote British exports.

The tariff was far less of an innovation, while in any case its effectiveness is much more debatable. There was a definite spirit of economic nationalism pervading the thoughts and actions of British policy-makers, one which although tempered by imperial reality was nevertheless very different from attitudes prevailing in the 1920s. Moreover, if we interpret Keynesian economic management as requiring that the needs of the domestic economy be acknowledged as paramount, then the 1930s witnessed two important developments. First, the increased independence of the British economy from the vagaries of the world economy was mirrored by a monetary policy which now directly served the needs of the domestic economy, not the external account as under the gold standard regime. Secondly, there was a strengthening of the controls over foreign investment, a course of action long sought by Keynes.

As regards the price stability objective, it is commonplace to argue that the case for full employment put by Keynes and his so-called disciples in the 1930s and 1940s ignored the danger of there later developing a serious unemployment–inflation trade-off. Misfounded as this accusation is, for Keynes was acutely aware of such a possibility (Harris 1948, 24–5), it is interesting that such has been the dismissal of the 'Treasury view' that no serious thought has been given to the possibility that this view actually foresaw, and wanted to avoid, such a trade-off. Ours is not the first generation to be obsessed with the fear of inflation. Reference has already been made to the influence of the continental hyperinflations on British policy-makers; mention should also be made of an additional searing experience, that of the inflationary boom and attendant labour unrest of 1919–20. With this episode representing the sole experience of full employment between the wars, policy-makers were understandably apprehensive about the political and inflationary consequences of any return to fuller employment.[2] Real wage resistance was pronounced between the wars, this despite the crushing of the general strike and the seemingly permanent excess supply of labour. Moreover, the behaviour of organized labour during the boom of 1936–7, a brief period during which demands for large wage increases and threats of industrial action suddenly re-emerged to dominate the industrial scene (*The Economist*, 3 April 1937, 1–2), can have done nothing to lessen these anxieties in the period immediately before the Second World War.

While there was no specific commitment to the achievement of a satisfactory rate of economic growth, government policy between the wars was directed towards promoting economic welfare in the broad sense. Their interpretation of this obligation had two important consequences for unemployment policy. First, however serious the unemployment problem, no remedial action should be taken which might entail disbenefits for those remaining in employment, always the majority of the labour force. There was thus an embargo on policies which might impair future growth prospects or current income. It was within such a spirit that public works policies were rejected, their possible disbenefits being particularly marked relative to unemployment benefit payments which could be easily presented as quite the most economical policy response to mass unemployment. Secondly, the existence of at least some measure of responsibility for promoting economic welfare, together with the undoubted political benefits from almost any attempt to combat unemployment, produced some developments of lasting worth. For example, a recognizably modern regional policy had evolved by 1939; this more by accident than by design, being the result of nothing more than a process of accretion.

While economic management in Britain had not yet assumed the form sought by Keynes and other advocates of deficit-finance, it had nevertheless changed radically between the First World War and the eve of the Second. The origins of demand management clearly lie in the later 1930s, though there was still no acceptance of the peacetime case for deficit-finance. This continued resistance can be discussed further at two levels. First, proximate causes, those that relate specifically to the interwar period and the then fiscal policy debate. Secondly, rather longer-term influences – recurrent themes in British economic policy – which make the interwar fiscal policy debate more comprehensible by placing it in a longer historical perspective. However, before embarking upon this discussion, let us return to a question first posed in chapter 1, that of the likely effectiveness of a Keynesian fiscal stimulus.

*   *   *

The verity of one of our initial propositions, that the history of the interwar fiscal policy debate has hitherto been largely a Keynesian history, should by now be clear. One consequence was that before Thomas (1975), no attention had been directed towards modelling the macroeconomic effects of any of the public works programmes proposed between the wars, their effectiveness merely being assumed. Thomas modelled a number of possible variants of the programmes proposed by Lloyd George and Keynes and Henderson in 1929. The results reported in table 9.1 are for a five-year programme of £100 million annual expenditure, a programme never actually proposed but none the less of interest as it would have stretched across the whole depression period, the time when a fillip to demand would have been of greatest assistance.

If Thomas's econometric model be accepted, then the results presented in table 9.1 do much to question the Keynesian case for public works between the wars. Clearly, the programme's disappointing results appear magnified by the interposition of the world depression. Nevertheless, it is also clear how preposterous was Lloyd George's claim that unemployment could be reduced to normal proportions within a year, that is even had it been possible to spend £100 million in the first year, itself a very debatable assumption.

With unemployment averaging 1.503 million amongst the total labour

Table 9.1 Effects of a 'Keynesian type' public works programme

	Total unemployment ('000)	Reduction in unemployment from the programme ('000)	Ratio (1)/(2)	Change in GNP from the £100m. increase in government expenditure (£m.)	Ratio of change in income to GNP
	(1)	(2)	(3)	(4)	(5)
1929	1,503	268	0.178	97.2	0.022
1930	2,379	300	0.126	108.3	0.025
1931	3,252	329	0.101	119.0	0.029
1932	3,400	346	0.102	125.0	0.030
1933	3,087	359	0.116	129.7	0.031

Sources: Derived from Thomas (1975, table 3; 1981, table 14.4).

force in 1929 (as against 1.250 million for the insured labour force), and taking Lloyd George's 'normal' unemployment as equivalent to Galenson and Zellner's (1957, table 2) estimated prewar unemployment rate of 4.7 per cent, a job deficiency of approximately 515,000 can be calculated. Lloyd George had claimed that unemployment would be reduced by 586,000 in the first year of the programme (table 8.1, p. 147). Yet, table 9.1 shows a predicted reduction of only 268,000 (though admittedly for a slightly different programme), a shortfall of over a quarter of a million jobs still remaining. Moreover, the Lloyd George estimate made no allowance for multiplier effects, merely for supply-side secondary direct employment from those industries supplying raw materials to the programmes.

The relative impotency of fiscal policy follows inevitably from the low value estimated for the government expenditure multiplier: 0.98 and 1.44 for the impact and long-run multipliers respectively. These are far less than contemporary estimates, which tended towards the range 1.5–3.0,[3] this because of the permanent income consumption function and lagged response of investment to profits used in Thomas's model. Contemporaries, for example, C. G. Clark (1938, 439–40), assumed that increments of wage income were spent on consumption within three months – this increasing the multiplier's value and the speed of its operation – rather than there being a longer adjustment period. Although the only modern econometric model available for interwar Britain, there has yet to be criticism of the specification or estimation of the consumption and investment functions by those researching within this field; we can therefore use Thomas's estimates with some confidence.

One further point about the multiplier's value merits comment. There is a certain irony about its low value, for one of the justifications for public works articulated by Keynes and others between the wars, was their partially self-financing character (in the form of reduced unemployment benefit outlays and increased taxation consequent upon greater employment); yet, of course, it was the very magnitude of these leakages – together with that into imports – which lessened the effectiveness of fiscal policy (T. Thomas 1975)!

It appears then that our answer to Keynes's and Henderson's question, 'Can Lloyd George do it?', must be firmly in the negative. If so, the further question arises, 'Could a larger public works programme have secured a return to a politically acceptable, and economically sustainable, high employment level?' First, what size of programme might have been required?[4]

With total unemployment reaching a peak of 3.4 million in 1932, Glynn and Howells (1980) investigated the government expenditure required to generate 2.8 million man-years of employment. With no pretence of providing a definitive result, merely an illustrative calculation, they employed a generous figure for the short-run multiplier (1.26), and a probable low figure for the marginal productivity of labour (£241.65), to obtain an estimate of £537 million as the *minimum* cost of providing such employment. If, however, Thomas's lower impact multiplier is used, and (say) a 5 per cent higher figure for the marginal productivity of labour, the sum required would have been a massive £725 million. These figures represent a demand injection of 12.6–17.0 per cent of 1932 GDP, 56.3–76.0 per cent of 1932/3 central government expenditure. As Glynn and Howells (1980, 42) note,

> Even before one asks where the funds to meet the [budget] deficit might have come from, the required amount can already be seen to be in the realms of political and economic fantasy. . . . In 1931 the prospect of a much smaller budget deficit had given rise to a major financial and political crisis.

We can return to these obstacles shortly. First, however, we should investigate the balance of payments implications of a substantial fiscal stimulus. We noted in chapter 2 the precarious external balance in the 1930s. Taking T. Thomas's (1981, 338, 342) estimated marginal propensity to import of 0.208, an increase in GNP of as much as £500 million would have resulted in additional imports of £104 million. It is difficult to conceive of this being accommodated, even with the freedom of the floating exchange rate after 1931, when the average balance on current account was already a £11.4 million deficit over 1929–37. If, in addition to this income effect, there was also a price effect – the massive increase in spending being manifest in higher prices as well as greater output – there would have been a loss of competitiveness and further adverse consequences for the trade balance. The higher level of employment would also very likely have resulted in some diversion to the home market of output previously destined for overseas. Moreover, it is not unduly pessimistic to predict that such a large programme would have created an atmosphere in which the combination of massive budget deficits and such adverse trade flows not only caused a capital outflow, but a capital flight of gigantic proportions. Therefore, as Arndt (1944, 134) noted, a substantial fiscal stimulus would have required for its success 'the transformation of the British economy into a largely State-controlled, if not planned, economic system'. Such dirigism was possible in Nazi Germany, the tightly controlled markets and insulated economy being a necessary accompaniment to deficit-financing (Overy 1982). For Britain, however, such developments were inconceivable.

In light of our earlier discussions of the confidence issue, we need say no more about the likely consequences of the pursuit of a large-scale public works programme for London's international financial standing and for private spending propensities, in particular domestic investment. Clearly, the programme would have been incompatible with the cheap money policy. Though the precise monetary implications are uncertain, the authorities experienced some difficulty in selling gilt-edged stock in the 1930s as part of their routine funding operations (Howson 1975, 95–107, 133–5); nor were their attempts to raise new funds overwhelmingly successful, as instanced by the issue of the first defence loan in 1937 which was 'a flop of the first magnitude' (*The Banker*, May 1939, 176, cited in Lees 1955, 69).

Reservations also need to be expressed about the scale of public works necessary to secure permanently high employment. Between 1929–38, annual public and semi-public fixed capital formation averaged £185.4 million (at 1930 prices), that of the private sector £463.8 million (calculated from Feinstein 1965, table 3.34). In such circumstances, even an annual public works programme as 'small' as £100 million appears large. What significance a £500 million programme, especially if such massive expenditures had to be repeated annually because of the failure of the original programme to have favourable pump-priming effects? It may be conjectured that the need to plan expenditure programmes of such magnitude would have advanced the nationalization debate (Barry 1965, chs 8–14), for the most probable strategy in the circumstances would have been the socialization of investment through (say) the reconstruction of the depressed staple industries. There would have resulted a transformation of the economy's operation, and a changing balance of political power, one of great significance for the Treasury.

On the eve of the Second World War the Treasury were still far from accepting Keynes's (1936, 128) contention that ' "wasteful" loan expenditure may nevertheless enrich the community on balance'; nor did they exhibit any inclination to modify their existing conduct of expenditure control in order to permit a more substantial unemployment policy. We noted in chapter 3 that the execution of a large-scale public works programme would have required a physical planning agency. The Treasury opposed such a course, for the establishment of an agency such as a National Investment Board would have created an alternative source of economic advice for ministers, thereby weakening Treasury control and its pre-eminent position. Thus, in part, opposition to large-scale public works was an administrative manoeuvre born out of the Treasury's acutely-developed sense of self-preservation.

Without a willingness to allow major economic and political changes, the obstacles to large-scale public works appear insuperable. This realism was eventually to have its effect upon Keynes: initially in the sense that *The Means to Prosperity* proposed a much smaller programme than that of *We Can Conquer Unemployment*; later, during the Second World War, when he had arrived at the view 'that if post-war unemployment should threaten, it would be better to take early, pre-emptive action, as this would minimize budgetary disturbance' (Booth 1984, 264).

*   *   *

A further consequence of the dominance of the Keynesian historiography of this period is that for too long the theoretical differences between the debate's participants have been given undue attention. As Skidelsky (1975b, 99) rightly notes, 'Because Keynes himself attacked the Treasury view on theoretical grounds, historians have assumed all too readily that the issues involved were issues of theory rather than of political culture.'

Such has been the misdirected focus of research in this area that very likely the general perception of this debate is one that is based upon little knowledge of the participants themselves. While it may be comforting to follow Keynes (1936, 383), to subscribe to the view that 'the ideas of economists and political philosophers, both when they are right and when they are wrong, are more powerful than is commonly understood', less rarefied forces must also be admitted to any explanation of historical change. Put crudely, while Lloyd George and Keynes were undoubtedly imaginative architects of alternative economic strategies, were they necessarily the best available sales representatives?

Lloyd George was disliked and mistrusted, especially by the two key politicians of the age – Baldwin and Neville Chamberlain (A. J. P. Taylor 1965, 269). As Blake (1976, 216) says:

> It was the paradox of the period that the public mood welcomed humdrum routine commonsense at precisely the moment when the problems of the day demanded something more than commonsense. Intellectual brilliance was at a discount when it should have been at a premium. Brains were too readily associated with personal corruption

and rackety private lives. What Lloyd George has to answer for is not his own dubious morals but the fact that they discredited him and indirectly his companions, some of the ablest men in public life, at just the time when the baffling questions of the inter-war years needed originality, energy, improvisation and adventure if they were to be answered.

Keynes was similarly tainted by his involvement with Lloyd George. Moreover, his arrogance and impatience with bureaucrats and politicians was responsible for the unsympathetic reception given to many of his policy prescriptions and theoretical writings,[5] the *General Theory* in particular, acceptance of which may have been unnecessarily delayed. In this respect, Phillips's comments on Keynes's (1939b) 'Crisis finance' articles are particularly interesting; for although he was in sympathy with much of Keynes's reasoning he felt compelled to make the observation that the articles were marked by 'Keynes' customary optimism, overemphasis and neglect of ulterior consequences. It is almost as though he sets out to instil distrust in his readers' (PRO 1939d, 1).

Mention should also be made of the complexion of interwar civil service administration, the administrative climate in which economic policies were debated and implemented. The point should be admitted that arguments couched in terms of administrative impracticability are the usual plea of a defensive bureaucracy, and no doubt this was partly the case for the Treasury in the 1930s. Nevertheless, when the Treasury were far from convinced of the fundamental correctness of the 'new' economics, both in theoretical terms and in its applicability to the current unemployment problem, there was an understandable reluctance to institute the major administrative reforms necessary for the adoption of large-scale public works. As was shown in chapter 3, this would have involved bringing a great volume of public investment under direct central control and establishing a planning agency to formulate long-term plans and supervise their execution, changes which would have had a profound influence on the structure and operation of British politics.

More generally, however valid Keynes's (1939a) specific accusations against the civil service, that it was ruled by those 'trained by tradition and experience and native skill to every form of intelligent obstruction', it is clear that the amateurism of the British civil service was becoming increasingly inappropriate to the range and complexity of problems confronting interwar bureaucracy and governments. It is to be regretted that the higher civil service, as it evolved under Fisher's direction, stood 'aloof from some of the most significant contemporary developments in the study of public administration', that it was 'far more concerned with developing the *esprit de corps* of the civil service than with administration *per se*' (Chapman and Greenaway 1980, 72, 112).

The questions under consideration also need to be seen in a wider context. An all-pervasive feature of the interwar fiscal policy debate was that the form of debate, by all parties concerned, was such as to obscure many of the real issues requiring analysis. This followed inevitably from the fact that the debate was conducted within a limited ambit: economic policy questions were approached from the 'Establishment' point of view, with a number of built-in assumptions which begged a large part of the arguments – assumptions, in particular, relating to the inviolability of the prevailing political system and the role of government. The Second World War caused an immediate and profound reappraisal of these assumptions. The emergency which overtook the whole nation was deemed to justify a radical modification of existing administrative and political systems. It could have been argued that the emergency which overtook the unemployed in the 1930s was just as pressing for them as anything that threatened the nation as a whole in the war, but of course no such arguments were articulated. Unemployment was deemed not to constitute such an emergency and thus did not justify any radical changes, changes which were a necessary precondition for a successful solution to Britain's unemployment problem.

The recurrence of mass unemployment in our own age, its dominance of political and economic debate, but failure to provoke a satisfactory response from government, must make more comprehensible the interwar period. Without suggesting any essential similarity between the two ages,[6] we can nevertheless identify certain recurrent themes in twentieth-century British economic policy: what we might term the diuturnity of orthodoxy.[7] Such an enquiry is fraught with all the usual problems of writing contemporary history; perhaps more so in this case. In considering the present we are inevitably thrust into the crucible of contemporary politics and policy analysis. Denuded of the protective clothing of balanced perspective provided by the passage of time, the temptation is ever present to draw parallels, to point to the repetition of error in history, when time and distance would in fact suggest alternative interpretations.

* * *

A natural starting point to our discussion is inflation: the fear of it in the interwar period, the actuality of it in the 1970s and 1980s. The Thatcher governments' economic strategy has consistently centred on the reduction of inflation to acceptable levels, thereby creating the conditions in which economic growth might take root and prove sustainable. Interwar governments, however, were more concerned about preventing inflation, the justification as later being the assumed benefits for the performance of the real economy, this notwithstanding the adverse effects of the downward price trend of 1920–34 and the fact that inflation would have eroded the real value of the greatly enlarged national debt and thus made budgetary policy both less difficult and less deflationary.

There were common political motives to both periods, and while rarely articulated they can be said to be at least as important as the supposed economic rationale for seeking to prevent or minimize inflation. As Higham and Tomlinson (1982, 11) have noted, 'governments do not adopt policy objectives independent of the means they believe necessary to realise those objectives.' Thus the inflation objective can be a convenient shield for governments whose ulterior motive is a politically-inspired desire to restrain public expenditure growth.

More broadly, concern about inflation has a simple and eminently logical appeal to societies needing, at times of crisis, comprehension of the root cause of their economic difficulties. This seems particularly true of Britain, for similar forces and sentiments underlie the continued appeal of budgetary orthodoxy, the subject to which we now turn.

Although Keynes (1936, xxi) believed it was his 'fellow economists, not the general public, whom [he] must first convince' of the correctness of the *General Theory*, his attack upon orthodox policies was broader in intent and effect. Indeed, as a proselytizer, he was probably at his most effective in his newspaper articles where he reached and influenced a much wider audience. But it is doubtful that even Keynes, with all his persuasive skills and dazzling literary gifts, could overthrow the balanced budget doctrine. For too long financial integrity had been perceived as the bedrock of British democracy. Something more fundamental was required. This profound change of opinion could only come through the practical experience of successful deficit-financing; it being the irony of history that this was to be provided by the Second World War when the rationale was not full employment as such but the maximum war effort. Indeed, this is the key to the whole question, for doubts about unbalanced budgets were only dispelled when deficit-financing could be seen to be successful, when it generated full employment without unacceptable political and economic costs.

It follows that, irrespective of whether there was a complete intellectual conversion to Keynesian demand management in the 1940s or not, were the practical success of deficit-finance to be in question, were the policy to be seen as imposing unacceptable costs (such as accelerating inflation), the balanced budget doctrine could quickly reappear because of its simple, attractive appeal as a base remedy for Britain's difficulties. The point at which the costs of deficit-finance were perceived as outweighing the benefits, and the exact significance of Callaghan's now famous address to the 1976 Labour Party Conference, will no doubt long exercise the minds of future historians. It is sufficient to note here that dissatisfaction with Keynesian demand management pre-dates 1976, or even 1973, the first OPEC price shock (Blackaby 1979).

Such dissatisfaction was essentially technical in its origins (Wass 1978). For example, from as early as the mid-1960s, serious doubts had formed about the trade-off between full employment and price and balance of payments stability, and there was concern about both the narrowness of existing demand management policy instruments and the frequency with which policy interventions proved destabilizing. Nevertheless, one might say that policy continued to be dominated by the long shadow cast by the interwar period; that these doubts had not yet crystallized into anything approaching an attempted theoretical refutation of Keynesian stabilization policies; and that, more importantly, the political costs of abandoning the commitment to full employment were *perceived* as electorally disastrous.

It was political forces, however, that gave momentum to the current reaction against deficit-finance and thus contributed towards the demise of Keynesian demand management. Of these, the most influential proved to be the opinion that the UK public sector had grown to an excessive size, that this not only explained the UK's poor postwar growth performance, but that if this process was permitted to continue economic weakness would increasingly be accompanied by political instability.

The economic aspects of this argument are, of course, associated with Bacon and Eltis's (1976) study *Britain's Economic Problem: Too few producers*; the political dimension developed later, but proved equally influential. Whilst Bacon and Eltis's prognosis has found little favour amongst academic economists, it has proved to have a much more robust political appeal. Moreover, this appeal has been strengthened by the growing body of 'public choice' literature which has sought to question the political assumptions underlying the managed economy (see, for example, Buchanan *et al.* 1978). Here, concern centres not only on the 'excessive' size of the public sector, but on the way in which politicians – operating without constitutional disciplines – have been able through their economic management to subordinate the long-term public interest to short-term political ends, and how this has resulted in a serious weakening of the British economy. As was shown in chapter 5, during the interwar period it was this very fear which at least partly explains why the balanced budget rule – a constitutional discipline – remained so entrenched and why officials and a wider political opinion appeared so impervious to the economic arguments of the developing Keynesian position.

In the sphere of budgetary policies, two additional broad similarities between our periods should also be noted. First, consider the following arguments used in defence of current government policies by Howe in the 1980 budget statement:

> Relaxed monetary and budgetary policies might bring higher output – even higher living standards – in the very short run, though even this is

questionable, but in reality they would simply fuel fresh inflation. Such policies would inevitably undermine the confidence of financial markets, industry and consumers. The action that would then be necessary to deal with the ensuing crisis would, equally certainly, destroy jobs and cut living standards still further.

(cited in Coutts *et al.* 1981, 83)

From this it appears that once more the maintenance of confidence has emerged to dominate the policy-making stage. The essentials of Howe's 1980 budget statement differ little from, say, Hopkins's 1930 evidence before the Macmillan Committee. In both periods, the state of confidence is judged to be an institutional factor beyond the authorities' control, one that both inhibits government from pursuing a stabilization policy and limits the effectiveness of such a policy in the unlikely event of its being adopted.

We should not be surprised by the re-emergence of maintaining confidence as a principal objective, not just because of the tenor of the current government's policies, but because the effectiveness of stabilization policies has, ultimately, always been dependent upon the willingness of the financial institutions to hold public debt. This in turn depends upon their broad support for government policies, the continuance of which – under present institutional arrangements – can never be assured by government (Tomlinson 1981a, 83–5).

Whatever the conclusions that one might draw about the wisdom of present institutional arrangements, there also remains a central point about the manner in which governments conduct their policies. Here we can identify an important and disturbing parallel between the interwar policy debate and the complexion of demand management since (say) 1976. In the earlier period, debate centred on the balanced budget target; in the more recent period, it has centred on the PSBR and £M3 targets. This has created a situation fraught with dangers. In Britain, perhaps more than in any other country, at times of serious disagreement about economic management, the logic of the ruling philosophy has been to set a single economic target, with the unfortunate tendency to ignore the fact that autonomous shocks make targets like balanced budgets or £M3 notoriously difficult to meet; but if not met, confidence is threatened because the atmosphere has been created whereby the target assumes a weight out of all proportion to the real role of that variable in economic performance. In a sense, therefore, governments almost create the conditions for their own failure.

As regards the second broad similarity between our two periods, consider the following statement:

> That existing financial difficulties make it necessary for the nation like the private individual to consider seriously what it can afford and not

merely what is desirable. Reviewed from this standpoint much expenditure is unwarrantable at the present time, which, under more favourable conditions, we should deem justifiable and even a wise investment of the national resources.

Only the rather dated prose style tells us that this statement is drawn from a document of the 1930s – in this case, the May report (HMSO 1931b, 220) – rather than the 1980s. Such has been the change in attitudes towards public expenditure that this statement could easily have been made by any one of the present Treasury ministers.

Once more public expenditure has begun to be seen as a 'luxury good', rather than as an important determinant of the level of aggregate demand, and as serving an essential supportive function in the process of economic growth. That this is so is clearly seen from the downward course of public investment over recent years, and the way in which the Treasury has justified public expenditure cuts since 1979. This reversion to earlier conceptions of the function of public expenditures is also evident in the present government's attitude towards employment generated by such expenditures. As in the interwar period, deficit-financing is currently dismissed by arguing that because the jobs so created do not add to productive capacity, they can only be temporary, and ultimately at the expense of jobs created by the private sector. Such views are far too extreme; far too simplistic; altogether suspicious, for Keynesian demand management is not just being rejected, but denigrated for its creation of 'illusory' employment as opposed to 'real' jobs, whatever these might be.

Another parallel between the two periods also suggests itself, that concerning the moral dimension of economic policy, in particular the 'hairshirt philosophy' referred to in chapter 6. This can be considered at two levels. First, the following description of the postwar Treasury is equally applicable to the interwar period:

> There is a strongly moralistic element in the Treasury predilection for cuts. It contains an appeal to the bourgeois/Puritan streak in all of us which believes that it is somehow wrong to spend and virtuous to refrain from spending.
>
> There is also something of the superstition of primitive medicine in that appeal, the notion that a medicine cannot be much good unless it tastes awful; and indeed there is much in common between the pre-scientific medicine of the past and the pre-scientific economics of the present.　　　　　　　　　　　　　　　　　　　　　　(Pollard 1982, 89)

Secondly, current policy statements, as with those of the 1930s, are replete with expressions such as courage, duty, fortitude, resolve. Why? The use of such language could be interpreted as a measure of the government's honesty, of its commitment to an economic strategy which it is convinced is correct. Alternatively, it could be seen as a rather disingenuous method of diverting criticism away from an economic policy whose intellectual foundations (if any) are being steadily eroded, but which can temporarily be bolstered by an appeal to non-economic criteria, to certain supposedly self-evident truths of human behaviour. Whichever, economists should roundly condemn any attempt to impute to economic policy these sorts of moral characteristics.

Such sins are further compounded when morality-of-policy arguments are applied to the unemployed themselves, the victims of the policy process. Here there is also a strong parallel between the two periods: the public abuse of so-called 'dole scroungers', and the attempt to redefine and lessen unemployment by changing the basis of measurement. There is also, of course, the neo-monetarist view that unemployment is greatly magnified by unemployment benefits, an opinion that mirrors attitudes of the 1930s.

* * *

We could continue, almost indefinitely, with such parallels. Instead, we can conclude this study with a discussion of why support for 'sound' finance has proved the most robust recurrent theme in twentieth-century British economic policy.

It is to be regretted that in Britain demands for sound finance, like support for the minimalist state, are too frequently articulated in terms of its being a morally unimpeachable principle. The evidence of fiscal window-dressing in the 1930s, and more recently creative accounting, the sale of public assets and fiscal relaxations largely contrived by less rigorous budgetary arithmetic than that of earlier years (see Devereux and Morris 1983; 1984), suggests that such advocacy is replete with hypocrisy and governmental mendacity. As Fisher noted in December 1935, 'It would seem, then, that "sound finance" includes some regard for expediency, and is something short of the absolute law and prophets' (PRO 1935i, 1).

It was noted earlier that we must take account of the personal characteristics of the participants in the interwar fiscal policy debate if we are to understand this episode fully. The more general point should now also be made: that economic debate in Britain is highly unsatisfactory, the form of debate unduly influencing the outcome. For example, the manner in which it was possible to reject the 1929 Liberal and 1983 Labour unemployment programmes strongly suggests the existence of certain insuperable barriers to the adoption of an 'alternative economic strategy'. Even if we discount media bias, and the fact that general elections are not the most propitious occasions at which to debate such matters, it is still true that policies which centre upon deficit-finance are almost uniquely easy to discredit. Their vilification can be effortlessly achieved, if a government so wishes, by appeal to fatuous traditional wisdoms such as: 'you can't pull yourself up by your own bootstraps', or no purpose is achieved 'by throwing money at the unemployment problem'. Orthodoxy can too easily appeal to base sentiments, whereas radical policy alternatives require optimism and imagination on the electorate's part – commodities traditionally in short supply in Britain, hardly ever apparent during depressions when the political response appears to be a retreat towards 'safety first' policies. It should not be forgotten that the British electorate have never sanctioned Keynesian demand management except within the context of cross-party support.

There were, of course, other more technical difficulties associated with the case for deficit-finance in the 1930s. While the weight of evidence strongly suggests that, *ceteris paribus*, an expansionary fiscal policy would have stimulated demand, such were the regional and industrial characteristics of the unemployment problem that the details of any fiscal stimulus would have required very careful planning. A centrally directed public works programme, such as that proposed by the Liberals in 1929, was thus insufficient and in part inappropriate for the task confronting policymakers. Moreover, given the business community's views about high direct taxation, it is clear that taxation as well as public expenditure could have been used to greater effect. That they were not was in part due to an influence, hitherto given insufficient weight in the literature on the interwar period, but one very familiar to our own age: that of technological unemployment. Common to both was a certain ambivalence about how unemployment might be eradicated: on the one hand, a certain confidence about market-based solutions, this normally deriving from a very superficial interpretation of Britain's industrial development over the past two centuries; on the other, a certain pessimism about government's seeming impotence, this normally deriving from more immediate political pressures. It was only towards the close of the interwar period that government broke free from such thinking and sought to combat unemployment more actively; a somewhat pessimistic antecedent for our own age.

The severity of the current depression was broadly predictable in 1979, for when the government assumed office committed to a period of monetary and fiscal disinflation it was inevitable that the automatic stabilizers would have to be overridden. It was equally inevitable, given the characteristics of the fiscal system, that this would exacerbate the resulting depression and heighten the costs of the experiment.

That such devastation can be wrought in furtherance of an economic philosophy, after our having supposedly 'eaten of the Fruit of the [Keynesian] Tree of Knowledge' (Samuelson 1970, 250), requires that we reconsider our current perspective upon the interwar period, a period when the Keynesian 'Tree of Knowledge' was supposedly taking root but had not yet borne fruit. It also requires a major effort to understand the preconditions for, and subsequent nature of, current monetarism, a philosophy too easily dismissed by critics (such as Stewart 1980) as merely:

> a form of retreat from the complexities of the modern world, a harking back to an era when the government was required only to provide a minimum of services . . . and to balance its own books, leaving it to the dynamic of industrial capitalism, unfettered by trade unions or by full parliamentary democracy, to produce wealth, and distribute it.

In light of current events we should now seriously consider the full implications of Matthews's (1968) paper, where it was argued that the achievement of full employment to the late 1960s owed more to the high-spending propensities of the private sector than to Keynesian demand management. We should also explore further the recent doubts expressed by Tomlinson (1981a) about whether there ever was a 'Keynesian revolution' in economic policy in Britain.[8] That influential opinion embraced monetarism with such alacrity should profoundly embarrass the economics profession whose defence of Keynesian demand management was less than ideal. It should not, however, paralyze thought. The process whereby Keynesian demand management was first discredited, and eventually completely rejected, must be understood if we are, in turn, to supplant crude monetarism in favour of a more acceptable and efficacious mode of economic management. To that end the 1930s fiscal policy debate here recounted can be used to good effect. This earlier episode illustrates clearly the strength of the political–psychological foundations of budgetary orthodoxy, the less than dominant role played by theoretical issues, and the ability of successive governments to avoid any commitment to wholeheartedly combating unemployment.

While our current predicament would undoubtedly confirm Santayana's aphorism, that 'Those who cannot remember the past are condemned to repeat it', at the same time we should also be concerned about the present deliberate distortion of recent history. The early 1980s have witnessed a most disturbing selective rewriting of postwar British financial history, this creating a popular image of deficit-finance as entirely discredited by the stagflation of the 1970s. Such ignorance and distortion aside, it is to be regretted that before the present monetarist policy experiment began the economics profession was not more vocal in its warnings, more prepared to make public its knowledge of the last 'great depression' and the likely consequences of eschewing deficit-finance for the pursuit of some suspect principle of monetary probity.

Finally, we should also protest about recent attempts to buttress current policies through a selective rewriting of the historical record of the interwar period. For example, it is quite unacceptable to argue the case for market efficiency now by appealing to the supposed existence of benefit-induced unemployment between the wars. It should never be forgotten that it was state action, in the form of military expenditures, which resolved interwar mass unemployment. Accordingly, it is quite disingenuous for market optimists to attempt to draw parallels between the 1930s and the 1980s, unless of course their motives are political and not economic.

APPENDIX I

DRAMATIS PERSONAE

Baldwin, Stanley (later Lord) – Prime Minister 1923–4, 1924–9, 1935–7; Lord President of Council 1931–5.

Bradbury, Lord (formerly Sir John) – Joint Permanent Secretary, Treasury 1913–19; principal British delegate to Reparation Commission 1919–25; member Committee on Finance and Industry 1929–31.

Bridges, E. E. (later Lord) – Principal Assistant Secretary, Treasury 1936–8; Secretary to Cabinet 1938–46; Permanent Secretary, Treasury 1945–56.

Chamberlain, Neville – Minister of Health 1923, 1924–9, 1931; Chancellor of the Exchequer 1923–4, 1931–7; Prime Minister 1937–40.

Churchill, Winston (later Sir) – Chancellor of the Exchequer 1924–9.

Fisher, Sir Warren – Permanent Secretary, Treasury and Head of Civil Service 1919–39.

Gregory, Sir Theodore – Cassel Professor of Economics, University of London 1927–37; member Committee on Finance and Industry 1929–31.

Grigg, P. J. (later Sir James) – Principal Private Secretary to successive Chancellors of the Exchequer 1921–30; Chairman, Board of Customs and Excise 1930, Board of Inland Revenue 1930–4.

Harrod, R. F. (later Sir Roy) – Lecturer in Economics, University of Oxford 1929–37.

Hawtrey, Sir Ralph – Director of Financial Enquiries, Treasury 1919–45.

Hayek, Professor F. A. von – Tooke Professor of Economic Science and Statistics, University of London 1931–50.

Henderson, H. D. (later Sir Hubert) – Editor, *The Nation & Athenaeum* 1923–30; Joint Secretary, Economic Advisory Council 1930–4; member Committee on Economic Information 1931–9; economic adviser, Treasury 1939–44.

Hopkins, Sir Richard V. N. – Chairman, Board of Inland Revenue 1922–7; Controller of Finance and Supply Services, Treasury 1927–32; Second Secretary 1932–42; Permanent Secretary 1942–5.

Inskip, Sir Thomas – Minister for the Co-ordination of Defence 1936–9.

Kahn, R. F. (later Lord) – Fellow of King's College, Cambridge since 1931.

Kaldor, Nicholas (later Lord) – Lecturer in Economics, London School of Economics.
Keynes, J. M. (later Lord) – Fellow, King's College, Cambridge 1909–46; Treasury 1914–19, 1940–6; member Committee on Finance and Industry 1929–31; Economic Advisory Council; Committee on Economic Information 1931–9.
Layton, Sir Walter (later Lord) – Editor, The Economist 1922–38.
Leith-Ross, Sir Frederick – Deputy Controller of Finance, Treasury 1925–32; Chief Economic Adviser to HM Government 1932–46.
Lithgow, Sir James – President, Federation of British Industries 1930–2.
Lloyd George, David – Prime Minister 1916–22; leader, Liberal Party.
MacDonald, J. Ramsay – Prime Minister 1924, 1929–35; Lord President of Council 1935–7.
MacGregor, Professor D. H. – Drummond Professor of Political Economy, University of Oxford 1922–45.
McKenna, Reginald – Chancellor of the Exchequer 1915–16; Chairman, Midland Bank 1919–43; member Committee on Finance and Industry 1929–31.
Macmillan, Harold (later Earl of Stockton) – Conservative MP 1924–9, 1931–45.
May, Sir George (later Lord) – Secretary, Prudential Assurance Co.; Chairman, Committee on National Expenditure 1931, Import Duties Advisory Committee 1932–9.
Meade, J. E. – Fellow and Lecturer in Economics, Hertford College, Oxford 1930–7; Economic Assistant, Economic Section, Cabinet Office 1940–5; Director 1945–7.
Mosley, Sir Oswald – Chancellor of Duchy of Lancaster 1929–30.
Niemeyer, Sir Otto – Controller of Finance, Treasury 1922–7.
Phillips, Sir Frederick – Principal Assistant Secretary, Treasury 1927–31; Deputy Controller 1931; Under Secretary 1932–9.
Pigou, Professor A. C. – Professor of Political Economy, University of Cambridge 1908–43.
Plant, Professor A. – Cassel Professor of Commerce, University of London 1930–65.
Robbins, Professor Lionel – Professor of Economics, London School of Economics 1929–61.
Robertson, D. H. – Reader in Economics, University of Cambridge 1930–8; member Committee on Economic Information 1936–9.
Robinson, E. A. G. (later Sir Austin) – Lecturer in Economics, University of Cambridge 1929–49.
Robinson, Joan – Assistant Lecturer in Economics, University of Cambridge 1931–7; Lecturer 1937–49.
Salter, Sir Arthur (later Lord) – Gladstone Professor of Political Theory and Institutions, University of Oxford 1934–44; Independent MP 1937–50.
Simon, Sir John (later Lord) – Secretary of State for Foreign Affairs 1931–5; Home Secretary 1935–7; Chancellor of the Exchequer 1937–40.
Snowden, Philip (later Lord) – Chancellor of the Exchequer 1924, 1929–31; Lord Privy Seal 1931–2.
Stamp, Sir Josiah (later Lord) – Chairman, London, Midland and Scottish Railway 1926–41; Committee on Economic Information 1931–9.
Stewart, P. M. (later Sir Malcolm) – Commissioner for the Special Areas (England and Wales) 1934–6.

APPENDIX II

THE ACTUAL AND ADJUSTED BUDGET DEFINITIONS

Reference was made in chapter 5 to a number of adjustments made to receipts (T_c), expenditure (G_c) and the budget balance (B_c) in order to obtain an unchanging, and economically more significant, definition of the budget balance (B). A brief discussion follows of the items constituting these adjustments.

I GOVERNMENT BORROWING

On the expenditure side of the account the consolidation of the social insurance funds and the removal of sinking fund payments needs no further explanation. The explanation of the other adjustments (set out in table II.1) is as follows.

1. Capital expenditure 'below the line': This, the only item in the budget accounts specifically shown as capital expenditure, covered expenditure on Post Office development, it being considered permissible to finance such expenditure by borrowing because the assets acquired were remunerative in an accepted accounting sense. Other capital items were incorporated in capital expenditure 'above the line', e.g. expenditure on road programmes.
2. Other borrowing: This includes two items: borrowing to meet interest on the encashment of savings certificates; and borrowing in 1932/3 to cover the cost of the War Loan conversion operation. Both items properly belong to expenditure, being charges that in normal circumstances would have been met within the budget.
3. Defence borrowing: This item constitutes borrowing under the Defence Loans Acts, 1937 and 1939, and needs to be incorporated as part of our adjustments since G_c only included defence expenditure financed out of revenue.

Table II.1 Expenditure adjustments: sinking fund payments and government expenditure charged to capital 1929/30–1939/40 (£m.)

	1929/30	1930/1	1931/2	1932/3	1933/4	1934/5	1935/6	1936/7	1937/8	1938/9	1939/40
Sinking fund (SF)	−47.7	−66.8	−32.5	−26.3	−7.7	−12.3	−12.5	−13.1	−10.5	−13.2	−7.2
Capital expenditure (CE)	+10.5	+11.0	+9.7	+7.5	+6.5	+7.5	+10.5	+13.5	+17.0	+22.6	+22.1
Other borrowing (OB)	+4.8	—	+8.4	+25.9	—	—	—	—	—	—	—
Defence borrowing (DB)	—	—	—	—	—	—	—	—	+64.9	+128.1	+491.7
Total adjustments	−32.4	−55.8	−14.4	+7.1	−1.2	−4.8	−2.0	+0.4	+71.4	+137.5	+506.6

Source: Financial Accounts.

Table II.2 Revenue adjustments: non-recurrent receipts included in 'Ordinary and Self-Balancing Revenue' 1929/30–1939/40 (£m.)

	1929/30	1930/1	1931/2	1932/3	1933/4	1934/5	1935/6	1936/7	1937/8	1938/9	1939/40
Old Exchange Account	—	—	−12.8	—	—	—	—	—	—	—	—
War Loan Depreciation Fund	—	—	—	—	−10.0	—	—	—	—	—	—
National Debt Commissioners – Death Duty Account	—	—	—	—	—	—	—	−5.8	−1.5	−1.5	−1.4
Road Fund	—	—	—	—	—	—	−4.5	−5.3	−3.6	—	—
Rating Relief Suspense Account	—	−16.0	−4.0	—	—	—	—	—	—	—	—
Profits of Bank of England note issue	—	−3.7	−0.6	−8.9	—	—	—	—	—	—	—
Enemy Debt Clearing Office – Surplus	−3.5	−3.5	−3.5	−3.0	—	—	−3.5	−0.7	—	—	—
Total adjustments	−3.5	−23.2	−20.9	−11.9	−10.0	—	−8.0	−11.8	−5.1	−1.5	−1.4

Sources: Financial Accounts; PRO T239/25–7, 'Treasury Register of Daily Receipts'.

II NON-RECURRENT REVENUE

These items (set out in table II.2), which came under the head 'Miscellaneous Revenue' in the financial accounts, can be considered under two headings.

1 Capital accounts:
    Old Exchange Account
    War Loan Depreciation Fund
    National Debt Commissioners – Death Duty Account
2 Miscellaneous funds:
    Road Fund
    Rating Relief Suspense Account
    Profits of Bank of England note issue
    Enemy Debt Clearing Office – Surplus

Items falling under the former heading were taken into receipts (T_c) for a variety of reasons, but in general the accounts had become obsolete and could be presented as containing capital sums which might be thus appropriated. In practice, these sums had usually been put to debt redemption, and thus the transactions were a convenient facade for masking fresh borrowing (see, for example, PRO 1931e; 1933h).

Under miscellaneous funds, account is taken of 'raids' on the capital balances of the Road Fund, the fictitious resources of the Rating Relief Suspense Account, which was merely an earmarking of past surpluses, and two miscellaneous items: profits of the Bank of England note issue and the surplus of the Enemy Debt Clearing Office, there being evidence that they were included according to necessity (PRO 1932g; 1936d).

APPENDIX III

THE ESTIMATION OF CONSTANT EMPLOYMENT RECEIPTS AND EXPENDITURE

I RECEIPTS

Central government receipts at constant employment (T^*) are shown in table III.1 according broadly to the five main categories of revenue.

1 Taxes on expenditure

(a) *Customs and Excise other than import duties.* Separate elasticities were calculated for taxes on spirits, beer, tobacco, sugar, hydrocarbon oils and a residual category, using a method adapted from that employed in previous studies (Bretherton 1937; Edelberg 1940). The first step was to take account of changes made in the rates of duty, by applying the estimates given in the budgets of the time of the effects of these changes on revenue, to obtain revenue series on a constant rate basis. An elasticity of revenue with respect to GDP at current prices was then calculated (table III.2), taking the change in revenue against the change in GDP between the two constant employment base years. Our results can be compared with those of Bretherton and Edelberg. The former took account of discretionary changes in calculating tax elasticities, constructing hypothetical tax yields which were then related to national income, for three periods: the upswing of the 1920s, the downturn of the early 1930s and the subsequent recovery phase (to 1935/6). Bretherton's indices of hypothetical yields for spirits, beer, tobacco and sugar conform well with our estimates on a constant rate basis, despite the fact that his starting point was 1922, not 1929, while his estimates of tax elasticities for the upswing and recovery phases correspond fairly closely with our results. Edelberg used the percentage employed (i.e. 100 per cent less the unemployment

Table III.1 Central government receipts at constant employment 1929/30–1939/40 (£m.)

	1929/30	1930/1	1931/2	1932/3	1933/4	1934/5	1935/6	1936/7	1937/8	1938/9	1939/40
1 Taxes on expenditure											
Customs and Excise	247.3	256.3	280.7	325.9	318.1	310.6	315.3	321.3	335.6	354.8	411.0
Motor vehicle licences	26.8	30.4	33.0	34.2	36.1	35.0	32.7	32.9	34.6	37.8	35.5
Stamp duties	25.7	30.0	30.0	30.0	30.0	30.0	30.0	30.0	30.0	30.0	30.0
Post Office surplus	9.2	10.1	11.5	10.9	13.1	12.3	11.7	11.0	10.5	9.5	3.8
Other	2.2	2.1	2.2	2.0	2.0	2.1	2.2	2.1	2.0	2.0	2.0
Total	311.2	328.9	357.4	403.0	399.3	390.0	391.9	397.3	412.7	434.1	482.3
2 Taxes on income											
Income and surtax	293.8	323.9	384.3	357.7	334.3	325.4	320.8	330.4	361.0	398.9	478.6
NDC	—	—	—	—	—	—	—	—	1.4	21.9	26.9
Other	2.3	3.0	2.5	2.2	1.8	2.3	1.3	1.0	1.0	0.9	0.6
Total	296.1	326.9	386.8	359.9	336.1	327.7	322.1	331.4	363.4	421.7	506.1
3 Taxes on capital											
Estate duties	79.8	82.7	87.9	87.9	87.9	88.0	88.0	88.0	89.0	89.0	94.2
4 National insurance contributions											
Unemployment	31.4	31.5	37.4	43.3	43.5	45.2	45.9	44.2	44.6	47.0	46.7
National health	26.4	27.6	28.9	29.6	28.9	29.0	28.9	29.4	30.2	31.7	31.9
Contributory pensions	24.5	25.0	25.5	25.5	25.6	25.6	27.0	31.9	33.1	34.1	33.9
Total	82.4	84.1	91.8	98.4	98.0	99.8	101.8	105.5	107.9	112.8	112.5
5 Miscellaneous revenue	127.9	142.3	105.8	87.3	86.2	81.3	92.7	101.3	95.6	99.0	110.1
6 *less* non-recurrent receipts	3.5	23.2	20.9	11.9	10.0	—	8.0	11.8	5.1	1.5	1.4
Total receipts (T^*)	893.9	941.7	1,008.8	1,024.6	997.5	986.8	988.5	1,011.7	1,063.5	1,155.1	1,303.8

Source: Data taken from *Financial Accounts* and adjusted on to a constant employment basis using the estimation procedures outlined below.

Table III.2 Elasticities of Customs and Excise duties with respect to GDP

Tax	Elasticity
Spirits	0.80
Beer	0.32
Tobacco	1.22
Sugar	0.27
Hydrocarbon oils	2.96
Other Customs and Excise	1.49

rate) as his cyclical index of activity, and related tax yields to employment to derive indirectly a measure of the income elasticity of demand, but did not correct for discretionary changes in tax rates. Consequently, there is little correspondence between our results and no further account is taken of them. Using the elasticities in table III.2 the actual yields were then adjusted to a constant employment basis by applying the ratio (Y^*/Y).

(b) Import duties. A similar method was used, but the adjustments were complicated by the fact that a general protective tariff was introduced in 1931–2 (increasing the revenue under this head from £4.8 million in 1931/2 to £28.8 million in 1932/3) which precluded direct comparison between our end years on a constant rate basis. Hence the actual values for 1930/1 and 1931/2 were roughly adjusted (by the ratio) to derive their constant employment values, while the yields for 1932/3 and subsequent years were adjusted to a constant rate basis, again using the official estimates of the effect of the authorities' discretionary action. An elasticity of revenue with respect to GDP was then calculated for the period 1932/3 to 1937/8, allowance being made for the extent to which GDP was below the constant employment level in 1932/3. The elasticity of import duty revenue with respect to GDP was found to be approximately 2.1.

(c) Motor vehicle licence duties. These duties were first recalculated on to a constant rate basis, and an elasticity of revenue with respect to GDP of approximately 2.1 was obtained, which corresponded closely with Bretherton's estimate.

(d) Stamp duties. Revenue from these miscellaneous taxes upon the transfer of assets was cyclically highly sensitive, with turning-points one year in advance of GDP, but largely insensitive to trend growth: revenue on a constant rate basis peaked in 1928/9 and 1936/7 at £30.1 million and £31 million respectively. It was assumed that at constant employment these duties would have yielded £30 million per annum, thus implying that stock exchange prices would have remained constant at constant employment – an approximate but not absurd assumption for a period during much of which the general price level is assumed to have fallen (in line with the actual course of prices), while output is assumed to have been rising. Since there was no clear relationship between changes in asset prices and variations in GDP it was decided to exclude this duty when calculating macro-marginal budget rates. A similar problem was encountered with estate duties.

(e) Post Office surplus. This was included as a revenue item since it was subject to government control, but was treated as autonomous.

(f) Other. A residual item of miscellaneous taxes which were small in magnitude (about £2 million per annum) and largely invariant to changes in income, and therefore not adjusted.

2 Taxes on income

(a) Income and surtax. Their constant employment values were obtained by calculating an aggregate tax elasticity relating changes in their yield at actual employment to changes in GDP,[1] which were then applied, using the ratio, to their actual values.

A number of general problems were encountered. First, income tax was levied one year and surtax two years in arrears (Hicks 1938, 303), so that separate elasticities had to be calculated taking into account the differential lags. Secondly, the official *ex ante* estimates of the change in revenue resulting from discretionary changes had to be used, but on occasion changes in revenue from year to year were associated with changes in GDP of the opposite direction. Fortunately, such occasions were rare.

The actual yields of income and surtax were adjusted to a constant rate basis for comparison with any two consecutive years.[2] Allowing for the lags, changes in yield were then related to changes in GDP and elasticities year by year were obtained. Ignoring the perverse results referred to above, means of observations were taken and found to be 1.60 for income tax and 3.71 for surtax.

The estimate for income tax almost exactly corresponds to Edelberg's estimate of 1.61 for the years 1929–37, despite the fact that his correlation analysis only took account of changes in the standard rate, and not changes in allowances, etc. Comparison with Bretherton's estimate is precluded because, unlike Edelberg, he did not lag receipts against GDP. Other contemporary evidence, however, suggests that an elasticity of 1.60 is of the right order of magnitude for a fully progressive income tax and given the technical details of its levy (Hicks 1938, 292, 300).

Verification of our surtax elasticity proved more difficult. Surtax introduced progression into income tax for the higher-income groups, the incomes of which were undoubtedly reduced by depressions and expanded by booms in greater proportion than those with moderate incomes (Stamp 1936). Thus one would expect a large, positive elasticity, but the result obtained (i.e. double that of income tax) is very high, primarily because of our observations for 1931/2 to 1932/3.[3] If these are omitted, the elasticity is reduced to 2.72; this revised elasticity was used in our adjustments, but since surtax was small in relation to total receipts the difference is not important.

(b) National Defence Contribution. This, a profits tax introduced in 1937, was first levied for the accounting period ending 1937/8. The technical details of the tax (see HMSO 1937) enable us to assume that its yield at constant employment would not have differed significantly from its actual yield. Hence no adjustment was made.

(c) Other. This class of revenue consisted of two profits taxes levied during and immediately after the First World War, which continued to yield small amounts during the period. Since they were levied on profits earned before 1929, adjustment is unnecessary.

3 Taxes on capital

This head comprises estate duties which showed a high cyclical sensitivity because asset prices fluctuated more than GDP, and the duties were progressive. As with stamp duties, estate duties were insensitive to trend growth: on a constant rate basis, the yield in our two base years was almost identical – £79.8 million in 1929/30 and £80.1 million in 1937/8. Consequently, the constant employment values were interpolated between the actual values for the two base years, taking into account rate increases in 1930/1 and 1939/40.

4 National insurance contributions

(a) Unemployment. A statistically significant relationship was found between private sector contributions to the Unemployment Fund and the level of GDP. The actual contributions were therefore adjusted by the ratio.[4]

(b) National Health and (c) Contributory Pensions. The same method was used and found to be satisfactory. Thus, for private sector contributions to all three schemes, a unitary elasticity with respect to GDP was implicitly assumed.

5 Miscellaneous revenue

This was the residual item in the revenue side of the account, covering a number of miscellaneous tax and non-tax receipts and the income of the Post Office (less the surplus, included in taxes on expenditure). These revenues varied markedly over the period, but this is explained by the fact that they included reparation receipts and the sale of war property during the years 1929/30 to 1931/2 and non-recurrent receipts which, as shown above, varied markedly. Removal of such items leads to a fairly stable revenue series, and hence these revenues were assumed to be autonomous.

II TEST OF ACCURACY OF REVENUE ESTIMATES

It is possible to cross-check our results for one year with some estimates published by Kaldor (1944) of the full employment yield of taxes in 1938, derived by a different approach. Kaldor estimated that the achievement of full employment (3 per cent unemployment) would have raised net national income by 10.7 per cent and been associated with an increase in central government receipts of 11.6 per cent. This gives an aggregate tax elasticity with respect to national income of 1.08, while our method (7.6–8.0 per cent unemployment) yielded a 3.1 per cent increase in revenue corresponding to an increase in GDP of 3.0 per cent, thus giving a marginally lower elasticity of 1.03.

The similarity between the two results provides corroborative evidence of the probable accuracy of the revenue side of our estimation procedure. The difference between the two aggregate tax elasticities is explained by:

1 Kaldor's estimate for direct taxes was (implicitly) on an accruals basis, whereas ours was on a payments basis, assuming a lag for income and surtax against GDP.

2 The major part of the growth of employment was assigned by Kaldor to a growth in incomes of the primary and secondary sectors so that, because of the productivity difference between these sectors and the service sector, output was increased significantly for a given increase in employment.
3 The significant difference between average and marginal shares of undistributed profits in income (7 and 23 per cent respectively) used by Kaldor resulted in a substantial proportion of the increase in income resulting from the attainment of full employment being put to a tax base whose elasticity with respect to income was markedly above the average for the fiscal system as a whole. Consequently, a given increase in incomes resulted in large increases in total receipts.

III EXPENDITURE

Transfer payments to the unemployed through the Unemployment Insurance Fund and transitional payments (later undertaken by the Unemployment Assistance Board) were the only items of endogenous expenditure adjusted,[5] although there were a number of other expenditures which were unemployment-related. These were not adjusted since their magnitude was small (reaching a peak of £11.5 million in 1931/2), and at our assumed rate of unemployment there would have remained a residual unemployment problem of some seriousness, necessitating expenditure on, for example, the depressed areas where unemployment rates were significantly in excess of the national average.

Outlay on unemployment benefits at constant employment were calculated as follows.[6] The total numbers unemployed and numbers claiming benefits were assumed at constant employment to have grown steadily year by year with the growth of the labour force (while the *numbers* unemployed increased, the unemployment *rate* remained within the range 10.8 to 11.1 per cent of the insured labour force). These figures were interpolated between the two base years to give their constant employment values. Three assumptions were then made.

1 Average benefits per claimant would have remained unchanged at constant employment.
2 The distribution of claimants between the two unemployment payments schemes would have remained unchanged.
3 The numbers claiming benefits as a ratio of the total numbers unemployed would have remained constant (at 0.83).

The results obtained by this method appear to pick up both discretionary changes and the effect of the growth in the numbers unemployed. Their reliability was tested by varying assumptions (2) and (3).

With regard to (2), the short-term unemployed essentially fell within the ambit of the unemployment insurance scheme while the long-term unemployed received their payments from the transitional payments/unemployment assistance scheme. The average cost per claimant was higher in the latter scheme, and hence a change in the average duration of unemployment could be expected to lead to a change in outlay on benefits.

Between 1929 and 1937, the two constant employment base years when unemployment rates were approximately similar, there was a marked increase in the

Table III.3 Central government expenditure: actual and constant employment 1929/30–1939/40 (£m.)

	1929/30	1930/1	1931/2	1932/3	1933/4	1934/5	1935/6	1936/7	1937/8	1938/9	1939/40
1 Total Ordinary and Self-Balancing Expenditure (G_c)	829.5	881.0	851.1	859.3	778.2	797.1	841.8	902.2	919.9	1,018.9	1,408.2
2 Expenditure adjustments	−32.4	−55.8	−14.4	+7.1	−1.2	−4.8	−2.0	+0.4	+71.4	+137.5	+506.6
3 Total benefits paid by social insurance funds	+155.9	+214.4	+239.8	+235.6	+221.0	+220.0	+222.9	+214.0	+220.7	+242.3	+220.1
4 Government contributions to social insurance funds	−76.5	−100.3	−116.3	−147.9	−141.3	−138.8	−143.0	−141.3	−144.8	−147.4	−144.7
5 Total expenditure at actual employment (G)	876.5	939.3	960.2	954.1	856.7	873.5	919.7	975.3	1,067.2	1,251.3	1,990.2
6 Adjustment to constant employment	—	−44.7	−58.1	−54.0	−33.4	−24.7	−17.0	−1.0	—	−15.5	+17.7
7 Total expenditure at constant employment (G^*)	876.5	894.6	902.1	900.1	823.3	848.8	902.7	974.3	1,067.2	1,235.8	2,007.9

Sources: *Financial Accounts*; table II.1; working notes to Feinstein (1972).

average duration of unemployment – the proportion of all applicants for unemployment benefits who had been unemployed for over 6 months (i.e. long-period unemployed) rose from 10.9 to 34.3 per cent (Beveridge 1944, table 8) – largely as a consequence of the intervening depression. If constant employment had been continuously achieved during these years it is likely that the observed duration of unemployment would have been rather different, and this might have affected outlay on unemployment benefits. To test this hypothesis, the ratio of unemployed receiving benefits under the insurance scheme was varied and it was found that the effect on total outlay was negligible: a 5 percentage points change in the ratio of claimants between the two schemes leading to an average change of only £0.52 million in total outlay on benefits at constant employment.

Assumption (3) was also found to have a minimal influence on our results: only in 1930/1 and 1938/9 would the constant employment outlay have been higher than our estimate if the actual ratio of claimants to total numbers unemployed had been left unadjusted, whilst for the rest of the period they would have been lower. The effect in each case was unimportant.

Total central government expenditure, at both actual and constant employment, is given in table III.3.

NOTES

CHAPTER 1 INTRODUCTION

1 Throughout the following chapters, the term the 'new' economics is used generally as consisting of the writings of Keynes from the late 1920s onwards; the work of the main disciples, Joan and Austin Robinson, Richard Kahn, Roy Harrod, James Meade and Nicholas Kaldor; and others such as Arthur Salter and Harold Macmillan who, while not themselves directly contributing to the developments in theoretical economics of the period, actively supported the new approach at a political level and were influential in its eventual official acceptance. An excellent account of the theoretical work of many of these economists is contained in Shackle (1967), while Harris (1948) and Davis (1971) look more broadly at Keynes and the 'new' economics.

CHAPTER 2 MASS UNEMPLOYMENT AND THE INTERWAR BRITISH ECONOMY

1 Such was the decline in the birth-rate in the 1930s that there arose widespread fears that the population might actually soon begin to fall (see Reddaway 1939 for a detailed discussion of population trends and their economic consequences). The 'population question' was of some importance to economic policy during the 1930s, a source of concern as regards the burden of the national debt and the potential of the economy for further growth.
2 The Ministry of Labour estimated in July 1929 that unemployment in the main staple trades accounted for approximately one-half of total unemployment amongst insured workers (cited in Aldcroft 1970a, 146). The greatest decline in employment occurred in the coal, textile and shipbuilding industries which released a total of 0.69 million workers between 1924–38, a fall in employment of 34.1 per cent (calculated from Aldcroft 1970a, table 22).
3 This paper has caused much controversy and misunderstanding – see Tomlinson (1978; 1982a) and Booth and Glynn (1980; 1982).

4 The Treasury's resolve to avoid deficit-financing was also strengthened by the fact that the debt position was considerably less favourable in Britain than in the US. Even with a doubling of the federal debt over 1932–9, largely as a consequence of the 'New Deal' policies, the debt/GDP ratio only rose from 0.334 to 0.446 (calculated from US Bureau of the Census 1975, I, 224; II, 1117), whereas in Britain, largely as a result of the heavy burden of war debts, the debt/GDP ratio averaged 1.53 over 1933/4–1938/9 (Middleton 1982, 54).
5 See HMSO (1931a, paras 306–19). Economists in the early 1930s pressed for a co-ordinated international reflation by a combination of monetary and fiscal measures, but such a policy never received unilateral governmental support, as instanced by the collapse of the 1933 World Economic Conference. It should be said, however, that the reluctance of governments to adopt this approach stemmed, not from doubts about its potential benefits, but from general uncertainty and domestic political pressures which made it difficult to abnegate the freedom to pursue an independent policy.
6 See, for example, Kahn (1931; 1933) and Keynes (1933). However, in the *General Theory*, Keynes (1936, 300–3) recognized that supply constraints might begin to operate before full employment was attained.
7 But see Glynn and Howells (1980) and Hatton (1982).

CHAPTER 3 THE TREASURY, ECONOMIC POLICY AND PUBLIC EXPENDITURE

1 Public expenditure as defined in table 3.1, p. 38. See table 3.2, p. 41, for the interwar data, OECD (1978, 12) for the postwar.
2 The sole exception was Sir Robert Horne, Chancellor from April 1921 to October 1922.
3 Newman (1972, 18). Her comments, strictly speaking, relate to the period 1918–25; nevertheless, the more detailed researches of Moggridge (1972) and Howson (1975) on this period would not lend support to her view.
4 For example, the failure of the 1929–31 Labour administration to tackle unemployment has traditionally been partially ascribed to Snowden's orthodoxy (e.g. Attlee 1954, 68–9, 72–3); for an opposing view, see McKibbin (1975).
5 There are also certain difficulties associated with the Cabinet papers as an historical source, in particular that the minutes of Cabinet meetings (PRO Cab23 papers) do not fully record disagreements between ministers (Roskill 1972, 476–7) while no record was made of the pre-budget meetings of the Cabinet.
6 Postwar inflations were not limited to the continental European countries, such as Germany. Indeed, the most rapid rate of inflation ever experienced by Britain in modern times occurred in the postwar boom of 1919–20. According to the Board of Trade wholesale price index the inflation rate was 42.5 per cent between April 1919 and April 1920 and at its worst (July 1919–February 1920) it reached 55.2 per cent on an annualized basis (data from Pigou 1947, appendix III, table IV). The experience of this inflation was to be a potent reminder throughout the interwar period of the consequences, *ceteris paribus*, of large-scale deficit-finance.

7 Mention should be made, however, of one sphere in which the general trend of an extension of the public sector did not operate to such a marked degree, that of employment (see Abramovitz and Eliasberg 1957). Public sector employment had expanded during the war, but as with expenditure, was curtailed in the immediate postwar period. Thereafter, public sector employment was only to rise marginally faster than total employment, increasing its share from 5.1 to 5.3 per cent over 1924–37 (Feinstein 1972, tables 57, 59, 60). There were, however, important compositional effects: employment in local government rose continuously, whereas employment in central government fell until the later 1920s and in the defence forces until the early 1930s.

8 See Mowat (1955, 129–31). The committee, established on 16 August 1921, was chaired by Sir Eric Geddes (formerly Minister of Transport), its terms of reference being 'to make recommendations to the Chancellor . . . for effecting forthwith all possible reductions in the National Expenditure on supply services, having regard especially to the present and prospective position of the Revenue'. Three reports were issued (HMSO 1922).

9 Figure 3.2 represents a slightly wider definition of public investment than that of table 3.4, the principal difference being the inclusion of public utilities (see Feinstein 1965, 46). Although many were private companies, their investment programmes were subject to some degree of governmental influence (Bretherton *et al.* 1941, ch. V).

10 The method adopted, at least initially, followed that of Price (1978, 124–8).

11 $Y = 0.118\ X_{t-1}^{1.4}$ $\qquad\qquad(R^2 = 0.41; DW = 0.97; t = 3.32)$
  (0.035)

where Y = public sector deviations and X = private sector deviations. Annual data were used for 1920–38, giving eighteen observations when account is taken of the one-year lag.

12 Of the various studies, Hicks (1938, 126–8) believed the effects of policy to be most destabilizing, while Bretherton *et al.* (1941, 359), Morton (1943, 331, 338) and Higgins (1946, ch. X), although critical of the policy stance, nevertheless tended towards the view that the effects of policy were generally near neutral.

13 Mention might also be made of the fact that after 1944 the full employment policy evolved from being a simple concern about using public investment to stabilize total investment to a more complex policy which sought also to stabilize demand in particular markets for investment goods, e.g. housing, plant and machinery (Price 1976, 52–3). The deficiencies of the data preclude a detailed analysis of this question for the interwar period, but from inspection of the figures for investment in dwellings (Feinstein 1965, table 3.34), the most important investment activity involving both the private and public sectors (and constituting an average of 29.5 per cent of GDFCF over 1920–38), it is clear that the activities of the public sector (in this case local authorities) were very often destabilizing. The difficulties caused by the unsatisfactory timing of many government investment projects not only generated adverse comment from economic and political critics but also prompted complaints from the building trades – see, for example, Building Industries National Council (1935).

14 This judgement of 1933 was made by Sir Charles Walker who had just retired as Deputy Secretary to the Admiralty (cited in Peden 1979b, 32).

15 See PRO (1933g, 1). Keynes was not unaware of this difficulty – see KP (1933, 2) – but seems to have taken no account of it.
16 Considerably more attention was given to these administrative constraints in the US than in the UK; for example, see the detailed studies of Woolman (1930), J. M. Clark (1935) and Gayer (1935).

CHAPTER 4 THE REVENUE DEPARTMENTS, TAXATION AND POLICY

1 Only Hicks (1938) has studied this general area in any depth, while Bretherton (1937) and Edelberg (1940) have studied taxation and the trade cycle.
2 See Griffith (1949) and Johnston (1965) for general accounts of the Inland Revenue, Crombie (1962) for Customs and Excise.
3 A number of Treasury officials had formerly served in Inland Revenue. Fisher had begun his career there and risen to Chairman in 1918, moving in 1919 to the Treasury as Permanent Secretary. Hopkins had followed a similar course, rising to Chairman by 1922 and then moving to the Treasury in 1927. More junior staff, such as E. Rowe-Dutton, had also served in the Inland Revenue. Nor was the movement of staff unidirectional: P. J. Grigg who had served in the Treasury (1918–30) moved first as Chairman of Customs and Excise (1930) and then to Inland Revenue (1930–4).
4 Chaired by Lord Colwyn, previously Chairman of the 1919–20 Royal Commission on the Income Tax (HMSO 1920), this committee had been established in March 1924 'to consider and report on the National Debt and on the incidence of existing taxation, with special reference to their effect on trade, industry, employment and national credit' (HMSO 1927a, viii).
5 The allowances were increased in 1931 and 1938, on both occasions as a partial offset to the increased standard rate of tax.
6 Some concessions, however, were made in 1937 (Dennison 1939, 89; Middleton 1985).

CHAPTER 5 THE BUDGET AND BUDGETARY POLICY: INTRODUCTION

1 Using the Treasury's internal receipts book (PRO T239/25–7) the exact date of a receipt can be pin-pointed. These registers show that, in general, the Treasury paid items into Miscellaneous Revenue in the third quarter of the financial year, thus reducing the central government deficit during the period when expenditure, irrespective of whether the final budget outturn was in balance, greatly exceeded revenue. If the budget forecast, however, was a deficit, although of an uncertain magnitude, receipts from items such as the profits of the Bank of England note issue and the Enemy Debt Clearing Office were taken in the final week of the financial year, their magnitude being varied (roughly) according to the sum necessary to balance the budget.
2 In modern parlance, there existed rational expectations of future taxes which deprived debt-financed government expenditure of all macroeconomic effect (see pp. 159–60 for a fuller discussion).
3 See, for example, Keynes (1937) and Meade (1937).

4 This problem was particularly acute with regard to the unemployment insurance system: 'Each successive Government has made changes in the scheme, which have been determined less by the need for the careful balancing of income and expenditure than by a desire to attract, or do as little as possible to repel, electoral support' (HMSO 1932a, 164).

5 See also Booth (1978) for the way in which the National Government, usually with Chamberlain as the motivating force, tried repeatedly to divorce policy questions from their political context. This was primarily achieved by creating administrative bodies, such as the Unemployment Assistance Board, which were quasi-independent of executive control.

6 For an early statement of this view, see Slichter (1934, 179–80); for recent critical analyses, see Currie (1978) and C. T. Taylor (1979).

7 See, however, R. M. Collins's (1981) study of the US business community which was much more vocal.

CHAPTER 6 BUDGETARY POLICY 1929–39

1 For a detailed serial discussion of the individual budgets, see Middleton (1981b, ch. 5).

2 See PRO (1931a; b) for clear evidence that the Cabinet discussed the possibility of cutting unemployment benefits as early as February 1931 (six months before the financial and political crisis).

3 Amongst the extensive literature on the 1931 crisis, the following accounts were of most use: Feiling (1946, 189–95), Clay (1957, 375–98), Bassett (1958), Skidelsky (1967, ch. 13) and Marquand (1977, ch. 25).

4 The individual budgets and budget debates from 1933 onwards are discussed in Sabine (1970), but readers should note that care must be exercised in using this work since it contains a great number of errors in its budget figures.

5 On assuming office in 1929 Snowden had also prepared estimates of the future budgetary situation, but this was a far less sophisticated exercise than that undertaken in 1932 (see PRO 1929b).

6 See, for example, a letter to *The Times* of 5 July 1932, signed by the leading economists of Cambridge, Oxford and eight other universities; and the further letter of 17 October 1932, signed by MacGregor, Pigou, Keynes, Layton, Salter and Stamp (see also the reply of 19 October signed by the LSE economists – Gregory, Hayek, Plant and Robbins, a letter which Robbins (1976, 88) now considers mistaken.

7 Strictly speaking this was beyond the terms of reference of the May Committee (HMSO 1931b, 4) which was charged with a review of 'Supply Services', not debt payments which were classified as 'Consolidated Fund Services'. This point, hitherto missed by students of the 1931 crisis, is important as further evidence that the Treasury were anxious to limit the scope of the debate about retrenchment.

8 See, for example, the two-day House of Lords debate at the end of June 1932 (*Hansard* 1932b; c); the Third Reading of the Finance Bill in the Commons earlier in the same month (*Hansard* 1932a); and the private members' economy report of later in the year (Mallet and George 1933, 474).

9 This change in policy explains the very negative reaction to the report of the Ray Committee on Local Expenditure (HMSO 1932c), a committee established in July 1932 to mollify more hawkish opinion, and which had recommended wide-ranging and controversial economies totalling £35–40 million. As with the May Committee, Ray treated the effects of the proposed economies as beyond its terms of reference.

10 Between 1935–7 the current balance deteriorated from a surplus of £23 million to a deficit of £47 million, a change of 1.4 percentage points of GDP. This deterioration primarily reflected the slow growth of exports (2 per cent) as compared with imports (6.2 per cent) – data from Feinstein (1972, tables 3, 5, 15). See PRO (1938f) for a detailed discussion by contemporary economists of the balance of payments implications of rearmament.

11 PRO (1939c; d). See also PRO (1939h, 6) for evidence of the Treasury's acceptance of the (Keynesian) savings–income relationship.

12 As Permanent Secretary to the Treasury Fisher's views obviously carried weight, but he was overruled on the budgets of 1936 and 1938, as well as 1939, indicating 'how limited Fisher's influence was on the purely fiscal aspects of policy' (Peden 1979a, 41).

13 On the eve of war the rearmament programme had grown to £2,100 million over 1939/40–1941/2, of which it was planned to borrow £1,190 million (PRO 1939f, 3–4).

CHAPTER 7 AN ASSESSMENT OF CHANGES IN FISCAL STANCE 1929–39

1 This chapter draws upon Middleton (1981a; 1984).

2 See Stein (1969, 185–6) and Okun and Teeters (1970, 78–9) for discussions of the development of this concept in the US during the Second World War.

3 See Lotz (1971, 4–7); and, for an example of a recent application of this method to an historical example, Pryor (1979).

4 A number of writers – for example, Lotz (1971, 14, 18) and Chand (1977, 411) – have suggested that discretion is required in using the constant employment balance measure because a change in the budget balance resulting from a given fiscal policy change measured at constant employment may differ from that measured at actual employment levels, i.e. the measure implicitly assumes that the ranking of budgets at constant employment is invariant to the degree of capacity utilization. But, as Chand says, if 'the tax structure underlying one budget is more progressive than that underlying another budget, the ranking at actual output levels could involve reversals from the full employment ranking, the likelihood of which increases, the further the economy is from its full employment level. Thus, what might appear to be a more expansionary budget at full employment could, in reality, be a more contractionary budget at actual employment levels.' This was not a problem in this study since the progressiveness of the tax structure did not change significantly over the period.

5 This is illustrated by a comparison of changes in the constant employment

balance as a percentage of GNP for three more recent years using different estimates based on different benchmark rates of unemployment:

Changes in constant employment budget balance as % of GNP

	1974–5	1975–6	1976–7
Treasury			
(5% unemployment)	–1.0	+2.7	+3.5
(3% unemployment)	–1.3	+2.7	+3.3
National Institute			
(2.6% unemployment)	+1.0	+2.4	+4.5
Ward and Neild			
(2–2.5% unemployment)	–0.9	+2.8	+2.7

Source: Calculated from Hartley and Bean (1978, table 1).

6 During the downturn of 1929–32 employment and output (at current prices) in the industrial sector fell by 10.5 and 16.8 per cent respectively, while in the service sector employment increased by 3.9 per cent but output fell by 7.1 per cent (Feinstein 1972, tables 9, 59).
7 The measures used, and the method of computation, follow the work of Ward and Neild (1978, ch. 3).
8 See, however, Broadberry (1984) and Middleton (1984).
9 In accordance with our definition of discretionary action (p. 125), b_t can be taken as a measure of the extent of fiscal drag in the system.
10 For example, Nevin (1955, 69, 76–82) partially attributes the recovery of bond prices in early 1932 – a recovery which aided the transition to cheap money – to the recovery of confidence engendered by the balancing of the budget and the formation of the National Government. Against these beneficial effects, however, must be placed the possibility that the 0.6 per cent fall in consumers expenditure over 1931–2 – as compared with a rise of 2.6 per cent over 1929–31 – resulted from the tightening of fiscal stance.
11 However, rearmament's opportunity cost should not be excluded from account: the export orders forgone as firms sought to satisfy rearmament demands. The magnitude of this effect remains uncertain.

CHAPTER 8 THE 'TREASURY VIEW' AND PUBLIC WORKS

1 See Hawtrey (1925), Hancock (1960; 1962), Winch (1972), J. Robinson (1976), Howson and Winch (1977), Skidelsky (1981) and Peden (1983a; 1984).
2 For a contemporary view, see Keynes (1929; 1933, 350); for later assessments, see Skidelsky (1967, 25), J. Robinson (1976, 71) and Hutchison (1978, 155).
3 Whilst there is little of substance in the charge that the Ministry of Labour were by their calculations attempting to 'explain away' the unemployment problem, in a rather different sense their arguments were somewhat disingenuous, viz. that their calculations were in terms of the insured workforce and thus ignored,

first, those not included in this category, and secondly, the effects of higher economic activity upon participation rates.
4 See, for example, Lavington (1921, 171-3) for the former, Pigou (1924a, pt II, ch. IX) for the latter.
5 See Hayek (1933, 20-1, 212ff; 1935, 98-9, 125, 128). Howson (1975, 91) records that in 1932 Phillips expressed his general approval of Hayek's theoretical position.
6 The following discussion draws upon Lonie (1980, 15-25) who uses both neoclassical loan fund analysis and an *IS-LM* approach in his investigation of the 'Treasury view'; the present author's findings accord closely with those of Lonie, and his work has encouraged me both to incorporate the *IS-LM* approach in this study and to broaden the compass of the analysis.
7 For a more comprehensive specification of the Keynesian and monetarist models, see Tobin (1974).
8 Dr K. G. P. Matthews of the University of Liverpool is researching in this area.
9 For studies of other national public works policies, see International Labour Office (1931; 1935), League of Nations (1934) and Royal Institute of International Affairs (1935).

CHAPTER 9 CONCLUSIONS

1 See Howson (1980) for an account of sterling's managed float, Redmond (1980) for the course of the effective exchange rate, and Capie (1978; 1983) for an assessment of the effectiveness of tariff protection.
2 At the upper turning-point in 1937 – when insured unemployment had fallen to 1.4 million – Phillips estimated that unemployment of $1\frac{1}{4}$ million was 'probably a normal figure (some 800,000 being the absolute minimum in the wildest boom)' (PRO 1937e). He did not indicate how the normal figure was to be achieved.
3 Kahn's (1931, 186) preferred value was 1.88, with a possible range 1.56–1.94; Keynes, who relied more upon intuition than detailed calculation, favoured the range 2–3, with a value certainly no less than $1\frac{1}{2}$ (1933, 341; 1936, ch. 10); C. G. Clark's (1938, 442) estimated values were 2.07 for 1929–33 and 3.22 for 1933–7; Stone and Stone (1938, table 4), who neglected the import leakage, obtained an estimate of 2.1; while Bretherton *et al.* (1941, 316) calculated income, employment and expenditure multipliers of 1.60–1.85, 1.18–1.58 and 1.03–1.39 for 1930–6 respectively. In none of these studies was the distinction drawn between impact and long-run multipliers.
4 Aldcroft (1984, ch. 3) also addresses this question.
5 As De Cecco (1977, 18–19) has noted, Keynes 'remained convinced till the last that only the dismal mediocrity of politicians, the shortsightedness of entrepreneurs, the imbecility of the rentier and incompetence and greed of bankers prevented Britain from reaching an age of plenty, a new and lasting renaissance'. Keynes was, however, on very good terms with Hopkins and Phillips (Robbins 1971, 187).
6 For a balanced view, see Tomlinson (1982b); see also Glynn and Booth (1983) and Lonie (1984).

7 The phrase, 'recurrent themes in British economic policy', is drawn from Ham (1981).
8 See Booth (1983; 1984) and Tomlinson (1984).

APPENDIX III THE ESTIMATION OF CONSTANT EMPLOYMENT RECEIPTS AND EXPENDITURE

1 This method has been used most successfully by Prest (1962).
2 This method was favoured because estimates of the effect of discretionary action for these taxes were probably more susceptible to inaccuracy the further away from the base year than estimates for other taxes.
3 Owing to the efforts of direct taxpayers in 1931/2 who had paid their surtax promptly, the yield was significantly above the estimate. With few arrears to collect the following year, the yield was considerably below the estimate. Thus, for a given change in GDP, there was an unrepresentative change in yield, and consequently the very high elasticity for 1931/2 to 1932/3 is spurious and should be left out of account.
4 This method was tested by standardizing contributions on to a 1931 constant rate basis, adjusting them by the ratio to derive constant employment values, and then, by regression analysis, relating them to constant employment GDP. The only year of any marked divergence from the relationship, 1939/40, is explained by the growth of the armed forces (which, under §41(1) of the Unemployment Insurance Act, 1920, did not contribute directly to the Unemployment Fund) and the decline of civil employment due to the demands of the war economy.
5 Benefits paid by the other social insurance schemes were assumed to be autonomous. Eligibility for health and pension benefits was largely unaffected by unemployment (Davison 1938, 60–1), while early retirement was not used as a means of mitigating unemployment.
6 The calculation of a satisfactory series for outlay on unemployment benefits presented innumerable difficulties. It proved impossible to derive a satisfactory statistical function relating the level of unemployment to outlay on unemployment benefits, nor was there a direct relationship with changes in GDP. It seems that a conflation of unemployment duration effects and numerous discretionary changes in benefit rates and eligibility for unemployment benefits were responsible for these difficulties.

BIBLIOGRAPHY

Place of publication is London unless otherwise stated.

1 UNPUBLISHED PAPERS

(i) Archives

CE Customs and Excise Papers, HM Customs and Excise Library, London:

(1929) F. L. C. Floud [Chairman, Board of Customs and Excise] to P. J. Grigg, 13 July.
(1934) A. D. Webb [Director, Intelligence Branch, Customs and Excise] to H. J. B. Lintott [Private Secretary to Chairman], 27 March.
(1938) A. D. Webb, 'Possible increases in duty', 6 February.

CP Neville Chamberlain Papers, University Library, Birmingham:

(1934a) NC2/23a, Diary, 6 February.
(1934b) NC2/23a, Diary, 16 March.
(1934c) NC18/1/864, Neville to Ida Chamberlain, 17 March.
(1935a) NC2/23a, Diary, 28 January.
(1935b) NC2/23a, Diary, 2 August.
(1935c) NC2/23a, Diary, 19 October.

FBI Federation of British Industries Papers, Confederation of British Industries Archives, London:

(1930) FBI Committees (June–December), 'Memorandum re. economy', 27 November.
(1931a) FBI/C/61, vol. 131, 'Meeting preliminary to deputation to Financial Secretary to the Treasury', 17 March.
(1931b) FBI/EA/GLENDAY/9, 'Draft report for the Economic Emergency Committee', 16 November.

KP J. M. Keynes Papers, Marshall Library, University of Cambridge:
(1931a) EA/1, H. D. Henderson to J. M. Keynes, 14 February.
(1931b) L/31, J. M. Keynes to J. R. MacDonald, 5 August.
(1933) A33₂, H. D. Henderson to J. M. Keynes, 28 February.

(ii) Public Record Office (PRO)

(1923) T160/639/F6064, 'Treasury control', 6 March.
(1928) T175/18, Economy in government expenditure – correspondence and memoranda.
(1929a) MT39/134, C. H. Bressey [Chief Engineer, Ministry of Transport Road Department] to Secretary, 21 March.
(1929b) Cab24/207, CP344(29), memorandum by the Chancellor of the Exchequer, 'The growth of expenditure', 29 November.
(1930a) T172/1690, P. Snowden to W. S. Churchill, 23 January.
(1930b) T175/26, F. W. Leith-Ross, 'Note on Mr Keynes' exposition to the Committee on Finance and Industry. Discussion of 20/02/30', undated.
(1930c) IR63/126, E. A. Gowers [Chairman, Board of Inland Revenue 1927–30] to P. Snowden, 24 February.
(1930d) T175/26, F. W. Leith-Ross, 'The assumptions of Mr Keynes', 27 February.
(1930e) T161/577/S34462/4, 'Progress of road programmes', memorandum by the Minister of Transport, 9 April.
(1930f) T175/26, R. V. N. Hopkins, 'The Liberal plan. Draft notes for evidence', undated (but internal evidence suggests early May).
(1930g) IR63/126, E. A. Gowers to P. Snowden, 4 July.
(1930h) IR63/130, E. A. Gowers to P. J. Grigg, 'Forecasts for 1930 and 1931', 6 October.
(1930i) Cab23/65, Cabinet 62(30)6, 22 October.
(1931a) Cab23/90B, CP31(31), memorandum by Minister of Labour, 'Unemployment insurance – emergency financial measures', 5 February.
(1931b) Cab23/66, Cabinet 12(31)2, 5 February.
(1931c) Cab23/66, Cabinet 13(31)4, 11 February.
(1931d) PRO30/69/677, J. M. Keynes to J. R. MacDonald, 5 March.
(1931e) T171/287, R. V. N. Hopkins to P. Snowden, undated (but about 19 March).
(1931f) T175/51, 'Chancellor of the Exchequer', undated and unsigned memorandum. (From the handwriting the author was almost certainly Hopkins, and internal evidence suggests a dating of 27 July.)
(1931g) PRO30/69/260, H. D. Henderson to J. R. MacDonald, 'The economy report', 7 August.
(1931h) PRO30/69/260, R. B. Howorth [Deputy Secretary to Cabinet 1930–42] to H. D. Henderson, 8 August.
(1931i) IR63/132, P. Thompson [Deputy Chairman, Board of Inland Revenue] to R. V. N. Hopkins, 10 August.
(1931j) IR63/132, 'Proposal for all round percentage increase of taxation', 13 August.
(1931k) IR63/132, A. L. Beck [Assistant Director, Statistics and Intelligence Branch, Inland Revenue], 'Memo. on increase and rate of I.T. and alteration of allowances', 16 August.

(1931l) IR63/132, R. V. N. Hopkins, 'Economy or taxation', undated (but about 17 August).
(1931m) IR63/132, W. Fisher, R. V. N. Hopkins, P. J. Grigg and A. J. Dyke [Deputy Chairman, Board of Customs and Excise] to P. Snowden, 18 August.
(1931n) Cab23/67, Cabinet 41(31)1, 19 August.
(1931o) Cab23/67, Cabinet 42(31)2A, 21 August.
(1931p) Cab23/67, Cabinet 44(31)1, 22 August.
(1931q) IR63/132, letter to Chancellor, 27 August.
(1931r) IR63/132, P. J. Grigg to J. D. B. Fergusson [Private Secretary to successive Chancellors of the Exchequer 1920–36], 17 September.
(1932a) Cab27/468, CP36(32), Cabinet Employment Policy Committee, Report, 25 January.
(1932b) T171/296, F. L. C. Floud [Permanent Secretary, Ministry of Labour] to R. V. N. Hopkins, 12 February.
(1932c) T171/296, R. V. N. Hopkins to W. Fisher and N. Chamberlain, 12 February.
(1932d) T171/296, note by Hopkins, 11 March.
(1932e) T171/296, R. V. N. Hopkins to W. Fisher and N. Chamberlain, 11 March; and marginal note by Chamberlain dated 13 March.
(1932f) T175/59, pt I, R. V. N. Hopkins to E. R. Forber [Chairman, Board of Customs and Excise 1931–4, Inland Revenue 1934–8], 15 March.
(1932g) T171/296, R. V. N. Hopkins, 'Budget estimate: 1932', 15 March.
(1932h) T171/296, F. L. C. Floud to J. D. B. Fergusson, 17 March.
(1932i) Cab24/229, CP105(32), note by the Treasury, 'Imperial defence policy', 17 March.
(1932j) T188/48, R. V. N. Hopkins to N. Chamberlain, 'Speculative forecast of 1935 on the basis of "Old Moore's Almanack"', 21 March.
(1932k) Cab23/70, Cabinet 19(32)2, 23 March.
(1932l) T171/296, note by Hopkins, 4 April.
(1932m) T171/296, P. J. Grigg to J. D. B. Fergusson, 11 April.
(1932n) T175/67, B. W. Gilbert [Assistant Secretary, Treasury], 'Memorandum on national expenditure', undated (but internal evidence suggests 2–3 May).
(1932o) T175/67, A. P. Waterfield [Principal Assistant Secretary, Treasury] to R. V. N. Hopkins, 3 May.
(1932p) T175/57, pt I, note by Phillips, 6 June.
(1932q) T172/1790, 'Notes on economy', undated (but internal evidence suggests early July).
(1932r) T171/309, F. Phillips, 'Budget forecasts', 29 October.
(1933a) T160/473/F12116/33/1, R. V. N. Hopkins to W. Fisher and N. Chamberlain, 7 February.
(1933b) T175/17, pt I, R. V. N. Hopkins to J. D. B. Fergusson, 15 February.
(1933c) T175/17, pt I, F. Phillips to R. V. N. Hopkins, 28 February.
(1933d) T175/17, pt I, F. Phillips, 'Mr. Keynes' first and second articles', 15 March.
(1933e) T175/17, pt I, F. Phillips, 'Questions for Keynes', undated (but internal evidence suggests 15–16 March).
(1933f) T171/309, F. Phillips and R. V. N. Hopkins, 'Budget 1933/4. Forecasts on basis of existing taxation', 18 March.
(1933g) T175/17, pt II, 'Mr. Keynes' first article in the "Times"', memorandum by R. V. N. Hopkins, 30 March.

(1933h) T171/309, Treasury memorandum, 'War loan depreciation fund', undated (but late March).
(1933i) T171/309, R. V. N. Hopkins to J. D. B. Fergusson, 6 April.
(1933j) T171/309, R. V. N. Hopkins, 'Arguments against unbalancing the budget', undated (but about 7 April).
(1933k) T188/72, F. Phillips to F. W. Leith-Ross, 'Recovery from the trade depression', 21 September.
(1933l) Cab23/77, Cabinet 68(33)5, 6 December.
(1933m) PRO30/69/1753, Ramsay MacDonald Diary, 6 December. (The contents of these diaries were, in MacDonald's words, 'meant as notes to guide and revive memory as regards happenings and must on no account be published as they are'.)
(1934a) T171/315, J. D. B. Fergusson to N. Chamberlain, 22 January.
(1934b) T171/315, 'Customs and Excise revenue in 1933–34 and preliminary estimate for 1934–35', 9 March.
(1934c) T171/317, J. D. B. Fergusson to N. Chamberlain, 14 December.
(1935a) T175/89, note by Phillips, 31 January.
(1935b) T171/317, note by Phillips, 11 February.
(1935c) T171/317, R. V. N. Hopkins to W. Fisher and N. Chamberlain, 12 February.
(1935d) T171/317, R. V. N. Hopkins to J. D. B. Fergusson and W. Fisher, 20 February.
(1935e) T161/672/S40504/09/2, F. Phillips to B. W. Gilbert and J. A. N. Barlow [Under Secretary, Treasury], 27 February.
(1935f) IR63/140, 'Inland Revenue estimate for 1935', 7 March.
(1935g) T171/317, L. Hore-Belisha [Minister of Transport] to N. Chamberlain, 12 April.
(1935h) T160/688/F14996/1, R. V. N. Hopkins to W. Fisher and N. Chamberlain, 7 October.
(1935i) T160/688/F14996/1, W. Fisher to Chancellor, 2 December.
(1935j) T171/324, note by Hopkins, 2 December.
(1936a) T171/324, F. Phillips, '1936/37 budget', 22 February.
(1936b) T171/324, R. V. N. Hopkins to W. Fisher and N. Chamberlain, 24 February; marginal note by Fisher.
(1936c) T171/324, F. Phillips, '1936/37 budget', 25 March; marginal note by Fisher.
(1936d) T171/315, A. P. Waterfield to R. V. N. Hopkins, 4 April.
(1936e) T171/324, note by Hopkins, 8 April.
(1936f) T172/1828, E. R. Forber to J. A. N. Barlow, 16 November.
(1936g) T172/1828, 'Note by Inland Revenue on taxation proposals in paragraph 30 of the third report of the Commissioner for the Special Areas', 16 November.
(1936h) T172/1828, R. V. N. Hopkins to Chancellor, 16 November.
(1936i) T177/25, F. Phillips to W. R. Fraser [Principal Assistant Secretary, Treasury], 'Financing the defence programme', 27 November.
(1937a) T171/332, note by Phillips, 18 January.
(1937b) T175/96, R. V. N. Hopkins to J. H. E. Woods [Private Secretary to successive Chancellors of the Exchequer 1936–40], 16 February.
(1937c) T171/332, note by Phillips, 10 March.

(1937d) T175/94, pt II, marginal note by Hopkins to note by Phillips, undated (but October–December).
(1937e) T161/783/S48431/3, note by Phillips, 29 October.
(1937f) Cab24/273, CP316(37), interim report by the Minister for Co-ordination of Defence, 'Defence expenditure in future years', 15 December.
(1937g) T171/340, R. V. N. Hopkins, 'Civil estimates 1938/9', 15 December.
(1937h) T161/855/S48431/01/2, R. V. N. Hopkins to W. Fisher and J. H. E. Woods, 20 December.
(1938a) Cab27/640, CP6(38), memorandum by the Chancellor of the Exchequer, covering reports by an interdepartmental committee, 20 January.
(1938b) T171/340, note by Chancellor of the Exchequer, 16 March.
(1938c) T171/340, R. V. N. Hopkins to J. A. Simon, 17 March.
(1938d) T175/104, pt II, R. V. N. Hopkins to W. Fisher and J. H. E. Woods, 7 July.
(1938e) T171/341, F. Phillips to R. V. N. Hopkins, 15 December.
(1938f) Cab58/30, EAC(SC)33, Committee on Economic Information, 26th report, 'Problems of rearmament', 16 December.
(1938g) T175/104, pt I, F. W. Leith-Ross, 'Twenty-sixth EAC report', 22 December.
(1939a) T171/341, W. Fisher to J. A. Simon, 'Budget 1939–40', 3 January.
(1939b) T171/341, J. A. Simon to R. V. N. Hopkins, 13 February.
(1939c) T175/104, pt II, note by Hopkins and Phillips, undated (but February).
(1939d) T177/47, F. Phillips to R. V. N. Hopkins, 24 April.
(1939e) T208/201, note by Phillips, 29 April.
(1939f) Cab24/287, CP149(39), 'Note on the financial situation', 3 July.
(1939g) PREM1/365, note by the Treasury, 18 July.
(1939h) T160/1289/F19426/3, report of Committee on Control of Savings and Investment, 11 August.
(1940) T171/349, 'Review of 1939–40', undated.
(1942a) T230/94, J. E. Meade to H. Clay [Economic adviser to Bank of England], 4 May.
(1942b) T230/94, R. V. N. Hopkins to H. Clay, 13 May.

2 SERIAL PUBLICATIONS

Commissioners of His Majesty's Customs and Excise, *Reports*, annual.
Commissioners of His Majesty's Inland Revenue, *Reports*, annual.
The Economist.
Financial Accounts of the United Kingdom, House of Commons paper, annual.
Financial Statements, House of Commons paper, annual.
Ministry of Labour, *Reports*, annual.
Ministry of Transport, *Reports of the Administration of the Road Fund*, annual.
The Times.

3 HANSARD (Parliamentary Debates, 5th ser.)

(1931a) 'Financial statement by the Chancellor of the Exchequer', House of Commons, 251, 27 April, 1391–1411.
(1931b) 'Financial statement by the Chancellor of the Exchequer', House of Commons, 256, 10 September, 297–313.

(1932a) Third Reading of Finance Bill, House of Commons, 266, 10 June, 2267–348.
(1932b) Debate on public expenditure, House of Lords, 85, 22 June, 67–126.
(1932c) Debate on public expenditure, House of Lords, 85, 29 June, 294–352.
(1933a) Statement by J. R. MacDonald, House of Commons, 274, 7 February, 13–15.
(1933b) Statement by S. Baldwin, House of Commons, 275, 1 March, 437–44.
(1933c) Statement by H. Macmillan, House of Commons, 276, 22 March, 346–55.
(1933d) 'Financial statement by the Chancellor of the Exchequer', House of Commons, 277, 25 April, 31–65.
(1934) 'Financial statement by the Chancellor of the Exchequer', House of Commons, 288, 17 April, 905–929.
(1935) 'Financial statement by the Chancellor of the Exchequer', House of Commons, 300, 15 April, 1617–38.
(1936) Statement by N. Chamberlain, House of Commons, 314, 3 July, 812–23.
(1937) Comment by A. V. Alexander upon the King's Speech, House of Commons, 328, 27 October, 201–2.
(1938) Statement by N. Chamberlain, House of Commons, 331, 10 February, 1229–32.
(1941) 'Financial statement by the Chancellor of the Exchequer', House of Commons, 370, 7 April, 1297–332.
(1979) Comment by E. Powell upon the budget speech, House of Commons, 968, 18 June, 948.

4 HMSO (Official reports and other government papers)

(1918) Committee on Currency and Foreign Exchanges After the War (Cunliffe Committee), *First Interim Report*, BPP 1918 (9182), vii, 853.
(1920) Royal Commission on the Income Tax (Colwyn Commission), *Report*, BPP 1920 (615), xviii, 97.
(1922) Committee on National Expenditure (Geddes Committee), *First Interim Report*, BPP 1922 (1581), ix, 1; *Second Interim Report*, BPP 1922 (1582), ix, 173; *Third Report*, BPP 1922 (1589), ix, 287.
(1927a) Committee on National Debt and Taxation (Colwyn Committee), *Report*, BPP 1927 (2800), xi, 371.
(1927b) Committee on National Debt and Taxation (Colwyn Committee), *Minutes of Evidence*, 2 vols.
(1928) Industrial Transference Board, *Report*, BPP 1928 (3156), x, 783.
(1929) *Memoranda on Certain Proposals Relating to Unemployment*, BPP 1928–9 (3331), xvi, 873.
(1931a) Committee on Finance and Industry (Macmillan Committee), *Report*, BPP 1930–1 (3897), xiii, 219.
(1931b) Committee on National Expenditure (May Committee), *Report*, BPP 1930–1 (3920), xvi, 1.
(1931c) *Memorandum on the Measures proposed by His Majesty's Government to secure Reductions in National Expenditure*, BPP 1930–1 (3952), xviii, 371.
(1931d) Committee on Finance and Industry (Macmillan Committee), *Minutes of Evidence*, 2 vols.
(1932a) Royal Commission on Unemployment Insurance (Gregory Commission), *Final Report*, BPP 1931–2 (4185), xiii, 393.

(1932b) Royal Commission on Unemployment Insurance (Gregory Commission), *Minutes of Evidence*, 2 vols.
(1932c) Committee on Local Expenditure (England and Wales) (Ray Committee), *Report*, BPP 1932–3 (4200), xiv, 1.
(1932d) Committee on Local Expenditure (Scotland) (Lovat Committee), *Report*, BPP 1932–3 (4201), xiv, 175.
(1934) Ministry of Labour, *Investigations into the Industrial Conditions in certain Depressed Areas*, BPP 1933–4 (4728), xiii, 313.
(1936) Ministry of Labour, *Third Report of the Commissioner for the Special Areas (England and Wales)*, BPP 1936–7 (5303), xii, 661.
(1937) *Charge of National Defence Contribution*, BPP 1936–7 (5485), xvii, 1139.
(1940) *Statistical Abstract for the United Kingdom, 1924–1938*, Cmd 6232.
(1941) *An Analysis of the Sources of War Finance and an Estimate of the National Income and Expenditure in 1938 and 1940*, BPP 1940–1 (6261), viii, 387.
(1944) Ministry of Reconstruction, *Employment Policy*, BPP 1943–4 (6527), viii, 119.
(1948) Central Statistical Office, *Annual Abstract of Statistics, 1935–46*, 84.
(1961) Control of Public Expenditure (Plowden Committee), *Report*, BPP 1960–1 (1432), xxi, 713.
(1971) Department of Employment and Productivity, *British Labour Statistics: Historical Abstract 1886–1968*.
(1976) Committee of Inquiry into Local Government Finance (Layfield Committee), app. 6, *The Relationship between Central and Local Governments: Evidence and Commissioned Work*.
(1978) *National Income and Expenditure 1967–77*.
(1982) *Corporation Tax*, Cmnd 8456.
(1983) Central Statistical Office, *Economic Trends*, 355.

5 BOOKS AND ARTICLES

Abramovitz, M. and Eliasberg, V. F. (1957) *The Growth of Public Employment in Great Britain*, Princeton, University Press/National Bureau of Economic Research.
Aldcroft, D. H. (1966) 'Economic progress in Britain in the 1920s', *Scottish Journal of Political Economy*, 13 (3), 297–316. Reprinted in D. H. Aldcroft and H. W. Richardson (eds) (1969) q.v. 219–38.
—— (1967) 'Economic growth in Britain in the inter-war years: a reassessment', *Economic History Review*, 2nd ser., 20 (3), 311–26. Reprinted in D. H. Aldcroft and P. Fearon (eds) (1969) q.v. 34–54.
—— (1969) 'The development of the managed economy before 1939', *Journal of Contemporary History*, 4 (4), 117–37.
—— (1970a) *The Inter-War Economy: Britain 1919–1939*, Batsford.
——(1970b) 'The impact of British monetary policy 1919–1939', *Revue Internationale d'Histoire de la Banque*, 3, 37–65.
—— (1984) *Full Employment: The elusive goal*, Brighton, Wheatsheaf Books.
Aldcroft, D. H. and Fearon, P. (eds) (1969) *Economic Growth in Twentieth-century Britain*, Macmillan.
—— and —— (eds) (1972) *British Economic Fluctuations 1790–1939*, Macmillan.

Aldcroft, D. H. and Richardson, H. W. (eds) (1969) *The British Economy 1870–1939*, Macmillan.
Alford, B. W. E. (1972) *Depression and Recovery? British economic growth 1918–1939*, Macmillan.
Allen, G. C. (1950) 'Economic progress, retrospect and prospect', *Economic Journal*, 60 (3), 461–80.
Amery, L. S. (1955) *My Political Life*, vol. III: *The Unforgiving Years 1929–1940*, Hutchinson.
Archibald, G. C. (1967) 'Regional multiplier effects in the UK', *Oxford Economic Papers* n.s., 19 (1), 22–45.
Armstrong Report (1980) *Budgetary Reform in the UK. Report of a Committee chaired by Lord Armstrong of Sanderstead*, Oxford, University Press/Institute for Fiscal Studies.
Arndt, H. W. (1944) *The Economic Lessons of the Nineteen-Thirties*, Oxford University Press.
Atkinson, A. B. and Stiglitz, J. E. (1980) *Lectures on Public Economics*, New York, McGraw-Hill.
Attlee, C. R. (1954) *As It Happened*, Heinemann.
Bacon, R. and Eltis, W. (1976) *Britain's Economic Problems: Too few producers*, Macmillan.
Baily, M. N. (1978) 'Stabilization policy and private economic behavior', *Brookings Papers on Economic Activity*, (1), 11–50.
Balogh, T. (1936) 'Economic policy and re-armament in Britain', *The Manchester School*, 7 (3), 77–90.
Barna, T. (1945) *Redistribution of Incomes through Public Finance in 1937*, Oxford, Clarendon Press.
Barro, R. J. (1974) 'Are government bonds net wealth?', *Journal of Political Economy*, 82 (6), 1095–117. Reprinted in R. J. Barro (1981) q.v. 243–65.
—— (1981) *Money, Expectations and Business Cycles: Essays in macroeconomics*, New York, Academic Press.
Barry, E. E. (1965) *Nationalisation in British Politics: The historical background*, Jonathan Cape.
Bassett, R. (1958) *Nineteen Thirty-One: Political crisis*, Macmillan.
Baumol, W. J. and Peston, M. H. (1955) 'More on the multiplier effects of a balanced budget', *American Economic Review*, 45 (1), 140–8.
Beck, G. M. (1951) *A Survey of British Employment and Unemployment 1927–45*, Oxford, University of Oxford Institute of Statistics.
Beer, S. H. (1956) *Treasury Control: The co-ordination of financial and economic policy in Great Britain*, Oxford, Clarendon Press.
Beloff, M. (1975) 'The Whitehall factor: the role of the higher civil service 1919–39', in C. Cook and G. Peele (eds) (1975) *The Politics of Reappraisal 1918–1939*, Macmillan, 209–31.
Benham, F. (1932) *Go Back to Gold*, Faber & Faber.
Benjamin, D. K. and Kochin, L. A. (1979) 'Searching for an explanation of unemployment in interwar Britain', *Journal of Political Economy*, 87 (3), 441–78.
—— and —— (1982) 'Unemployment and unemployment benefits in twentieth-century Britain: a reply to our critics', *Journal of Political Economy*, 90 (2), 410–36.

Beveridge, W. H. (1936) 'An analysis of unemployment – I', *Economica* n.s., 3 (4), 357–86.
—— (1937a) 'An analysis of unemployment – II', *Economica* n.s., 4 (1), 1–17.
—— (1937b) 'An analysis of unemployment – III', *Economica* n.s., 4 (2), 168–83.
—— (1944) *Full Employment in a Free Society*, George Allen & Unwin.
Blackaby, F. T. (ed.) (1978) *British Economic Policy 1960–74*, Cambridge, University Press.
—— (1979) 'The economics and politics of demand management: a review of British experience', in S. T. Cook and P. M. Jackson (eds) (1979) q.v. 185–97.
Blake, R. (1976) *The Conservative Party from Peel to Churchill*, Fontana/Collins.
Blinder, A. S. and Solow, R. M. (1974) 'Analytical foundations of fiscal policy', in A. S. Blinder and R. M. Solow *et al.* (1974) *The Economics of Public Finance*, Washington D.C., Brookings Institution, 3–115.
Booth, A. E. (1978) 'An administrative experiment in unemployment policy in the 'thirties', *Public Administration*, 56 (2), 139–57.
—— (1983) 'The "Keynesian revolution" in economic policy-making', *Economic History Review*, 2nd ser., 36 (1), 103–23.
—— (1984) 'Defining a "Keynesian revolution"', *Economic History Review*, 2nd ser., 37 (2), 263–7.
Booth, A. E. and Glynn, S. (1975) 'Unemployment in the interwar period: a multiple problem', *Journal of Contemporary History*, 10 (4), 611–36.
—— and —— (1979) 'The public records and recent British economic historiography', *Economic History Review*, 2nd ser., 32 (3), 303–15.
—— and —— (1980) 'Interwar unemployment: restatement and comments', *Journal of Contemporary History*, 15 (4), 761–8.
—— and —— (1982) 'Interwar unemployment – two views', *Journal of Contemporary History*, 17 (3), 550–5.
Bretherton, R. F. (1937) 'The sensitivity of taxes to fluctuations of trade', *Econometrica*, 5 (2), 171–83.
Bretherton, R. F., Burchardt, F. A. and Rutherford, R. S. G. (1941) *Public Investment and the Trade Cycle in Great Britain*, Oxford, Clarendon Press.
Bridges, E. E. (1950a) *Treasury Control*, Athlone Press.
—— (1950b) *Portrait of a Profession: The civil service tradition*, Cambridge, University Press.
—— (1966) *The Treasury*, 2nd edn, George Allen & Unwin.
Brittan, S. (1964) *The Treasury under the Tories 1951–1964*, Harmondsworth, Penguin Books.
Broadberry, S. N. (1982) 'Unemployment in interwar Britain: a disequilibrium approach', University of Oxford, unpublished D. Phil. dissertation.
—— (1983) 'Unemployment in interwar Britain: a disequilibrium approach', *Oxford Economic Papers* n.s., 35 (3), 463–85.
—— (1984) 'Fiscal policy in Britain during the 1930s', *Economic History Review*, 2nd ser., 37 (1), 95–102.
Brown, E. C. (1956) 'Fiscal policy in the 'thirties: a reappraisal', *American Economic Review*, 46 (5), 857–79.
Brown, J. A. (1940) 'The 1937 recession in England', *Harvard Business Review*, 18 (4), 248–60.

Buchanan, J. M., Burton, J. and Wagner, R. E. (1978) *The Consequences of Mr Keynes: An analysis of the misuse of economic theory for political profiteering, with proposals for constitutional disciplines*, Institute of Economic Affairs.

Buchanan, J. M. and Wagner, R. E. (1977) *Democracy in Deficit: The political legacy of Lord Keynes*, Academic Press.

Building Industries National Council (1935) *Report on Long-Term Public Works Policy*.

Buiter, W. H. and Miller, M. (1981) 'The Thatcher experiment: the first two years', *Brookings Papers on Economic Activity*, (2), 315–67.

Burkhead, J. (1954) 'The balanced budget', *Quarterly Journal of Economics*, 68 (2), 191–216.

Burns, E. M. (1941) *British Unemployment Programs 1920–1938*, Washington D.C., Committee on Social Security, Social Science Research Council.

Buxton, N. K. (1975) 'The role of the "new" industries in Britain during the 1930s: a reinterpretation', *Business History Review*, 49 (2), 205–22.

Cairncross, A. K. and Eichengreen, B. J. (1983) *Sterling in Decline: The devaluations of 1931, 1949 and 1967*, Oxford, Basil Blackwell.

Campbell, J. (1977) *Lloyd George: The goat in the wilderness 1922–1931*, Jonathan Cape.

Capie, F. (1978) 'The British tariff and industrial protection in the 1930s', *Economic History Review*, 2nd ser., 31 (3), 399–409.

—— (1983) *Depression and Protectionism: Britain between the wars*, George Allen & Unwin.

Chand, S. K. (1977) 'Summary measures of fiscal influence', *International Monetary Fund Staff Papers*, 24 (2), 405–47.

Chapman, R. A. and Greenaway, J. R. (1980) *The Dynamics of Administrative Reform*, Croom Helm.

Chester, D. N. (1951a) *Central and Local Government: Financial and administrative relations*, Macmillan.

—— (1951b) 'The central machinery for economic policy', in D. N. Chester (ed.) (1951) *Lessons of the British War Economy*, Cambridge, University Press, 5–33.

Chester, D. N. and Willson, F. M. G. (eds) (1968) *The Organization of British Central Government 1914–1964*, 2nd edn, George Allen & Unwin.

Chubb, B. (1952) *The Control of Public Expenditure: Financial committees of the House of Commons*, Oxford, Clarendon Press.

Clark, C. G. (1932) 'The state and economic policy', *Public Administration*, 10 (3), 261–9.

—— (1938) 'Determination of the multiplier from national income statistics', *Economic Journal*, 48 (3), 435–48.

Clark, J. M. (1935) *Economics of Planning Public Works*, Washington D.C., National Planning Board, Federal Emergency Administration of Public Works.

Clay, H. (1957) *Lord Norman*, Macmillan.

Collins, M. (1982) 'Unemployment in interwar Britain: still searching for an explanation', *Journal of Political Economy*, 90 (2), 369–79.

Collins, R. M. (1981) *The Business Response to Keynes 1929–1964*, New York, Columbia University Press.

Conservative Party (1931) 'Tariff committee report', Conservative Research Department, unpublished. (There is a copy of this document in the archives of Customs and Excise.)

Cook, S. T. and Jackson, P. M. (eds) (1979) *Current Issues in Fiscal Policy*, Oxford, Martin Robertson.

Corner, D. C. (1956) 'Exports and the British trade cycle: 1929', *The Manchester School*, 24 (2), 124–60.

Coutts, K., Tarling, R., Ward, T. and Wilkinson, F. (1981) 'The economic consequences of Mrs Thatcher', *Cambridge Journal of Economics*, 5 (1), 81–93.

Cripps, T. F. and Tarling, R. J. (1974) 'An analysis of the duration of male unemployment in Great Britain 1932–73', *Economic Journal*, 84 (2), 289–316.

Crombie, J. (1962) *Her Majesty's Customs and Excise*, George Allen & Unwin.

Cross, C. (1966) *Philip Snowden*, Barrie & Rockliff.

Cross, R. (1982) 'How much voluntary unemployment in interwar Britain?', *Journal of Political Economy*, 90 (2), 380–5.

Currie, D. A. (1978) 'Macroeconomic policy and government financing: a survey of recent developments', in M. J. Artis and A. R. Nobay (eds) (1978) *Studies in Contemporary Economic Analysis*, vol. 1, Croom Helm, 65–99.

Daly, M. E. (1979) 'Government policy and the depressed areas in the inter-war years', University of Oxford, unpublished D. Phil. dissertation.

Davis, J. R. (1971) *The New Economics and the Old Economists*, Ames, Iowa State University Press.

Davison, R. C. (1938) *British Unemployment Policy: The modern phase since 1930*, Longmans.

De Cecco, M. (1977) 'The last of the Romans', in R. Skidelsky (ed.) (1977) *The End of the Keynesian Era: Essays on the disintegration of the Keynesian political economy*, Macmillan, 18–32.

Dennison, S. R. (1939) *The Location of Industry and the Depressed Areas*, Oxford University Press.

Devereux, M. P. and Morris, C. N. (1983) 'Budgetary arithmetic and the 1983 budget', *Fiscal Studies*, 4 (2), 29–42.

—— and —— (1984) 'The Chancellor's arithmetic', *Fiscal Studies*, 5 (2), 63–72.

Dimsdale, N. H. (1981) 'British monetary policy and the exchange rate 1920–1938', *Oxford Economic Papers* n.s., Supplement, 33 (2), 306–49.

Dow, J. C. R. (1964) *The Management of the British Economy 1945–60*, Cambridge, University Press.

Dowie, J. A. (1968) 'Growth in the inter-war period: some more arithmetic', *Economic History Review*, 2nd ser., 21 (1), 93–112. Reprinted in D. H. Aldcroft and P. Fearon (eds) (1969) q.v. 55–79.

—— (1975) '1919–20 is in need of attention', *Economic History Review*, 2nd ser., 28 (3), 429–50.

Edelberg, V. (1940) 'Flexibility of the yield of taxation – some econometric investigations', *Journal of the Royal Statistical Society*, 103 (2), 153–79.

Einzig, P. (1959) *The Control of the Purse: Progress and decline of Parliament's financial control*, Secker & Warburg.

Feiling, K. (1946) *The Life of Neville Chamberlain*, Macmillan.

Feinstein, C. H. (1965) *Domestic Capital Formation in the United Kingdom 1920–1938*, Cambridge, University Press.

Feinstein, C. H. (1972) *National Income, Expenditure and Output of the United Kingdom 1855–1965*, Cambridge, University Press.
Feldstein, M. (1982) 'Government deficits and aggregate demand', *Journal of Monetary Economics*, 9 (1), 1–20.
Finer, S. E. (1956) 'The Federation of British Industries', *Political Studies*, 4 (1), 61–84.
Floud, R. and McCloskey, D. (eds) (1981) *The Economic History of Britain since 1700*, vol. 2: *1860 to the 1970s*, Cambridge, University Press.
Fogarty, M. P. (1945) *Prospects of the Industrial Areas of Great Britain*, Methuen.
Friedman, M. (1968) 'The role of monetary policy', *American Economic Review*, 58 (1), 1–17.
Fry, G. K. (1969) *Statesmen in Disguise: The changing role of the Administrative Class of the British Home Civil Service 1853–1966*, Macmillan.
Galenson, W. and Zellner, A. (1957) 'International comparison of unemployment rates', in National Bureau of Economic Research, *The Measurement and Behavior of Unemployment*, Princeton, University Press, 439–581.
Garside, W. R. (1980) *The Measurement of Unemployment: Methods and sources in Great Britain 1850–1979*, Oxford, Basil Blackwell.
Gayer, A. D. (1935) *Public Works in Prosperity and Depression*, New York, National Bureau of Economic Research.
Gibbs, N. H. (1976) *Grand Strategy*, vol. 1: *Rearmament Policy*, History of the Second World War, United Kingdom Military Series, HMSO.
Gilbert, B. B. (1970) *British Social Policy 1914–1939*, Batsford.
Glynn, S. and Booth, A. E. (1983) 'Unemployment in interwar Britain: a case for re-learning the lessons of the 1930s?', *Economic History Review*, 2nd ser., 36 (3), 329–48.
Glynn, S. and Howells, P. G. A. (1980) 'Unemployment in the 1930s: the "Keynesian solution" reconsidered', *Australian Economic History Review*, 20 (1), 28–45.
Godfrey, L. (1975) *Theoretical and Empirical Aspects of the Effects of Taxation on the Supply of Labour*, Paris, OECD.
Godley, W. A. H. and Shepherd, J. R. (1964) 'Long-term growth and short-term policy. The productive potential of the British economy, and fluctuations in the pressure of demand for labour, 1951–1962', *National Institute Economic Review*, 29, 26–38.
Grant, A. T. K. (1967) *A Study of the Capital Market in Britain from 1919–1936*, rep., Cass.
Griffith, W. (1949) *A Hundred Years: The Board of Inland Revenue 1849–1949*, Somerset House.
Grigg, P. J. (1948) *Prejudice and Judgement*, Jonathan Cape.
Haberler, G. (1939) *Prosperity and Depression: A theoretical analysis of cyclical movements*, Geneva, League of Nations.
Ham, A. (1981) *Treasury Rules: Recurrent themes in British economic policy*, Quartet Books.
Hancock, K. J. (1960) 'Unemployment and the economists in the 1920s', *Economica* n.s., 27 (3), 305–21.
—— (1962) 'The reduction of unemployment as a problem of public policy 1920–29', *Economic History Review*, 2nd ser., 15 (2), 328–43. Reprinted in S. Pollard (ed.) (1970) q.v. 99–121.

Hansen, B. (1969) *Fiscal Policy in Seven Countries 1955-1965*, Paris, OECD.
Hargreaves. E. L. (1930) *The National Debt*, Edward Arnold.
Harris, S. E. (ed.) (1948) *The New Economics: Keynes' influence on theory and public policy*, Dobson.
Harrod, R. F. (1951) *The Life of John Maynard Keynes*, Macmillan.
Hartley, N. and Bean, C. (1978) 'The standardized budget balance', *Government Economic Service Working Paper*, no. 1, HM Treasury.
Hatton, T. J. (1977) 'Excess demand in the labour market 1861-1939', University of Warwick, unpublished paper.
—— (1980) 'Unemployment in Britain between the world wars: a role for the dole', University of Essex, Department of Economics discussion paper.
—— (1982) 'Unemployment in the 1930s and the "Keynesian solution": some notes of dissent', University of Essex, Department of Economics discussion paper.
—— (1983) 'Unemployment benefits and the macroeconomics of the interwar labour market: a further analysis', *Oxford Economic Papers* n.s., 35 (3), 486–505.
Hawtrey, R. G. (1925) 'Public expenditure and the demand for labour', *Economica*, 5 (1), 38–48.
Hayek, F. A. (1933) *Monetary Theory and the Trade Cycle*, trans. N. Kaldor and H. M. Croome, Jonathan Cape.
—— (1935) *Prices and Production*, 2nd edn, Routledge.
—— (1944) *The Road to Serfdom*, Routledge & Kegan Paul.
—— (1979) *Law, Legislation and Liberty*, vol. III: *The political order of a free people*, Routledge & Kegan Paul.
Heath, T. L. (1927) *The Treasury*, Putnam.
Heclo, H. and Wildavsky, A. (1974) *The Private Government of Public Money: Community and policy inside British politics*, Macmillan.
Heertje, A. (1977) *Economics and Technical Change*, New York, John Wiley.
Hicks, U. K. (1938) *The Finance of British Government 1920-1936*, Oxford University Press.
—— (1953) 'The budget as an instrument of policy 1837-1953', *Three Banks Review*, 18 (2), 16–34.
—— (1963) *British Public Finances: Their structure and development 1880-1952*, rev. edn, Oxford University Press.
Higgins, B. (1946) *Public Investment and Full Employment*, Montreal, International Labour Office.
Higham, D. and Tomlinson, J. (1982) 'Why do governments worry about inflation?', *National Westminster Bank Quarterly Review*, (2), 2–13.
Hopkins, R. V. N. (1930) 'Evidence', 22 May, in HMSO (1931d) q.v. II, 13–26.
—— (1931) 'Evidence', 29 January, in HMSO (1932b) q.v. I, 381–91.
Hornby, W. (1958) *Factories and Plant*, History of the Second World War, United Kingdom Civil Series, HMSO and Longmans.
Howson, S. (1974) 'The origins of dear money 1919-20', *Economic History Review*, 2nd ser., 27 (1), 88–107.
—— (1975) *Domestic Monetary Management in Britain 1919-38*, Cambridge, University Press.
—— (1980) *Sterling's Managed Float: The operations of the Exchange Equalisation Account 1932-39*, Studies in International Finance no. 46, Princeton, University, International Finance Section.

Howson, S. (1981) 'Slump and unemployment', in R. Floud and D. McCloskey (eds) (1981) q.v. 265–85.
Howson, S. and Winch, D. (1977) *The Economic Advisory Council 1930–1939: A study in economic advice during depression and recovery*, Cambridge, University Press.
Hutchison, T. W. (1968) *Economics and Economic Policy in Britain 1946–1966: Some aspects of their interrelations*, George Allen & Unwin.
—— (1977) *Keynes versus the 'Keynesians'. . . ? An essay in the thinking of J. M. Keynes and the accuracy of its interpretation by his followers*, Institute of Economic Affairs.
—— (1978) Review of Howson and Winch (1977), *Economic History Review*, 2nd ser., 31 (1), 155–6.
Ilersic, A. R. (1955) *Government Finance and Fiscal Policy in Post-War Britain*, Staples Press.
International Labour Office (1931) *Unemployment and Public Works*, Geneva, International Labour Office.
—— (1935) *Public Works Policy*, P. S. King.
Irish, M. (1980) 'Unemployment in interwar Britain: a note', University of Bristol, unpublished paper.
Jennings, W. I. (1959) *Cabinet Government*, 3rd edn, Cambridge, University Press.
Johnston, A. (1965) *The Inland Revenue*, George Allen & Unwin.
Jones, M. E. F. (1983) 'Benefit-induced unemployment in the regions 1929–38: another look at Benjamin and Kochin', paper presented to Economic History Society Conference 'Young Researchers' Session', University of Kent at Canterbury.
JPE (1982) Papers by M. Collins, R. Cross, D. Metcalf *et al.*, P. A. Ormerod and G. D. N. Worswick, and D. K. Benjamin and L. A. Kochin, q.v. *Journal of Political Economy*, 90 (2), 369–436.
Kahn, R. F. (1931) 'The relation of home investment to unemployment', *Economic Journal*, 41 (2), 173–98.
—— (1933) 'Public works and inflation', *Journal of the American Statistical Association*, Supplement, 22 (1), 168–73.
—— (1978) 'Some aspects of the development of Keynes's thought', *Journal of Economic Literature*, 16 (2), 545–59.
Kaldor, N. (1944) 'The quantitative aspect of the full employment problem in Britain', in W. H. Beveridge (1944) q.v. appendix C.
Kaldor, N. and Trevithick, J. (1981) 'A Keynesian perspective on money', *Lloyds Bank Review*, 139, 1–19.
Kalecki, M. (1943) 'Political aspects of full employment', *Political Quarterly*, 14 (4), 322–31.
Keynes, J. M. (1929) 'The Treasury contribution to the White Paper', *The Nation and Athenaeum*, 18 May.
—— (1931) 'Some consequences of the economy report', *The New Statesman and Nation*, 15 August. Reprinted in Keynes (1972) q.v. 141–5.
—— (1933) *The Means to Prosperity*. Reprinted in Keynes (1972) q.v. 335–66.
—— (1936) *The General Theory of Employment, Interest and Money*, The Collected Writings of John Maynard Keynes, vol. VII (1973), Macmillan/St Martin's Press.
—— (1937) 'How to avoid a slump', *The Times*, 12–14 January. Reprinted in T. W. Hutchison (1977) q.v. 65–73.

—— (1939a) 'Democracy and efficiency', *The New Statesman and Nation*, 28 January.
—— (1939b) 'Crisis finance', *The Times*, 17-18 April.
—— (1972) *Essays in Persuasion*, The Collected Writings of John Maynard Keynes, vol. IX, Macmillan/St Martin's Press.
—— (1973) *The General Theory and After*, pt II: *Defence and Development*, The Collected Writings of John Maynard Keynes, vol. XIV, ed. D. E. Moggridge, Macmillan/St Martin's Press.
Keynes, J. M. and Henderson, H. D. (1929) *Can Lloyd George Do It? – The pledge examined*. Reprinted in Keynes (1972) q.v. 86-125.
Keynes, M. (ed.) (1975) *Essays on John Maynard Keynes*, Cambridge, University Press.
Laursen, L. and Metzler, L. A. (1950) 'Flexible exchange rates and the theory of employment', *Review of Economics and Statistics*, 32 (4), 281-99.
Lavington, F. (1921) *The English Capital Market*, Macmillan.
LCES (1972) *The British Economy: Key statistics 1900-1970*, Times Newspapers/London and Cambridge Economic Service.
League of Nations (1934) *National Public Works*, Geneva, League of Nations.
—— (1936) *Public Finance 1928-1935*, pt V, Geneva, League of Nations.
—— (1937) *Public Finance 1928-1935*, pts XI, XII, XXXIV, Geneva, League of Nations.
Lees, D. S. (1955) 'Public departments and cheap money 1932-38', *Economica* n.s., 22 (1), 61-80.
Leijonhufvud, A. (1968) *On Keynesian Economics and the Economics of Keynes: A study in monetary theory*, Oxford University Press.
Lewis, W. A. (1949) *Economic Survey 1919-1939*, George Allen & Unwin.
Liberal Industrial Inquiry (1928) *Britain's Industrial Future*, Ernest Benn.
Liberal Party (1929) *We Can Conquer Unemployment*, Cassell.
—— (1930) *How to Tackle Unemployment: The Liberal plans as laid before the government and the nation*, Press Printers.
Lloyd George, D. (1935) *Organising Prosperity*, Ivor Nicholson & Watson.
Lomax, K. S. (1964) 'Growth and productivity in the United Kingdom', *Productivity Measurement Review*, 38, 5-22. Reprinted in D. H. Aldcroft and P. Fearon (eds) (1969) q.v. 10-33.
London Chamber of Commerce (1925) 'Evidence', 5 May, in HMSO (1927b) q.v. II, 516-30.
Lonie, A. A. (1980) 'The economic basis of the "Treasury view" vintages 1929 and 1930', University of Dundee, unpublished paper.
—— (1984) 'The "Treasury view" and Mrs Thatcher', *Three Banks Review* (forthcoming).
Lotz, J. (1971) 'Techniques of measuring the effects of fiscal policy', *OECD Economic Outlook: Occasional Studies*, (July), 3-31.
Lucas, R. E. (1976) 'Econometric policy evaluation: a critique', in K. Brunner and A. H. Meltzer (eds) (1976) *The Phillips Curve and Labor Markets*, Carnegie-Rochester Conference Series on Public Policy, vol. 1, Amsterdam, North Holland, 19-46.
McCrone, G. (1969) *Regional Policy in Britain*, George Allen & Unwin.
McKibbin, R. (1975) 'The economic policy of the second Labour government 1929-1931', *Past and Present*, 68 (3), 95-123.

Malinvaud, E. (1977) *The Theory of Unemployment Reconsidered*, Oxford, Basil Blackwell.
Mallet, B. and George, C. O. (1933) *British Budgets, Third Series, 1921-22 to 1932-33*, Macmillan.
Marquand, D. (1977) *Ramsay MacDonald*, Jonathan Cape.
Matthews, R. C. O. (1964) 'Some aspects of post-war growth in the British economy in relation to historical experience', *Transactions of the Manchester Statistical Society*. Reprinted in D. H. Aldcroft and P. Fearon (eds) (1969) q.v. 80-100.
—— (1968) 'Why has Britain had full employment since the war?', *Economic Journal*, 78 (3), 555-69.
Matthews, R. C. O., Feinstein, C. H. and Odling-Smee, J. C. (1982) *British Economic Growth 1856-1973*, Oxford, Clarendon Press.
Meade, J. E. (1937) *An Introduction to Economic Analysis and Policy*, 2nd edn, Oxford University Press.
Metcalf, D., Nickell, S. J. and Floros, N. (1982) 'Still searching for an explanation of unemployment in interwar Britain', *Journal of Political Economy*, 90 (2), 386-99.
Middlemas, K. and Barnes, J. (1969) *Baldwin: A biography*, Weidenfeld & Nicolson.
Middleton, R. (1981a) 'The constant employment budget balance and British budgetary policy 1929-39', *Economic History Review*, 2nd ser., 34 (2), 266-86.
—— (1981b) 'Fiscal policy and economic management in the 1930s', University of Cambridge, unpublished Ph.D. dissertation.
—— (1982) 'The Treasury in the 1930s: political and administrative constraints to acceptance of the "new" economics', *Oxford Economic Papers* n.s., 34 (1), 48-77.
—— (1983) 'The Treasury and public investment: a perspective on interwar economic management', *Public Administration*, 61 (4), 351-70.
—— (1984) 'The measurement of fiscal influence in Britain in the 1930s', *Economic History Review*, 2nd ser., 37 (1), 103-6.
—— (1985) 'Unemployment in the north east during the interwar period', in R. A. Chapman (ed.) (1985) *Public Policy Studies: The north east of England*, Edinburgh, University Press (forthcoming).
Midland Bank (1932) 'Errors and omissions – can half a policy pay?', *Midland Bank Monthly Review*, (April-May), 1-3.
Mills, T. C. and Wood, G. E. (1977) 'Money substitutes and monetary policy in the UK 1922-1974', *European Economic Review*, 10 (1), 19-36.
Moggridge, D. E. (1970) 'The 1931 financial crisis – a new view', *The Banker*, 120 (534), 832-9.
—— (1972) *British Monetary Policy 1924-1931: The Norman Conquest of $4.86*, Cambridge, University Press.
Moggridge, D. E. and Howson, S. (1974) 'Keynes on monetary policy 1910-1946', *Oxford Economic Papers* n.s., 26 (2), 226-47.
Morgan, E. V. (1952) *Studies in British Financial Policy 1914-1925*, Macmillan.
Morton, W. A. (1943) *British Finance 1930-1940*, Madison, University of Wisconsin Press.
Mowat, C. L. (1955) *Britain Between the Wars 1918-1940*, Methuen.
Musgrave, R. A. (1964) 'On measuring fiscal performance', *Review of Economics and Statistics*, 46 (2), 213-20.

Neild, R. R. (1963) *Pricing and Employment in the Trade Cycle: A Study of British manufacturing industry 1950–1961*, Cambridge, University Press.

Nevin, E. (1955) *The Mechanism of Cheap Money: A Study of British monetary policy 1931–1939*, Cardiff, University of Wales Press.

Newman, N. (1972) 'The role of the Treasury in the formation of British economic policy 1918–25', University of Durham, unpublished Ph.D. dissertation.

OECD (1978) *Public Expenditure Trends*, OECD Studies in Resource Allocation, no. 5, Paris, OECD.

Okun, A. M. and Teeters, N. H. (1970) 'The full employment surplus revisited', *Brookings Papers on Economic Activity*, (1), 77–110.

Ormerod, P. A. and Worswick, G. D. N. (1982) 'Unemployment in interwar Britain', *Journal of Political Economy*, 90 (2), 400–9.

Overy, R. J. (1982) *The Nazi Economic Recovery 1932–38*, Macmillan.

Parker, R. A. C. (1981) 'British rearmament 1936–9: Treasury, trade unions and skilled labour', *English Historical Review*, 96 (2), 306–43.

Patinkin, D. (1976) 'Keynes and econometrics: on the interaction between the macroeconomic revolutions of the interwar period', *Econometrica*, 44 (6), 1091–123.

Peacock, A. T. and Wiseman, J. (1967) *The Growth of Public Expenditure in the United Kingdom*, 2nd edn, George Allen & Unwin.

Peden, G. C. (1979a) 'Sir Warren Fisher and British rearmament against Germany', *English Historical Review*, 94 (1), 29–47.

—— (1979b) *British Rearmament and the Treasury 1932–1939*, Edinburgh, Scottish Academic Press.

—— (1980) 'Keynes, the Treasury and unemployment in the later nineteen-thirties', *Oxford Economic Papers* n.s., 32 (1), 1–18.

—— (1983a) 'Sir Richard Hopkins and the "Keynesian revolution" in employment policy 1929–1945', *Economic History Review*, 2nd ser., 36 (2), 281–96.

—— (1983b) 'The Treasury as the central department of government 1919–1939', *Public Administration*, 61 (4), 371–85.

—— (1984) 'The "Treasury view" on public works and employment in the interwar period', *Economic History Review*, 2nd ser., 37 (2), 167–81.

Phelps Brown, E. H. and Shackle, G. L. S. (1939) 'British economic fluctuations 1924–38', *Oxford Economic Papers*, 2 (2), 98–134.

Pigou, A. C. (1924a) *The Economics of Welfare*, 2nd edn, Macmillan.

—— (1924b) 'Evidence', 5 May, in HMSO (1927b) q.v. I, 39–58.

—— (1947) *Aspects of British Economic History 1918–1925*, Macmillan.

Pilgrim Trust (1938) *Men Without Work. A report made to the Pilgrim Trust*, Cambridge, University Press.

Pollard, S. (ed.) (1970) *The Gold Standard and Employment Policies between the Wars*, Methuen.

—— (1973) *The Development of the British Economy 1914–1967*, 2nd edn, Edward Arnold.

—— (1982) *The Wasting of the British Economy: British economic policy 1945 to the present*, Croom Helm.

Prest, A. R. (1962) 'The sensitivity of the yield of personal income tax in the United Kingdom', *Economic Journal*, 72 (3), 576–96.

Price, R. W. R. (1976) 'Local authority finance and the management of the economy', in HMSO (1976) q.v. 48–80.

—— (1978) 'Public expenditure', in F. T. Blackaby (ed.) (1978) q.v. 77–134.

Pryor, Z. P. (1979) 'Czechoslovak fiscal policies in the great depression', *Economic History Review*, 2nd ser., 32 (2), 228–40.

Recktenwald, H. C. (ed.) (1978) *Secular Trends of the Public Sector*, Proceedings of the 32nd Congress of the International Institute of Public Finance (Edinburgh 1976), Paris, Editions Cujas.

Reddaway, W. B. (1939) *The Economics of a Declining Population*, George Allen & Unwin.

Redmond, J. (1980) 'An indicator of the effective exchange rate of the pound in the nineteen-thirties', *Economic History Review*, 2nd ser., 33 (1), 83–91.

Richardson, H. W. (1961) 'The new industries between the wars', *Oxford Economic Papers* n.s., 13 (3), 360–84. Reprinted in D. H. Aldcroft and H. W. Richardson (eds) (1969) q.v. 264–88.

—— (1965) 'Over-commitment in Britain before 1930', *Oxford Economic Papers* n.s., 17 (2), 237–59. Reprinted in D. H. Aldcroft and H. W. Richardson (eds) (1969) q.v. 190–218.

—— (1967) *Economic Recovery in Britain 1932–39*, Weidenfeld & Nicolson.

—— (1972) 'The role of consumption in interwar fluctuations', in D. H. Aldcroft and P. Fearon (eds) (1972) q.v. 161–87.

Robbins, L. (1971) *Autobiography of an Economist*, Macmillan.

—— (1976) *Political Economy: Past and Present. A review of leading theories of economic policy*, Macmillan.

Robinson, A. (1978) *Parliament and Public Spending: The Expenditure Committee of the House of Commons 1970–76*, Heinemann.

Robinson, J. (1976) *Economic Philosophy*, Harmondsworth, Penguin Books.

Roseveare, H. (1969) *The Treasury: The evolution of a British institution*, Allen Lane.

Roskill, S. (1972) *Hankey, Man of Secrets*, vol. II: *1919–1931*, Collins.

Royal Institute of International Affairs (1935) *Unemployment: An international problem*, Oxford, University Press.

Sabine, B. E. V. (1966) *A History of Income Tax*, George Allen & Unwin.

—— (1970) *British Budgets in Peace and War 1932–45*, George Allen & Unwin.

Samuelson, P. A. (1970) *Economics*, 8th edn, New York, McGraw-Hill.

Sayers, R. S. (1956) *Financial Policy 1939–45*, History of the Second World War, United Kingdom Civil Series, HMSO and Longmans.

—— (1967a) *A History of Economic Change in England 1880–1939*, Oxford University Press.

—— (1967b) 'The timing of tax payments by companies', *Three Banks Review*, 75, 24–32.

—— (1976) *The Bank of England 1891–1944*, 3 vols, Cambridge, University Press.

Schedvin, C. B. (1970) *Australia and the Great Depression: A study of economic development and policy in the 1920s and 1930s*, Sydney, University Press.

Schumacher, E. F. (1944) 'Public finance – its relation to full employment', in Oxford Institute of Statistics, *The Economics of Full Employment*, Oxford, Basil Blackwell, 85–125.

Shackle, G. L. S. (1967) *The Years of High Theory: Invention and tradition in economic thought 1926–1939*, Cambridge, University Press.

BIBLIOGRAPHY

Shann, E. O. G. and Copland, D. B. (1931) *The Crisis in Australian Finance 1929–1931: Documents on budgetary and economic policy*, Sydney, Angus & Robertson.

Shaw, G. K. (1979) 'The measurement of fiscal influence', in S. T. Cook and P. M. Jackson (eds) (1979) q.v. 44–60.

Shay, R. P. (1977) *British Rearmament in the Thirties: Politics and profits*, Princeton, University Press.

Shirras, G. F. and Rostas, L. (1942) *The Burden of British Taxation*, Cambridge, University Press.

Silverman, H. A. (1931) *Taxation: Its incidence and effects*, Macmillan.

Skidelsky, R. (1967) *Politicians and the Slump: The Labour Government of 1929–31*, Macmillan.

—— (1975a) *Oswald Mosley*, Macmillan.

—— (1975b) 'The reception of the Keynesian revolution', in M. Keynes (ed.) (1975) q.v. 89–107.

—— (1981) 'Keynes and the Treasury view: the case for and against an active unemployment policy 1920–1939', in W. J. Mommsen (ed.) (1981) *The Emergence of the Welfare State in Britain and Germany 1850–1950*, Croom Helm, 167–87.

—— (1983) *John Maynard Keynes*, vol. 1: *Hopes Betrayed 1883–1920*, Macmillan.

Slichter, S. H. (1934) 'The economics of public works', *American Economic Review*, Papers and Proceedings, 24 (1), 174–85.

Snowden, P. (1934) *An Autobiography*, vol. 2: *1919–1934*, Ivor Nicholson & Watson.

Stamp, J. (1936) 'The influence of the price level on the higher incomes', *Journal of the Royal Statistical Society*, 99 (4), 627–60.

Stein, H. (1969) *The Fiscal Revolution in America*, Chicago, University Press.

Stewart, M. (1972) *Keynes and After*, 2nd edn, Harmondsworth, Penguin Books.

—— (1980) 'This Milton's paradise spells nothing but loss', *Times Higher Education Supplement*, 27 June.

Stone, R. (ed.) (1977) *Inland Revenue Report on National Income 1929*, Cambridge, University, Department of Applied Economics.

Stone, R. and W. M. (1938) 'The marginal propensity to consume and the multiplier: a statistical investigation', *Review of Economic Studies*, 6 (1), 1–24.

Stone, R. and Rowe, D. A. (1966) *The Measurement of Consumers Expenditure and Behaviour in the United Kingdom 1920–1938*, vol. II, Cambridge, University Press.

Sykes, J. (1939) *A Study in English Local Authority Finance*, P. S. King.

Taylor, A. J. P. (1965) *English History 1914–1945*, Oxford, Clarendon Press.

Taylor, C. T. (1979) 'Crowding out: its meaning and significance', in S. T. Cook and P. M. Jackson (eds) (1979) q.v. 86–107.

Thirlwall, A. P. (1969) 'Types of unemployment: with special reference to "non demand-deficient" unemployment in Great Britain', *Scottish Journal of Political Economy*, 16 (1), 20–49.

Thomas, M. (1983) 'Rearmament and economic recovery in the late 1930s', *Economic History Review*, 2nd ser., 36 (4), 552–79.

Thomas, T. (1975) 'Econometric history and the interwar period: "Could Lloyd George have done it?"', Econometric Society Third World Congress, unpublished paper.

Thomas, T. (1976) 'Aspects of UK macroeconomic policy during the interwar period: a study in econometric history', University of Cambridge, unpublished PhD dissertation.
—— (1981) 'Aggregate demand in the United Kingdom 1918–45', in R. Floud and D. McCloskey (eds) (1981) q.v. 332–46.
Tobin, J. (1974) 'Friedman's theoretical framework', in R. J. Gordon (ed.) (1974) *Milton Friedman's Monetary Framework: A debate with his critics*, Chicago, University Press, 77–89.
—— (1980) *Asset Accumulation and Economic Activity: Reflections on contemporary macroeconomic theory*, Oxford, Basil Blackwell.
Tomlinson, J. (1978) 'Unemployment and government policy between the wars: a note', *Journal of Contemporary History*, 13 (1), 65–75.
—— (1981a) 'Why was there never a "Keynesian revolution" in economic policy?', *Economy and Society*, 10 (1), 72–87.
—— (1981b) *Problems of British Economic Policy 1870–1945*, Methuen.
—— (1982a) 'Interwar unemployment – two views', *Journal of Contemporary History*, 17 (3), 545–50.
—— (1982b) 'Unemployment and policy in the 1930s and 1980s', *Three Banks Review*, 135, 17–33.
—— (1984) 'A "Keynesian revolution" in economic policy-making?', *Economic History Review*, 2nd ser., 37 (2), 258–62.
Trevithick, J. (1978) 'Keynes, Robertson and the crowding-out debate', University of Cambridge, unpublished paper.
Tunzelmann, G. N. von (1982) 'Structural change and leading sectors in British manufacturing 1907–68', in C. P. Kindleberger and G. di Tella (eds) (1982) *Economics in the Long View: Essays in honour of W. W. Rostow*, vol. 3: *Applications and Cases, Part II*, Macmillan, 1–49.
US Bureau of the Census (1975) *Historical Statistics of the United States, Colonial Times to 1970*, 2 vols, Washington D.C., US Government Printing Office.
Ward, T. S. and Neild, R. R. (1978) *The Measurement and Reform of Budgetary Policy*, Heinemann Educational Books/Institute for Fiscal Studies.
Wass, D. (1978) 'The changing problem of economic management', in Central Statistical Office, *Economic Trends*, 293, 97–104.
Williams, D. (1963) 'The 1931 financial crisis', *Yorkshire Bulletin of Economic and Social Research*, 15 (2), 92–110.
Williamson, P. (1982) '"Safety first": Baldwin, the Conservative Party and the 1929 general election', *Historical Journal*, 25 (2), 385–409.
Winch, D. (1972) *Economics and Policy: A historical study*, rev. edn, Collins/Fontana.
Wood, J. B. (1972) *How Much Unemployment? The methods and measures dissected*, Institute of Economic Affairs.
Woods, J. (1954) 'Treasury control', *Political Quarterly*, 25 (4), 370–81.
Woolman, L. (1930) *Planning and Control of Public Works*, New York, National Bureau of Economic Research.
Worswick, G. D. N. (ed.) (1976) *The Concept and Measurement of Involuntary Unemployment*, George Allen & Unwin.
Youngson, A. J. (1969) *Britain's Economic Growth 1920–1966*, 2nd edn, George Allen & Unwin.

INDEX

In some cases, sub-sub-entries are listed in page order to give chronological sequence.

accelerated depreciation, 74–5
Aldcroft, D. H., 8, 13, 20–1, 28, 114, 126, 133, 137, 204 n. 2, 211 n.4 (ch. 9)
 and Richardson, H. W., 18–19, 20–1, 27–8
Alford, B. W. E., 9, 21
Allen, G. C., 10
Amery, L. S., 33
Archibald, G. C., 30
Armstrong Report on Budgetary Reform, 51
Arndt, H. W., 8, 86, 133, 137, 179
asset prices, 131, 198, 200
Atkinson, A. B. and Stiglitz, J. E., 71
Attlee, C. R., 205 n. 4 (ch. 3)
Australian Premiers' Plan, 59
automatic stabilizers, 43, 123, 131–2, 142–3
 and budgetary equilibrium, 3, 39, 96, 188
 definition of, 129
 Keynes, J. M. on, 112
autonomous expenditures, 129, 130, 131

Bacon, R. and Eltis, W., 71, 184
Baily, M. N., 159–60
balance of payments
 effect of depression on, 27–8, 101
 external constraint, 27–8, 143, 154, 174–5, 178–9
 and gold standard, 101, 154
 and London's financial position, 28, 179
 policy, 174–5
 and public works, 178–9
 and rearmament, 116, 117, 118, 120, 210 n. 11

 and 'Treasury view', 160–1, 163–4
 see also exports; imports
balanced budget multiplier, 95, 124, 156
 see also fiscal policy multiplier; multiplier
balanced budget rule, 142, 159
 documentary evidence for, 37
 and expenditure growth, 83–92
 'Treasury view' on misunderstood, 87–8
 see also budgetary orthodoxy
balanced budgets
 definition of, 79
 and characteristics of fiscal system, 39, 132
 and fiscal window-dressing, 80–3
Baldwin, S., 180, 191
Balfour Committee on Industry and Trade, 71
Balogh, T., 141
bankers' ramp, 100
Barna, T., 69
Barro, R. J., 158, 159
Barry, E. E., 179
Baumol, W. J. and Peston, M. H., 124
Beck, G. M., 14
Beer, S. H., 35
Beloff, M., 37
benefit–wage ratio
 and cyclical macro-marginal budget rate, 132
 and unemployment, 9, 19–20, 187, 190
Benham, F., 110
Benjamin, D. K. and Kochin, L. A., 8, 9, 19–20., 132
Beveridge, W. H., 12, 16–17, 29, 89, 203
Blackaby, F. T., 3, 183

Blake, R., 180–1
Blinder, A. S. and Solow, R. M., 123
Booth, A. E., 35, 171, 180, 208 n. 5 (ch. 5), 212 n. 8
 and Glynn, S., 3, 11, 16
Bradbury, J., 91, 191
Bretherton, R. F., 66, 196, 198, 199, 207 n. 1 (ch. 4)
 and Burchardt, F. A. and Rutherford, R. S. G., 94, 138, 141, 169, 206 nn. 9, 12, 211 n. 3 (ch. 9)
Bridges, E. E., 35, 36, 37, 48–9, 120, 191
Brittan, S., 31
Broadberry, S. N., 7–9, 124, 160, 210 n. 8
Brown, E. C., 125–6
Brown, J. A., 27
Buchanan, J. M., Burton, J. and Wagner, R. E., 85, 88, 184
Buchanan, J. M. and Wagner, R. E., 88
budget accounts, definitions of, 78–80, 123–5, 193–5
budget balance
 at actual employment, 78–9, 96–7, 98, 101, 103, 106, 108, 122–3, 125, 129, 133–9, 143
 adjusted, 79–81, 96–7, 101, 124–5, 129, 134–9, 143, 193–5
 at constant employment, 123–43, 196–203
 conventionally defined, 78–80, 193
 response of to income variations, 96–7, 127–32
budgetary history, 3, 96–109
 traditional view of interwar, 79, 133–4, 143
 see also under budgetary policy; fiscal stance
budgetary orthodoxy
 Chamberlain's, 35, 103–5, 114–15
 Conservative Governments' (1979–), 188
 and financial community, 94–5, 164
 influence of US 'New Deal' on, 27, 160
 nineteenth-century principles of, 83–5
 political foundations of, 87–8
 relaxation of, 104, 113–15, 120
 revival of, 88–9, 183–4
 Snowden's, 35, 100, 114
 Treasury papers on, 37
 see also balanced budget rule
budgetary policy
 changing nature of, 96, 113–15, 117–20
 conservatism of, 33, 59, 103, 114–15
 effects of, 78, 133–6, 142–3
 incremental nature of, 107
 influence of political factors on, 89, 105
 Keynesian objectives of, 6, 142
 during sub-periods: boom and slump (1919–22), 38–9, 174; depression (1929–33), 96–102, 109–14, 133–4, 136–8; recovery (1933–7), 102–7, 114–15, 134, 138–40; rearmament and recession (1937–9), 107–9, 115–20, 134, 140–2; deflation (1967–70), 136; depression (1979–), 142–3, 184–5
 traditional objectives of, 78, 133, 142
 see also fiscal stance
budgets
 (1930), 97, 98
 (April 1931), 98, 99
 (September 1931), 59–61, 85, 98, 99–101, 105, 113, 137, 142, 143, 166
 (1932), 98, 102
 (1933), 87–8, 102, 103, 104, 105, 114–15, 159
 (1934), 103, 105
 (1935), 103, 105
 (1936), 103, 107
 (1937), 107, 108
 (1938), 108, 118, 120
 (April 1939), 108, 118, 119, 120
 (September 1939), 108
 (1941), 4
 (1980), 184–5
Building Industries National Council, 206 n. 13
Buiter, W. H. and Miller, M., 3, 143
Burkhead, J., 84
Burns, E. M., 30
business community
 and confidence, 87, 94–5
 on role of state, 95, 171
 on taxation, 71–5, 95, 188
 trade cycle consciousness of, 94–5
 in US, 208 n. 7 (ch. 5)
 see also company sector
Buxton, N. K., 20

Cabinet, 36, 113, 116
 committees, 35, 60, 168–9
 financial control, 49, 51
 and financial crisis (1931), 59, 100
 position of Chancellor of the Exchequer, 35
Cairncross, A. K. and Eichengreen, B. J., 101
Callaghan, L. J., 183
Campbell, J., 146
Capie, F., 211 n. 1
capital allowances, 61, 74–6
capital levy, 60
central government
 borrowing powers, 51
 control over local government, 51–4, 55–6
 grants to local authorities, 41–2, 44–5, 52–4, 55
central government expenditure
 capital account, 41, 42–3, 45–6
 at constant employment, 201–3
 current account, 41, 42–3
 cuts in, 32, 38, 39, 43–4, 63, 99–100, 109–13
 debt interest, 41, 42

central government expenditure—*continued*
  growth of, 41, 42
  prices and, 43, 127–9
  social expenditure, 41
  stabilizing effectiveness of, 43, 133–43
  transfer payments, 41, 42
  see also public expenditure
Chamberlain, N., 3, 33, 35, 91, 103–5, 113–15, 167, 180, 191
Chancellors of the Exchequer, 37, 82
  Camberlain, N., 33, 35, 91, 103–5, 113–15, 167, 180, 191
  Churchill, W. S., 33–4, 82, 90, 91, 113, 191
  Horne, R., 33
  influence of Treasury officials on, 33–4, 119
  powers of, 34–6
  and revenue departments, 57–9, 82–3
  Simon, J. A., 119, 192
  Snowden, P., 35, 100, 114, 192, 208 n. 5 (ch. 6)
Chand, S. K., 123, 209 n. 4
Chapman, R. A. and Greenaway, J. R., 181
cheap money, 102, 114–15, 137, 140, 168, 179
Chester, D. N., 36, 51, 54
  and Willson, F. M. G., 33
Chubb, B., 49
Churchill, W. S., 33–4, 82, 90, 91, 113, 191
City of London, *see* financial community
civil expenditure, 109, 117, 121
civil service, higher
  administrative ethos of, 4, 181
  consensus within, 35–7
  conservatism of, 181
  corps d'élite of, 35, 70, 181
  Fisher, W. and, 32, 35, 50, 70, 181
  Keynes, J. M. on, 181
Clark, C. G., 52, 177
classical economics, 84, 86, 149, 158
Collins, R. M., 208 n. 7 (ch. 5)
Colwyn Committee on National Debt and Taxation, 71–3
commodity taxes, 68, 197–8
  see also taxes on expenditure
company sector
  response of to fiscal policies, 94, 159–60
  taxation of, 63–4, 66–7, 71–7, 95
  see also business community
confidence
  and crowding-out, 85–6, 94–5, 162–4, 179, 185
  and financial crisis (1931), 95, 137, 178
  and financial orthodoxy, 94–5, 109
  intangibility of, 95, 137, 163
  as policy objective, 119, 137, 168, 185
  and taxation, 73, 88, 119
  and 'Treasury view', 149, 162–4, 168
Conservative Governments (1979–), 2–3, 100–1, 142–3, 182–3, 184–5, 186, 188
Conservative Party, 91, 100, 146

constant employment budget balance, 4, 78, 122–5, 134–43
  see also fiscal stance
consumers expenditure, 23, 25
  at constant employment, 127
  and fiscal policy, 210 n. 10
  and taxation, 63–4, 68
  and terms of trade, 67–8
Cook, S. T. and Jackson, P. M., 124
Corner, D. C., 24
corporate incomes, *see* company sector
counter-cyclical expenditure control, 46, 51, 51–6, 168–70
Coutts, K., Tarling, R., Ward, T. and Wilkinson, F., 185
creative accounting, *see* fiscal window-dressing
Cripps, T. F. and Tarling, R. J., 16
crowding-out
  definitions of, 92–3
  Keynes, J. M. on, 85–6, 148, 156–7, 167–8, 171–2
  psychological, 93, 149, 162–3, 171
  super, 165
  and 'Treasury view', 93–4, 145, 147–9, 153–5, 156–8, 161–5, 167–8
  with unemployment, 86, 93, 147, 153, 157–8
Cunliffe Committee on Currency and Foreign Exchanges After the War, 38
Customs and Excise, 57, 61–2, 68

Daly, M. E., 14
debt interest, 39, 41, 42, 79, 86, 102, 104, 111, 114, 137, 139
debt management policy, 34
  aggregate demand and, 86
  and cheap money, 102, 114
  and defence borrowing, 179
  funding operations, 105, 114, 179
De Cecco, M., 211 n. 5 (ch. 9)
defence borrowing, 107–9, 179, 193
  amount of, criteria for, 117–18
  decision to commence, 107, 115–16
  as precedent for public works, 170
  see also rearmament
defence departments, 43, 49–50, 51, 109, 117
defence expenditure
  economy campaigns and, 43
  pressures for increased, 85, 109
  rearmament programme and, 106–9, 115–21, 141
  summary figures of, 140
  Treasury control of, 49–50, 51, 116–17
  see also rearmament
deficient demand, 1, 12, 16, 21, 29–30, 55, 144, 150, 160
deficit-financing, 132, 166, 176
  and debt-burden, 86, 205 n. 4 (ch. 2)
  opposition to (since mid-1970s), 143, 159–60, 183–4, 186, 187–8

deficit-financing—*continued*
  and rearmament, 109, 115, 119, 141, 169–70, 173
  and regional problem, 16, 30, 143, 188
  traditional antipathy towards, 84, 89, 183–4
  and unemployment, 3, 12, 29–30, 144
  see also demand management; Keynes, J. M.
demand management
  and interwar real economy, 7–9, 10–30
  origins of Keynesian, 1, 44, 77, 96, 119–20, 172–6
  post-1945, 2, 47, 54, 136, 142–3
  recent reaction against Keynesian, 142, 183–4, 186, 189
  and selective measures, 18, 29–30, 143
  see also deficit-financing; fiscal policy debate; Keynes, J. M.
Dennison, S. R., 170
depression, *see under* trade cycle
de-rating of industry, 45, 74
Devereux, M. P. and Morris, C. N., 187
Dimsdale, N. H., 114
direct taxation, 67, 73, 97
  see also taxes on income
discretionary action, definition of, 125
'displacement effect', 63
Dow, J. C. R., 54
Dowie, J. A., 20, 39

economic growth
  and interwar economic historiography, 7–9, 20–1
  measurement of, 21
  and state action, 175–6
  and taxation, 70–7, 84
  technical progress and, 13–15, 20, 188
  and unemployment, 175, 188
economic optimists
  new, 7–9, 19–20, 132, 190
  old, 7–9, 18–19, 20–1, 27
economic pessimists
  new, 7–9, 19, 160
  old, 7, 8, 18
economic policy(-ies)
  and administrative constraints, 36, 54–6, 180
  co-ordination of, 52
  external constraint on, 27–8, 143, 178–9
  general consensus on, 32, 35–7
  implementation lags, 55
  interpretation of foundations of, 4–5, 32, 34, 36–7, 149
  Keynesian objectives, 142, 174, 175
  moral dimension of, 114–15, 186–7
  recurrent themes in, 182–8
economic statistics, 7, 70, 78–9, 123, 171
economics profession, 3, 56, 104, 169, 183, 189
The Economist, 101, 109, 118, 137, 141, 169, 170, 175

economy campaigns
  'Geddes axe', 32, 39, 43, 99
  later 1920s, 43–4
  May Committee, 32, 43, 99–100, 109–13
  post-First World War, 38, 43
Edelberg, V., 196–8, 199, 207 n. 1 (ch. 4)
Einzig, P., 51
employment, 11–13, 15–16, 20, 22, 206 n. 7
  see also unemployment
Employment Policy White Paper (1944), 4, 89, 173
  see also full employment
endogenous expenditures, 33, 120, 127, 201
estate duties, 128, 131, 198, 200
  see also taxes on capital
exchange rate policy, 28, 101, 174–5
expenditure ratio, *see under* public expenditure
exports, 23, 24, 26, 27–8, 117, 164, 210 n. 11
  see also balance of payments
external balance, *see* balance of payments

Federation of British Industries (FBI), 3, 73–4, 95
Feinstein, C. H., 2, 11–13, 22, 23, 25, 28, 38, 41, 42, 43, 46, 47, 62, 63, 64, 97, 99, 126, 130, 135, 179, 202, 206 nn. 7, 9, 13, 209 n. 10, 210 n. 6
Feldstein, M., 159
financial community
  confidence of, 94–5, 101, 109, 118, 119, 162–3
  and financial crisis (1931), 100
  London's position and, 28, 94–5, 179
  opposition to deficit-financing, 94–5, 163, 179
  and standards of financial conduct, 94–5, 100
financial crisis (1931)
  abandonment of gold standard, 86, 101, 112, 142
  influence upon later policies, 94
  and Labour Government (1929–31), 99–100, 111–13
  May Committee and, 99–100, 109–13
  and revenue departments, 59–61
financial departments, *see* revenue departments; Treasury
fine-tuning, 55
Finer, S. E., 73
First World War
  expansion of state activities, 37
  and national debt, 39, 41, 60, 86
  public expenditure growth, 37–8, 73, 173
  taxation, 62–3
  and Treasury control, 34, 49
'fiscal constitution', 85, 115, 184
fiscal drag, 131
fiscal impotence, 158–60

fiscal influence, measurement of, 43, 122–5
fiscal leverage, 124
fiscal policy, *see* budgetary policy
fiscal policy debate
  economic–theoretical dimension of, 4–6, 36–7, 83–95, 145–65, 167–8, 176–9
  Keynesian history of, 2, 4–7, 32, 176, 180
  political–administrative dimension of, 5–7, 36–7, 51–6, 84–5, 87–92, 95, 149–55, 162–3, 165–6, 168–71, 180–2, 183–90
  and real economy, 7–9, 12, 18, 19, 27–30, 175, 177–8
  unsatisfactory form of, 182, 185, 187–8
  see also Keynes, J. M.; 'Treasury view'
fiscal policy multiplier, 156, 163, 164–5
  see also balanced budget multiplier; multiplier
fiscal stance
  definition of, 125
  and fiscal window-dressing, 83, 95, 136
  during sub-periods: boom and slump (1919–22), 38–9; depression (1929–33), 24, 133, 136–8, 143; recovery (1933–7), 103, 133, 138–40; recession and rearmament (1937–9), 133, 140–2; deflation (1967–70), 136; depression (1979–), 142–3
  see also budgetary policy
fiscal system, characteristics of, 39, 124, 127–32
fiscal window-dressing, 115
  and budgetary stability, 80, 85, 97, 101, 104
  extent of, 80–3, 136, 187, 193–5
  public knowledge of, 82
  rationale for, 80
  on revenue account, 58, 81–3, 104
  and spending departments, 81, 101, 104
Fisher, W., 31–2, 34, 35, 37, 50, 70, 119, 181, 187, 191, 207 n. 3 (ch. 4)
Fogarty, M. P., 15
foreign investment, 153, 164, 175
free market economy, 6, 7, 84, 95, 143, 174, 187
Friedman, M., 89, 158
Fry, G. K., 34
full employment
  acceptance of costs of, 183–4
  assumption of 'Treasury view', 5, 93–4, 149, 156–7
  commitment to, 173, 174
  and demand management, 1–2, 119–20, 159, 184, 189
  and economic growth, 71, 175–6, 184
  and inflation, 6, 175
  White Paper (1944), 4, 89, 173
functional finance, 89

Galenson, W. and Zellner, A., 177
Garside, W. R., 12

Geddes Committee on National Expenditure, 43
general elections, 90, 105, 145, 149, 170, 187
Germany, 24, 92, 111, 179
Gilbert, B. B., 53
Glynn, S. and Booth, A. E., 211 n. 6 (ch. 9)
Glynn, S. and Howells, P. G. A., 178, 205 n. 7
Godfrey, L., 71
Godley, W. A. H. and Shepherd, J. R., 126
gold standard, 154
  abandonment of, 24, 86, 101
  as policy constraint, 112, 166, 174
  protection offered by, 91–2
  return to, 33–4, 38, 86, 91
government, *see* Liberal Governments (1906–14); Labour Government (1929–31); National Governments (1931–45); Labour Governments (1974–9); Conservative Governments (1979–)
Grant, A. T. K., 7
Gregory, T., 191, 208 n. 6 (ch. 6)
Grigg, P. J., 91, 163, 191, 207 n. 3 (ch. 4)

Haberler, G., 158
Ham, A., 212 n. 7
Hancock, K. J., 156
Hansen, B., 67
Hargreaves, E. L., 60
Harris, S. E., 148, 175
Harrod, R. F., 5, 88, 191, 204 n. 1 (ch. 1)
Hartley, N. and Bean, C., 210 n. 5
Hatton, T. J., 8, 9, 16, 19, 205 n. 7
Hawtrey, R. G., 37, 191, 210 n. 1
Hayek, F. A., 90, 155, 158, 191, 208 n. 6 (ch. 6), 211 n. 5 (ch. 8)
Heath, T. L., 34
Heclo, H. and Wildavsky, A., 32, 50–1
Heertje, A., 14
Henderson, H. D., 113, 148–9, 152–3, 155, 165, 176–8, 191
Hicks, U. K., 44, 51, 66, 68, 72, 79, 82, 84, 85, 137, 138, 150, 199, 206 n. 12, 207 n. 1 (ch. 4)
Hicks neutrality, 14
Higgins, B., 206 n. 12
Higham, D. and Tomlinson, J., 183
Hopkins, R. V. N., 36, 37, 61, 82, 99, 107, 109, 113, 119, 154–5, 161–3, 185, 191, 207 n. 3 (ch. 4), 211 n. 5 (ch. 9)
Hornby, W., 117
Horne, R., 33
Howe, R. E. G., 184–5
Howson, S., 20, 29, 39, 60, 101, 102, 114, 120, 166, 173, 179, 205 n. 3, 211 n. 5 (ch. 8), n. 1 (ch. 9)
  and Winch, D., 114, 166, 168, 171, 210 n. 1
Hutchinson, T. W., 32, 166

Ilersic, A. R., 70
Import Duties Advisory Committee, 91
import duties, 64, 68, 198
  see also tariffs; taxes on expenditure
imports, 23–4, 27–8, 69, 117, 118, 164, 178
  see also balance of payments
income tax, 59, 60–1, 67
  assessment of, 66, 199
  business community and, 70–3, 95
  at constant employment, 197, 199
  cyclical sensitivity of, 66, 67, 99, 138, 199
  and fiscal window-dressing, 58, 82–3
  growth of revenue from, 63
  incidence of, 71–3
  as recovery instrument, 33, 73, 77, 95
  standard rate of, 63
  see also taxes on income
indirect taxation, 67, 69, 99
  see also taxes on expenditure
industrial policy, 18, 76–7
industry(-ies)
  construction, 26
  consumer goods, 16, 18
  de-rating of, 45, 74
  export, 24, 26, 28, 30, 117, 141
  'new', 15, 18, 20
  'old–new' debate, 9, 20–1
  producer goods, 16, 117, 141
  rationalization of, 74–6
  rearmament, 117, 141
  and regional problem, 15–18, 29–30
  service, 18, 20, 126
  staple, 15–21, 30, 75, 170
  state assistance to, 18, 75–6
  and taxation, 70–7
  'Treasury view' and, 154, 162
inflation
  British experience (1919–20) of, 6, 37–8, 91–2
  and budget deficits, 86–8
  Conservative Governments (1979–) and, 182–3
  continental experience of, 86, 92, 205 n. 6 (ch. 3)
  fear of, 6, 91–2, 163, 175, 182–3
  and labour market, 86
  and labour unrest, 6, 175
  and national debt, 182–3
  political causes of, 87, 90, 91–2
  public works and, 86, 162, 163
  and rearmament, 117
  and recovery (1932–7), 26, 29, 175
  –unemployment trade-off, 6, 175
  see also prices
Inland Revenue
  and fiscal window-dressing, 58, 82–3
  and national income statistics, 70
  revenue forecasting, 69–70
  role in budgetary process, 57–62
  on tax shifting, 72
  taxation policy of, 60–1, 75–6

inner Britain, 15, 16
  see also regional problem
Inskip, T., 116, 191
investment
  autonomous fluctuations in, 45, 122
  demand function, 93, 157, 161
  level of, 23, 25, 45–7, 137, 179
  private, 45, 154–5, 179
  public, see public investment
  taxation and, 66–7, 71–6
Irish, M., 19
IS–LM analysis, 155–65

Jennings, W. I., 35
Johnston, A., 58
Jones, M. E. F., 19

Kahn, R. F., 92, 104, 154, 192, 204 n. 1 (ch. 1), 205 n. 6 (ch. 2), 211 n. 3 (ch. 9)
Kaldor, N., 192, 200–1, 204 n. 1 (ch. 1)
  and Trevithick, J., 144
Keynes, J. M., 192
  on civil service, 181
  conduct of fiscal policy debate, 5, 30, 33, 172, 180, 181, 183
  and confidence, 162, 172
  and crowding-out, 85–6, 148, 156–7, 167–8, 171–2
  General Theory (1936), 4, 19, 155, 166, 171–2, 179, 180, 181, 183, 205 n. 6 (ch. 2), 211 n. 3 (ch. 9); acceptance of, 4, 181
  on gold standard, 91, 112
  and Henderson, H. D., 148–9, 152–3, 155, 165, 176–8
  on inflation, 86, 175
  on May report (1931), 112
  Means to Prosperity (1933), 5, 87, 104–5, 114–15, 166–7, 180, 205 n. 6 (ch. 2), 210 n. 2, 211 n. 3 (ch. 9)
  on Memoranda (1929), 156
  and multiplier, 54, 104, 148, 178, 211 n. 3 (ch. 9)
  papers, 3
  presuppositions of Harvey Road, 88
  –Robertson debate, 167–8
  on tax cuts, 33
  and Treasury: common ground with, 171–2; influence on, 1, 4, 166, 209 n. 11, 211 n. 5 (ch. 9)
  on 'Treasury view', 5, 86, 148
Keynesian policies
  estimated effectiveness of, 176–9
  monetarist criticisms of, 89, 144, 158
  'new classical' criticisms of, 158–60
  'public choice' criticisms of, 88–9, 184
  see also demand management; fiscal policy debate; Keynes, J. M.
Keynesian revolution, 5, 89, 90, 144, 189
Keynesians
  interwar economic historiography, 2, 4–5, 143, 149, 176, 180

Keynesians—*continued*
  Keynes and, 172
  on 'Treasury view', 144

Labour Government (1929–31), 59, 97–100, 113, 165–6, 205 n. 4 (ch. 3)
Labour Governments (1974–9), 113, 183
Labour Party, 40, 56, 113, 146, 183, 187
'Land fit for Heroes', 38
Laursen, L. and Metzler, L. A., 67
Lavington, F., 211 n. 4 (ch. 8)
Layton, W., 192, 208 n. 6 (ch. 6)
LCES, 13
League of Nations, 111
Lees, D. S., 179
Leijonhufvud, A., 172
Leith-Ross, F. W., 37, 192
Lewis, W. A., 8
Liberal Governments (1906–14), 37, 48
Liberal Industrial Inquiry, 56, 146
Liberal Party
  and National Investment Board, 56
  public works programme (1929), 6, 145–55, 161–3, 176–7, 180, 187–8
  on taxation of *rentier* incomes, 60
  see also Lloyd George, D.
Liberal Summer School, 5, 146
liquidity preference, 93, 149, 163, 165
liquidity trap, 155–6
Lithgow, J., 73, 192
Lloyd George, D., 192
  election programme (1929), 145–6, 176–8, 180
  on Labour's public works (1929–31), 166
  mistrust of, 180–1
  'New Deal', 35, 91, 105, 166–7
  Treasury criticism of, 33, 109
  on unemployment, 6
  see also Liberal Party
local government
  Act (1929), 42, 45, 47, 52, 56
  autonomy, 44, 51–2
  central control of, 44–5, 51–4, 55–6
  central grants to, defects of system, 53–4
  de-rating, 45, 74
  finances, weaknesses of, 44–5, 52, 53–4
  fragmentation of, 52
  and Housing and Town Planning Act (1919), 53
  and local income tax, 45
  and public works, 45, 53–4, 55–6, 137–8, 152, 165, 169
  rate income, 45, 52
local government expenditure
  capital account, 41, 45–6, 51
  central control of, 44–5, 51–4, 55–6
  'concentration process', 44
  current account, 41, 51
  direct command of resources, 44
  growth of, 42, 44–5
  stabilizing effectiveness of, 137–8
  see also public expenditure

Lomax, K. S., 18
London Chamber of Commerce, 71–2
Lonie, A. A., 211 n. 6 (ch. 8), n. 6 (ch. 9)
Lotz, J., 123, 209 nn. 3, 4
Lucas, R. E., 158, 159

McCrone, G., 17
MacDonald, J. R., 112, 192
MacGregor, D. H., 192, 208 n. 6 (ch. 6)
McKenna, R., 91, 192
Macmillan, H., 33, 192, 204 n. 1 (ch. 1)
Macmillan Committee, 36, 154, 161, 205 n. 5 (ch. 2)
macro-marginal budget rates, 128–32
  see also tax elasticities
Malinvaud, E., 7
Mallet, B. and George, C. O., 63
managed economy
  economic authorities and the, 91–2, 120, 174
  origins of, 96, 119–20, 173–6
  'public choice' critique of, 88–9, 184
market clearing, *see* 'new classical macroeconomics'
Matthews, K. G. P., 211 n. 8
Matthews, R. C. O., 1–2, 8, 12, 13, 189
  and Feinstein, C. H. and Odling-Smee, J. C., 13–14, 21–2, 132
May, G., 192
May Committee on National Expenditure, 43
  Henderson, H. D. on, 113
  Hopkins, R. V. N. on, 113
  Keynes, J. M. on, 112
  majority report, 110–11
  minority report, 110–11
  orthodoxy of, 109–13
  on public expenditure growth, 90, 110–11
  rationale for expenditure cuts, 110–11, 185–6
  recommendations, 59, 99;
    macroeconomic consequences of, 112–13, 133, 134, 137, 143
  role in financial crisis (1931), 99–100, 113
  and taxation, 59, 99, 100
  terms of reference of, 208 n. 7 (ch. 6)
Meade, J. E., 192, 204 n. 1 (ch. 1), 207 n. 3 (ch. 5)
Memoranda on Certain Proposals Relating to Unemployment (1929), 93–4, 149–54, 160, 161
Metcalf, D., Nickell, S. J. and Floros, N., 132
Middlemas, K. and Barnes, J., 107
Middleton, R., 17, 45, 51, 56, 142, 166, 205 n. 4 (ch. 2), 207 n. 6, 208 n. 1, 209 n. 1, 210 n. 8
Mills, T. C. and Wood, G. E., 156
Ministry of Labour
  conflicts with Treasury, 50, 83, 101
  and *Memoranda* (1929), 92, 150–1

Ministry of Labour—*continued*
  on multiplier, 151
  on public works, 92, 150–1
  unemployment data, 16, 204 n. 2, 210 n. 3
Ministry of Transport, 52
  conflict with Treasury, 50, 104
  on public works, 152–3
miscellaneous revenues, 65, 66, 194, 195, 200
Moggridge, D. E., 34, 101, 205 n. 3
monetarism, *see* monetarist counter-revolution
monetarist counter-revolution
  and Conservative Governments (1979–), 2–3, 189
  disillusionment with fiscal policy, 89, 158
  'new classical' criticisms of, 158
  'Treasury view' as antecedent for, 144, 171–2
monetary policy
  accommodating fiscal policy, 93, 165, 167–8
  cheap money, 102, 114, 140, 142, 168
  influence of Keynes on, 166
  in *IS–LM* models, 156, 158, 165
  and monetary targets, 185
  and rearmament, 116, 179
  and recovery policy, 114, 133, 140, 142, 175
  stance of, 24
  v. fiscal instruments, 89–90, 142
money demand function, 155, 156, 157, 161, 171
Morgan, E. V., 38
Morton, W. A., 206 n. 12
Mosley, O., 166, 192
motor vehicle licence duties, 68, 120, 198
  see also taxes on expenditure
multiplier
  Kahn, R. F. and, 104, 154, 211 n. 3 (ch. 9)
  Keynes, J. M. and, 54, 104, 148, 178, 211 n. 3 (ch. 9)
  and regional problem, 30
  'Treasury view' on, 151, 154–5, 163, 164–5
  values for, 95, 163, 164–5, 165, 177–8
  see also balanced budget multiplier; fiscal policy multiplier
Musgrave, R. A., 124

national debt
  burden of, 42, 59–60, 182–3, 205 n. 4 (ch. 2)
  charge on budget, 102, 114, 137
  payments on US war debt, 102, 114
  preoccupation with, 84, 86
  sinking funds, 100, 114, 139
  and War Loan conversion, 102, 104, 114, 137
  see also debt management policy

National Defence Contribution, 64, 67, 199
National Governments (1931–45), 99, 100, 166–7, 208 n. 5 (ch. 5), 210 n. 10 (ch. 7)
national income statistics, 70, 171
national insurance, *see* social insurance funds
National Investment Board, 56, 180
Neild, R. R., 126
Nevin, E., 93, 210 n. 10
'new classical macroeconomics', 143, 144, 158–60
'New Deal', *see under* Lloyd George, D.; United States
'new' economics, 56, 95
  exponents of, 4
  and Keynesian revolution, 4–5
  Treasury and, 32, 83, 89, 90, 115, 121, 181
Newman, N., 34, 37, 205 n. 3
Niemeyer, O., 91, 192

Okun, A. M. and Teeters, N. H., 123, 209 n. 2
'Old Moore's Almanack', 104, 105–7
Ormerod, P. A. and Worswick, G. D. N., 19
outer regions, 14, 15–16
  see also regional problem
output
  at constant employment, 125–7
  cyclical fluctuation of, 22, 23, 24
  –employment elasticity, 132
  price elasticity of demand for, 14
  trend growth of, 21–2
  see also trade cycle
Overy, R. J., 179

Parker, R. A. C., 117
Parliament, 34, 51, 85, 104, 113, 169–70
Patinkin, D., 171
Peacock, A. T. and Wiseman, J., 44, 63, 138
Peden, G. C., 32, 49, 50, 116, 117, 166, 171, 209 n. 12
personal incomes, taxation of, 63–4, 66
  see also under taxes on income
Phelps Brown, E. H. and Shackle, G. L. S., 26
Phillips, F., 37, 82, 89–90, 118–19, 167, 181, 192, 211 n. 5 (ch. 8), nn. 2, 5 (ch. 9)
Pigou, A. C., 72, 192, 205 n. 6 (ch. 3), 208 n. 6 (ch. 6), 211 n. 4 (ch. 8)
Pilgrim Trust, 17, 20
Plant, A., 192, 208 n. 6 (ch. 6)
Plowden Committee on Control of Public Expenditure, 54
political–business cycles, 90
political neutrality, 6, 89–91
Pollard, S., 78, 92, 186
population, 13, 40, 85, 86

Prest, A. R., 212 n. 1
Price, R. W. R., 47, 54, 100, 206 nn. 10, 13
prices
    and budget balance, 127–9
    and national debt, 59–60, 84, 86, 182–3
    and public expenditure, 37–8, 43, 127–9
    relative, 155
    and taxation, 64, 66, 67, 68, 71–2, 129
    and trade cycle, 29
    trend of, 24, 182
    see also inflation
productivity
    at constant employment, 126–7
    interwar growth of, 10, 13, 21
    and labour displacement, 13–15
    and technical progress, 14
    and unemployment, 13–15, 188
profits, 25, 63–4, 71–3, 75–6, 118
Pryor, Z. P., 209 n. 3
'public choice economics', 88–9, 184
public corporations, 46, 56
public expenditure
    cuts in, 32, 38, 39, 43–4, 63, 99–100, 109–13
    debt interest, 39, 41, 42, 102, 114, 137
    definition of, 38
    direct command of resources, 39, 173
    and economic growth, 73–4, 95, 184, 186
    effects of unemployment on, 40, 90, 99, 130–2
    Federation of British Industries on, 73–4
    forces for growth of, 38–40, 44, 87, 90, 111
    growth, elasticity measure of, 32, 40–1
    as luxury good, 186
    as ratio to GDP, 37–9
    and social reform, 37, 38, 40, 90
    stabilizing effectiveness of, 39, 43, 45–7, 133–43
    subsidies and grants, 39
    trends in, 23, 37–47
    see also central government expenditure; fiscal stance; local government expenditure; public investment
public investment
    counter-cyclical adjustment of, 53–7, 137–8, 168–70, 176, 179
    forward planning of, 169
    and nationalization, 179
    postwar, 47, 54, 186
    and private investment, 46–7, 154–5
    social rate of return on, 154
    stabilizing effectiveness of, 45–7, 137–8, 141, 176–9
    trends in, 38, 41, 45–7
    unnecessary restraint of, 147
    see also public works
Public Record Office papers, 3, 34, 37, 72
public sector, enlargement of,
    effects on economic growth, 84, 184
    implications for fiscal policy, 39, 173
    magnitude, 37–8, 62–3, 70

public sector borrowing requirement (PSBR), 142–3, 185
public sector employees' salaries, 105, 127–9
public sector employment, 206 n. 7
public works, 6–7, 54–6, 144–72
    and balance of payments, 154, 163–4, 178–9
    changes in 'Treasury view', on, 166–71
    and confidence, 92–5, 149, 162–3
    counter-cyclical, 54–6, 169–70
    debates: (1929), 145–65, 176–8; (1933), 104, 114, 166–7; (1935), 35, 91, 105, 166–7
    and demobilization problem, 151
    and economic growth, 175–6
    employment-creation of, 146–7, 152, 176–8
    and 'illusory' employment, 186
    in *IS–LM* models, 155–65
    under Labour Government (1929–31), 165–6, 169
    labour supply for, 150–1, 176–7
    local authority, 45, 53–4, 55–6, 137–8, 152, 165, 169
    and monetary policy, 114, 147–8
    and multiplier, 148, 154–5, 177–8
    under National Governments (1931–45), 166–70
    physical planning of, 56, 152–3, 179–80
    rearmament as, 141, 162, 170, 173
    self-liquidating, 148, 178
    speed of execution of, 56, 145, 147, 152–3, 165–6
    and Treasury expenditure control, 55
    see also public investment; 'Treasury view'
purchase tax, 68
see also taxes on expenditure

quantity theory of money, 156

rational expectations, 158–60, 207 n. 2 (ch. 5)
Ray Committee on Local Expenditure, 209 n. 9
real wage resistance, 160, 175
real wages, 10, 67
rearmament
    and balance of payments, 116, 117, 118, 120, 210 n. 11
    as 'balance of risks', 116
    and budgetary policy, 3–4, 63, 107–9, 115–21, 134, 141–2, 162, 173
    and demand management, 117–20, 141–2, 169, 173–4
    effect upon real economy, 119–20, 121, 141–2, 174, 190
    expenditure: control of, 49–50, 109, 116–17, 141; increase in, 106–7, 140, 209 n. 13
    financing of, 106, 115–16

rearmament—*continued*
  opposition to, 107
  as trade cycle instrument, 141, 169–70, 173
  see also defence borrowing; defence expenditure
receipts
  automatic growth of, 68, 127–32
  at constant employment, 196–201
  course of, 62–7
  'displacement effect', 63
  effect of First World War on, 38, 62–3
  elasticity of, 68, 127–32
  structure of, 64–8
  see also taxation
recession, *see under* trade cycle
Recktenwald, H. C., 63
recovery (1932–7), *see under* trade cycle
recovery policy, 101, 104–5, 113, 114, 166–7, 169–70
  see also unemployment policy
Reddaway, W. B., 204 n. 1 (ch. 2)
Redmond, J., 211 n. 1
relation, international co-ordination of, 28
regional policy, 75–6, 143, 176
regional problem, 14–18, 19, 24, 30, 75, 143, 188
rentier incomes, taxation of, 59–60, 110–11
retrenchment, *see* economy campaigns
revenue departments
  conflicts with Treasury, 58–62, 82–3
  and financial crisis (1931), 59–61
  and forecasting, 69–70, 104
  functions and responsibilities, 57–9
  role in budgetary process, 57–62
  and tax policy, 59–61, 67, 72, 75–7
revenue forecasting
  accuracy of, 69
  and budgetary policy, 69, 82–3
  cautiousness of, 58, 70
  over medium term, 69, 104
  and national income statistics, 70
  of taxes on expenditure, 61–2
  of taxes on income, 62, 69
  and Treasury, 58, 61–2, 70
  see also 'Old Moore's Almanack'
'Ricardian equivalence theorem', 159
Richardson, H. W., 8, 24, 26, 27, 29, 68, 78, 133, 138
Robbins, L., 192, 208 n. 6 (ch. 6), 211 n. 5 (ch. 9)
Robertson, D. H., 167, 192
Robinson, A., 33
Robinson, E. A. G., 192, 204 n. 1 (ch. 1)
Robinson, J., 4, 192, 204 n. 1 (ch. 1)
Roseveare, H., 48
Roskill, S., 205 n. 5 (ch. 3)
Rowe-Dutton, E., 207 n. 3 (ch. 4)
Royal Commission on the Income Tax, 74, 207 n. 4
Royal Commission on Unemployment Insurance, 208 n. 4 (ch. 5)

Sabine, B. E. V., 63, 142, 208 n. 4 (ch. 6)
Salter, A., 192, 204 n. 1 (ch. 1), 208 n. 6 (ch. 6)
Samuelson, P. A., 188–9
Sargent, T. J., 158
Say's law, 94
Sayers, R. S., 23, 60, 66, 102
Schedvin, C. B., 59
Schumacher, E. F., 85
Second World War
  and Keynesian revolution, 4–5, 170–1, 183, 189
  unemployment on eve of, 142
Shackle, G. L. S., 204 n. 1 (ch. 1)
Shann, E. O. G. and Copland, D. B., 59
Shaw, G. K., 123
Shay, R. P., 116, 117
Shirras, G. F. and Rostas, L., 68–9, 70
Silverman, H. A., 72
Simon, J. A., 119, 192
sinking funds, 79, 80, 81, 100, 114, 139, 193
Skidelsky, R., 5, 100, 146, 148, 180
skilled labour, shortages of, 26, 117
Slichter, S. H., 208 n. 6 (ch. 5)
Smith, A., 84
Snowden, P., 35, 100, 114, 192, 208 n. 5 (ch. 6)
social expenditure, 41, 82, 111
social insurance funds
  and budget definitions, 78–80, 81, 99, 138–9, 193
  contributions to, 66, 138–9, 200
  expenditures: at constant employment, 201–3; cyclical sensitivity of, 99, 201
  political manipulation of, 208 n. 4 (ch. 5)
social policy, 38, 111
Special Areas (England and Wales), 75–6
spending departments, Treasury control of, 44, 47–51, 109, 116–17
  see also Treasury control
stabilization policy, *see* demand management
Stamp, J., 192, 199, 208 n. 6 (ch. 6)
stamp duties, 128, 131, 198, 200
  see also taxes on expenditure
Stein, H., 93–4, 209 n. 2
Stewart, M., 2, 4, 189
Stewart, P. M., 75, 192
Stone, R., 70
  and Rowe, D. A., 68
  and Stone, W. M., 211 n. 3 (ch. 9)
structural change, 9, 20
structural problem, 15–16, 18, 75
Supplementary Estimates, 51, 83, 101, 113
supply
  aggregate, elasticity of, 29
  constraints, 29–30, 117
  labour, 12–13, 71, 150–1
'supply cycle', 51
surtax, 59, 60–1, 67
  assessment of, 66, 199
  at constant employment, 197, 199

Treasury control—*continued*
  post-First World War reform of, 32, 34, 49
  of rearmament, 49–50, 116–17, 120–1
  and stabilization policies, 51, 53, 179–80
  strains of First World War on, 49
'Treasury view'
  on budget deficits, 87–9
  changes in, 166–71, 209 n. 11
  and classical economics, 5, 85, 93–4, 149, 153, 156, 171
  on confidence, 162–3, 172
  on crowding-out, 93–4, 145, 147–9, 153–5, 156–8, 161–5, 167–8
  Hopkins, R. V. N. on, 36, 154, 161–3
  on industry, 154, 162
  inflation and the, 153, 175
  IS–LM models of, 155–65
  Keynes, J. M. on, 148, 156–7
  Keynes's influence on, 1, 166
  and Keynes–Robertson debate, 167–8
  on Liberal programme (1929), 149–55, 160–5
  on *Means to Prosperity* (1933), 87–8, 114–15, 159
  and *Memoranda* (1929), 93, 149–54, 160, 161
  on monetary policy, 89–90, 153, 165, 167–8
  on multiplier, 151, 154–5, 163
  on 'normal channels of trade', 151, 154–5, 161–2
  political–administrative aspects of, 149, 152
  and real resources, 92, 116, 120
  renewed interest in, 144
  Ricardian analysis of, 93–4, 153
  theoretical foundations of, 36–7, 145, 149
  on unemployment, 149, 150–1, 154–5, 160, 211 n. 2
  verdicts on, 2, 4, 144
  see also public works
Trevithick, J., 167–8
TUC, 60
Tunzelmann, G. N. von, 8

unemployment
  benefit-induced, 9, 19–20, 132, 187, 190
  at constant employment, 125–6, 201
  cyclical course of, 11–12, 25, 139
  duration of, 11, 16–17, 30, 139, 201–3
  economic loss from, 12
  and employment, 12–13, 15
  frictional, 11
  at industrial level, 15
  –inflation trade-off, 6, 175
  and labour supply, 13
  and Live Register, 16, 150–1
  national insurance returns for, 11–12
  'natural rate' of, 158
  non-Keynesian, 12
  and output, 22, 132
  population and, 13
  and public expenditure, 40, 90
  and regional problem, 14–18, 19, 29–30
  on eve of Second World War, 141–2
  structural, 13, 29–30
  in sub-periods: (pre-1914), 12, 13, 16, 177; (interwar), 2, 4, 7–9, 10–18, 24–7, 104, 113, 125, 132, 138–9, 141–2, 145, 150–1, 154, 166, 174, 175, 176–7, 182; (post-1945), 2, 12, 132; (1979–), 2, 182
  technological, 13–15, 19, 188
  Treasury estimate of 'normal', 211 n. 2
  trend course of, 13
  voluntary, 9, 19–20, 187
Unemployment Assistance Board, 201, 208 n. 5 (ch. 5)
unemployment benefits
  administration of, 138–9, 208 n. 5 (ch. 5)
  and budgetary stability, 80, 99
  at constant employment, 201–3
  cuts in (1931), 99–100, 110–11
  and cyclical macro-marginal budget rate, 131–2
  growth of outlay on, 40, 99
  and induced unemployment, 9, 19–20, 132, 187, 190
  restoration of 1931 cuts, 105
  v. public works, 175–6
Unemployment Insurance Fund, 99, 138–9, 201
unemployment policy, 91, 145–6, 175–6
  see also recovery policy
United States
  business community, 208 n. 7 (ch. 5)
  depression in, 24
  fiscal policies, 27, 111, 125, 160
  foreign lending, 23–4
  monetarist counter-revolution in, 89
  national debt, 205 n. 4 (ch. 2)
  'New Deal', 27, 160, 205 n. 4 (ch. 2)
  UK war debt to, 102, 114

War Loan conversion operation, 102, 104, 137, 193
Ward, T. S. and Neild, R. R., 67, 122, 125, 131–2, 136, 210 n. 7
Wass, D., 184
wear and tear allowances, *see* capital allowances
'Whitehall view', 35, 36, 150
Williamson, P., 149
Winch, D., 4, 32, 86, 89, 95, 104, 143, 150, 153, 154, 168
Wood, J. B., 12
Wood, K., 4
Woods, J., 35
World Economic Conference, 205 n. 5 (ch. 2)
Worswick, G. D. N., 11

Youngson, A. J., 8, 154, 166

surtax—*continued*
  cyclical sensitivity of, 66, 67, 99, 138, 199
  and fiscal window-dressing, 58, 82–3
  see also taxes on income
Sykes, J., 52

tariffs
  and insulation of domestic economy, 28, 174–5
  introduction of (1931–2), 64, 91
  and recovery policy, 102, 133
  revenue from, 68, 198
tax base, 63, 64, 68, 75, 104
tax elasticities, 68, 127, 129, 132
  see also macro-marginal budget rates
tax exhaustion, 75
taxation
  avoidance/evasion of, 60
  business community on, 70–3, 95
  and capital allowances, 61, 63, 74–6
  disincentive effects of, 71
  and economic growth, 70–7, 84
  effect on higher-income cohorts, 59–61
  equity considerations, 59–60
  international comparisons of, 70–1
  per capita, 70
  progressive structure of, 63, 66, 209 n. 4
  as recovery instrument, 33, 43, 77, 95, 188
  role in budgetary process, 57–62
  and savings, 71, 72
  see also receipts
taxes on capital, 62, 65, 66, 200
  see also capital levy; estate duties
taxes on expenditure
  ad valorem duties, 67, 129
  base for, 64, 68
  at constant employment, 127, 129, 196–9
  effective rates of, 63, 64, 129
  and prices, 67, 129
  specific duties, 64, 67, 129
  and terms of trade, 67–8
  trends in, 62, 63, 64, 65
  see also commodity taxes; import duties; indirect taxation; motor vehicle licence duties; purchase tax; stamp duties
taxes on income
  burden of, 70–2
  at constant employment, 197, 199
  of corporate sector, 63, 64, 66–7, 71–7, 129
  cyclical sensitivity of, 129, 138, 199
  disincentive effects of, 71
  effective rates of, 63, 64, 129
  elasticity of, 129
  of personal sector, 63, 64, 71, 129
  and savings, 71, 72
  trends in, 62, 64–6
  see also direct taxation; income tax; National Defence Contribution; surtax

Taylor, A. J. P., 180
terms of trade, 25, 67–8
TFP, *see* productivity
Thatcher administrations, *see* Conservative Governments (1979–)
Thirlwall, A. P., 29
Thomas, M., 141
Thomas, T., 12, 124, 176–8
The Times, 10, 104, 208 n. 6 (ch. 6)
Tobin, J., 158, 159, 160, 211 n. 6 (ch. 8)
Tomlinson, J., 7, 185, 189, 204 n. 3, 211 n. 6 (ch. 9)
trade cycle
  consciousness, 94–5
  episodes: recession (1920–1), 16, 19, 38–9, 43, 174; depression (1929–32), 2–3, 16, 19, 23–5, 27–8, 43; recovery (1932–7), 24–6, 27, 43; recession (1937–8), 25, 26–7, 43, 169–70, 173, 174; depression (1979–), 2–3, 142–3, 188
  GDP and components, 22–5
  historical comparisons of, 2–3, 22, 55, 132
  and unemployment, 11–12, 22, 25
  see also output
Treasury
  cautiousness of, 31, 32, 33, 36, 50–1
  conservatism of, 4, 31, 33, 85, 115
  disputes within, 119
  and expenditure growth, 32, 48–51, 87–90, 116–17, 121
  and fiscal window-dressing, 80–3
  and Fisher, W., 31–2, 34, 35, 37, 50, 70, 119, 181, 187, 191
  'hairshirt philosophy' of, 115, 186
  institutional position of, 3, 7, 31, 33–5, 78
  interpretations of, 32
  Keynes's influence on, 1, 112, 114–15, 154, 166–71, 173, 175, 176, 179, 180–1
  and local government, 52
  officials, commonality of background, 37
  papers, 34, 36–7
  policy, moralism of, 186
  and rearmament, 49–50, 107–9, 115–21
  responsiveness of to external pressures, 32
  and revenue departments, 57–62, 69–70, 104
  and taxation, 72, 75–6
  widening of responsibilities, 34
Treasury control
  Accounting Officer and, 49
  and 'candle-ends', 48
  and conflicts with spending departments, 50, 83, 101, 104
  and departmental financial responsibility, 34, 49
  and expenditure growth, 32, 49–50
  Gladstonian era of, 32, 48–9, 84–5
  maxims of, 50–1